Red Kant: Aesthetics, Marxism and the Third *Critique*

Also available from Bloomsbury

Aesthetic Theory, Theodor W. Adorno
Cinema I, Gilles Deleuze
Cinema II, Gilles Deleuze
The Aesthetic in Kant, James Kirwan
The Bloomsbury Companion to Kant, edited by Gary Banham,
Dennis Schulting and Nigel Hems
The Dialectics of Aesthetic Agency, Ayon Maharaj
The Kant Dictionary, Lucas Thorpe
The Politics of Aesthetics, Jacques Rancière

Red Kant: Aesthetics, Marxism and the Third *Critique*

Michael Wayne

B L O O M S B U R Y

LONDON · NEW DELHI · NEW YORK · SYDNEY

Bloomsbury Academic

An imprint of Bloomsbury Publishing Plc

50 Bedford Square
London
WC1B 3DP
UK

1385 Broadway
New York
NY 10018
USA

www.bloomsbury.com

Bloomsbury is a registered trade mark of Bloomsbury Publishing Plc

First published 2014

British Library Cataloguing-in-Publication Data
A catalogue record for this book is available from the British Library.

ISBN: HB: 9781472511348
ePDF: 9781472505118
ePub: 9781472508683

Library of Congress Cataloging-in-Publication Data
A catalog record for this book is available from the Library of Congress.

Typeset by Integra Software Service Pvt. Ltd.

In Memory of Maurice, My Dad

Nothing that is beautiful will harm the workers

Lavena Saltonstall, garment worker,
Cotton Factory Times, 1914

Contents

Introduction

In the twilight of reason, a turn to the philosophy of the aesthetic may seem like a luxury that we can ill afford. Yet that very scepticism concerning the relevance of aesthetic questions already concedes the split between the social and the individual, the public and the private, the political and the personal, which is so fundamental to the dominant order. Despite its commodification in mass formats and the hierarchical access to its more 'refined' forms, the aesthetic, as a philosophical concept and as a particular branch of cultural practice, is fundamentally about reconnecting those components of our being that have been fissured by an evolving capitalist system. As a guide to exploring the aesthetic as the reconnecting tissue of social life, we can begin by offering a definition of the aesthetic as a *critical communicative act in a sensuous-imaginative form*.

Firstly, it is a communicative act in which the act of communication is central and elaborated with a high degree of complexity. The rise of design across everyday goods indicates an aesthetic sensibility permeating our ordinary object world. But here the aesthetic is subordinate to other functional ends and this limits its communicative architecture. The aesthetic liberated from other functional purposes allows for communicative acts of great dialogic complexity that reach deep into our collective social being and across time and space, although certainly not in an unchanging, fixed abstractly universal sense. Thus as a communicative practice, the aesthetic is distinct from cultural practices understood more broadly, that is from an anthropological perspective. Cultural practices of all kinds are meaningful and socially grounded, from haircuts to Halloween, and the establishment of cultural studies was founded on this broad anthropological principle. But while the aesthetic is a communicative act not all communicative acts are aesthetic. On this characteristic alone we could scarcely differentiate the aesthetic from other modes of communication, such as the daily news media or an advert, which typically have, relative to the aesthetic, a contracted reach into our social being.

When the aesthetic is working aesthetically, it is also a *critical* form of communication, which is to say that it is in some way a commentary on our social being that steps outside dominant or typical enunciations. The aesthetic is, potentially, a cognitively rewarding experience for what it tells us about what we did not know or what we did not want to know or what we knew but had 'forgotten' or what we know but which we had consigned to some private sphere of our lives as one of those truths that simply cannot be acknowledged in a public sphere subordinated to power, or finally, what we know only in an abstract external way but had lost the capacity to *feel*, to live or experience in some way. For the aesthetic is embodied in our sensuous being and is not merely a cerebral affair and when it is working aesthetically it can counter the socially induced and carefully crafted *anesthetics* to feeling and cognition about the world around us and its problems.

The aesthetic is a mode of cultural practice that is inextricably sourced in and gives licence to our imaginative powers. It is in this sense a special kind of laboratory for testing, experimenting, speculating and hypothesizing but with materials that have a great deal of plasticity, even though these materials always retain some important and substantive links with empirical reality and logical relations as much as social reality. The imaginative dimension of the aesthetic is not an untethered flight of fancy, but a reciprocal and dynamic relationship between what is and what could be, a utopian anticipation of a reconciliation of the division between the social and the creative that despite all the propaganda to the contrary remains absolutely entrenched.

In many ways what follows is an unpacking of these three dimensions of the aesthetic: the communicative, the critical and the sensual-imaginative *form* of the aesthetic. More specifically, it is an unpacking of the surprising connection between the conceptual genealogy of the aesthetic as developed by Immanuel Kant (1724–1804) and later Marxist theory. Yet Kant has a reputation which many liberal and conservative scholars are eager to protect: the reputation that he is a bourgeois philosopher. It is a reputation which many Marxist critics have been only too willing to accept and accordingly identify Kant's philosophy with some of the fundamental structures (so debilitating for critical thought) of the bourgeois epoch: formalism, elitism, idealism, dualism and a static a-historical universalism. These are not unreasoned charges to lay at Kant's door and in many substantive ways his philosophy is marked by all of these features. Yet this Marxist orthodoxy on Kant needs challenging because ultimately it cannot tell the whole story. Indeed Kant's own turn to the aesthetic is precisely an attempt to overcome these problems within the architecture of his philosophy.

In an important essay 'Red Kant' (to which I owe the title of this book), Robert Kaufman has amusingly put the dominant Marxist narrative:

Hegel made Marxism possible, Kant was Marxism's irredeemably bourgeois-idealist Other. Hegel, stood on his head rather than his feet (or was it the other way around?), became Marx; Kant, head at both ends, could only lie down and be buried.

Kaufman (2000: 687)

This is particularly true within Anglophone Marxism, which continues to be dominated, as most cultural theory is, by the intellectual hegemony of the French. But it is not universally true. As perhaps one might expect, Marxist-inflected German philosophy of culture is far more receptive to Kant than in the Anglophone world, but such work is translated far less into English than the latest work from Paris. Meanwhile, elsewhere, Chinese aesthetic Marxism has been the occasion for productive engagements with Kant, as Liu Kang has shown us (Kang 2000).

My aim in this book is to carve out a Marxist reading of Kant's third *Critique*, which is at least new within the English language and from a position that is distinct from Kantian-Marxism. Kantian-Marxism is one of three broad traditions, which have interpreted his work as a whole. There is firstly the dominant conservative or liberal bourgeois tradition, which has claimed Kant as their own. In their hands, Kant is a powerful philosophical weapon in the field of knowledge, morality and aesthetics. There is a minority radical current *within* this bourgeois tradition that has emerged in the wake of the linguistic turn in cultural theories during the twentieth century and which has returned to Kant having gone through post-structuralism, or even Marxism. Its standard bearers are Deleuze, Lyotard and Rancière in France, and de Man and latterly Shaviro in America. The second camp is the minority Kantian-Marxist tradition which, I shall argue, is not sufficiently critical of the positivism and dualism of Kant's first *Critique*. Like the bourgeois tradition, Kantian-Marxism does not really perceive any kind of break from the first to the third *Critique* and generally soft-pedals on the contradictions in Kant's thought. In terms of writing a history of philosophical thought, Kantian-Marxism too readily assimilates Kant's thought to Marxism, as if it were a ready-made precursor to Marx. This is too simple a genealogical story. The third traditional way of reading Kant is the 'orthodox' Marxist reading alluded to by Kaufman and which is happy to accept the bourgeois tradition's classification of Kant as one of their own and criticize him on those grounds. If anything the orthodox Marxist tradition sees the third *Critique* in less positive terms than the first. The latter, according to the orthodox Marxist position, at least offers the outlines of an account of the possibility for objective knowledge. While the Kantian and Kantian-Marxist tradition downplay Kant's internal contradictions, the orthodox Marxist interpretation of Kant freezes Kant's contradictions into a static structure that trapped his thought completely. What is missing is a sense of an internal dynamic and momentum in Kant's thought, a sense of development and mutation that at least partially pushes past and reconfigures these contradictions in the movement from the first to the third *Critique*.

I have identified three positions on Kant: the bourgeois (itself split between its mainstream and 'radical' wings), the Kantian-Marxist and the orthodox Marxist. We can also identify three broad traditions of bourgeois aesthetic theory (and each has influenced Marxist theory). These traditions correspond to three categories of aesthetic practices, although the problems associated with the aesthetic *theories* are not to be conflated with the aesthetic *practices* themselves. Firstly, there is the classical high culture conceptualization of the aesthetic – with its elitism, traditionalism and status quo orientation more or less openly declared. It would be a great mistake to conflate the socially engineered appropriation by elites of what is called 'high culture' with the culture itself, however. Secondly, there is the avant-garde conceptualization of the aesthetic, which begins with Nietzsche and later flows into deconstruction, post-structuralism and postmodernism, and which nourished – despite its radical political attack on harmony, depoliticized beauty and order – a powerful irrationalism or at least relativism that has even, in the stimulating but problematic work of Bruno Latour, entered into the philosophy of natural science (1999). This tidal wave of 'aestheticization' has been enough to make Habermas, for example, very critical of the role of the aesthetic in philosophy (Habermas 1987). Both the classical and the avant-garde theoretical traditions find in Kant some theoretical sustenance, with Kant's conception of beauty and the sublime typically supporting the classical and the avant-garde positions, respectively. Thirdly, there is the tradition of aesthetic populism, still fighting a battle that is largely won, often uncritically aligned with the capitalist culture industries whose products it enthusiastically celebrates in a manner barely differentiated from fan culture and the output of corporate marketing departments and largely responsible for a massive trivialization of whole disciplines, such as film and television studies. Again, it would be a great mistake to conflate the problems associated with such theoretical appropriations with the cultural practices themselves, which deserve the *serious* attention they are patently not getting in some quarters.

Significantly, genuinely popular culture (as opposed to its industrial-corporate production), the culture of the working class that is the product of lived experience and self-organized leisure time, has had comparatively little theorization as a (re) source for the aesthetic, even though it has historically fed into both classical and avant-garde practices and continues to feed into (or be appropriated by) the corporate media culture. Work in a broadly Marxist ethnographic tradition – the foundational moment of Cultural Studies in the UK – by Hebdige (1979), Willis (1981), McGrath (1996) and latterly by feminist writers engaging with class (e.g. Walkerdine and Lucey 1989 and Munt 2000) represents some significant exceptions to an otherwise neglected area. Much of this tradition has been abandoned in the West today on the assumption that the working class does not exist or that distinct working-class cultures have been wholly absorbed into mass culture. This judgment, however, speaks more of the distance of the intellectuals from the working class – one of the great fundamental and largely unrecognized problems of contemporary politics in the West – than it does of the relationship between the working class and corporate culture. The long history of an autonomous working-class culture and self-education charted by Jonathan Rose (2001) may have been transformed by deindustrialization but is unlikely to have disappeared completely. The other significant theoretical stream that cannot be assimilated to the three bourgeois traditions identified earlier has its roots in the convergence of modernism with mass socialist politics and Marxist theory between the October Revolution of 1917 and the outbreak of the Second World War in 1939. The ghosts of that particular conjuncture still haunt us today.

Faced with the deeply problematic models of the classical, avant-garde and populist *assessments* of the aesthetic, as well as the problematic class distinctions evoked by classical and the avant-garde practices on the one hand and the apparent seamless absorption of the popular into the commodity form on the other, it might be tempting to retreat from the aesthetic altogether as anything other than the terrain of the enemy. Mainstream cultural theory has indeed collapsed the aesthetic into culture more generally, sometimes motivated by good anti-elitist or even occasionally materialist impulses, but with the end result of eliminating what is exceptional about the aesthetic vis-à-vis the main dynamics of the social order, or alternatively cultural theory has rescued the aesthetic only as high art. While ideology critique remains indispensable, it is also the case that when the aesthetic acts aesthetically, it mobilizes capacities and possibilities that make it indispensable for developing a culture open to radical social change. Some of the important concepts that emerge from a consideration of Kant's aesthetic that will help us re-evaluate it include the imagination, both the productive and reproductive imagination, the schema, aesthetic ideas, the technically practical, determinative judgment and crucially reflective judgment, indeterminacy, singularity, formal purposiveness, technic and beauty. Certainly we shall need to reconstruct the dominant way in which Kant's aesthetic of beauty is usually perceived, as subjective, divorced from concepts, disinterested in social engagement and prone to aesthetic formalism. A common complaint for critics of Kantian-inspired beauty is that it is blind to 'pain' and instead valorizes 'perfection, repletion, and wholeness' (Alberro 2004: 28). Indeed, but the standard conceptualizations of Kant's philosophy of the aesthetic push it away from the social. And it is my contention that the significance of Kant's aesthetic turn in the third *Critique* is precisely that it constitutes a reaching towards the category of the social that was missing from Kant's earlier philosophical architecture. This hypothesis, certainly against the grain of bourgeois and Marxist scholarship, means recovering a non-bourgeois version of Kant from the usual object of criticism. The mental shift which a return to and reworking of Kantian categories produces vis-à-vis the dominant terminology of cultural theory is, I think, productive. There is a materialist kernel in Kant's work that is strangely missing from great swathes of cultural theory. However, this kernel must be rescued from the bourgeois materialist frameworks (of naturalism and psychologism, for example) that suffuse contemporary Kantian aesthetics. Yet the trajectory of Kant's own thought, from the first to the third *Critique*, provides us with the resources to rethink Kant in historical materialist terms and indeed to see in Kant important precursors to Marx. Kant's concept of subreption, for example, will be understood here as a forerunner to Marx's concept of commodity fetishism. Insofar as the absence of the social was the product of Kant's epoch, a social order that paradoxically disavows its own sociality, then the project of the third *Critique* remains relevant to us today, when that same (although now mutated) social order has so definitively passed beyond whatever claim it once had to advancing human progress. Insofar as the third *Critique* tries to articulate what had been hitherto inexpressible in Kant's philosophy through an engagement with the aesthetic, we can perhaps today recover a historical and materialist understanding of the aesthetic via Kant. Yet beyond understanding the aesthetic, this book hopes to show that a Marxist defence of creativity and the imagination is not a quixotic enterprise.

***

I would like to thank the following people who have at some point given feedback on the work in this book. Mark Bould, Martin Gaughan, Ben Highmore, Esther Leslie, Alberto Toscano, Jason Toynbee, Greg Tuck and Joel Wainwright. Of course they are not responsible for any errors of judgment that remain. Finally, my thanks to Colleen Coalter at Bloomsbury for her support.

1

Disinterring Kant

For Kant, the term 'critique' means less to call into question than to establish the universal principles for how something is possible. The *Critique of Pure Reason* investigates the principles by which we can objectively know the world. *The Critique of Practical Reason* investigates the principles by which we can act morally in the world. The *Critique of Judgment* investigates the principles by which we can respond in the register of the aesthetic to the world. The problem for Kant is that the principles by which we can rationally know the world and the principles by which we can act morally within the world seem to leave little room for each other, an embarrassing contradiction which bourgeois scholarship is keen to gloss over, despite the fact that Kant very openly hopes to show in the third *Critique* that the power of aesthetic judgment may act as a way of mediating between the fissured halves of his philosophical architecture.

We may define bourgeois scholarship on Kant as constitutionally unable to interrogate the historical and class-conditioned nature of Kant's work or its own interpretations. Needless to say, this is not simply a matter of filling in the social and historical context of Kant, but rather seeing how Kant's context inscribes itself into every line of philosophy that he wrote. This inscription of the social into discourse must begin by combating the massive homogenization which bourgeois scholarship casts over Kant, turning the very heterogeneous philosophical materials that can be gleaned within his work into an unproblematic unity. Kant's philosophical architecture is best characterized as a polyphonic structure whose tensions and contradictions give off many different notes, whose very discordance should be a matter of great interest. Kant was writing at a time when he could develop in embryonic form the most extraordinary seeding of intellectual traditions that would subsequently in their later historical elaboration separate out and confront one another in often antagonistic terms, their differences hardening into the mutually exclusive divisions of intellectual labour and internecine academic warfare that came to characterize bourgeois intellectual life. But in Kant, these embryonic methodologies, such as phenomenology, empiricism, rationalism, logical positivism, linguistics, cognitive psychology, moral philosophy, socio-biology and vitalism, still coexist uneasily but with a productive frisson within the same philosophical framework. So it would be strange if one could not also detect within such a heterogeneous field some of the proto-forms of Marxist thought itself. I will argue that we can indeed detect anticipations of what would later become key concepts in Marxism, such as dialectics, praxis, the social individual, mimesis, production, mediation and the metabolic exchange with nature. Taken as a whole, Kant's thought is like a dramatic staging at the level of philosophy of the main contours and contradictions of bourgeois society, a staging which stress-tests the limited horizons of bourgeois thought in much the same way that the great Marxist literary theorists such as Raymond Williams, Terry Eagleton, Pierre Macherey and Fredric Jameson taught us to approach literary works as generative products that enact the contradictory impulses of their era. Yet Anglophone Marxism has very largely taken a disappointingly unproductive 'orthodox' position on Kant's aesthetic philosophy and as a result has cut itself off from or disavowed its genealogical relationship to an important philosophical resource. Of course there is a basis to the interpretation of Kant as a bourgeois philosopher, something that Kantian-Marxism, from Goldmann through to Colletti and Karatani, tends to deny. However, this bourgeois dimension to Kant's philosophical architecture is radically unstable, and an anti-bourgeois Kant is just as readily discernable within the third *Critique*.

The immense gulf

The bourgeois tradition of analytic philosophy tends to view Kant's *oeuvre* as one in which the second and third *Critique*s add the domains of moral reason and aesthetics to the first, thus *completing* Kant's system. This mentality of adding and completing fails to appreciate the extent to which all Kant's *Critiques* were motivated by a profound unease and troubling sense of the contradictions within his work. The third *Critique* is deeply troubling for the analytic tradition. It is not a text that has erased the marks of its own process of production (e.g. it was published after the first edition with two introductions) or a text that is tidily sewn up and finished. It comes across as a work in progress, zigzagging unexpectedly into new terrain (there is no explicit rationale for the unexpected introduction of the sublime), formulating different sometimes contradictory perspectives (on the conceptuality or non-conceptuality of the beautiful, for example) and returning anxiously to issues which earlier we had been told were settled (the section on the 'Dialectic of Aesthetic Judgment' appears to decisively reformulate Kant's Deduction of Pure Taste in relation to moral reason). For the bourgeois reception of Kant, where a lack of conceptual clarity is symptomatic of a failure of logical thinking on the part of the individual concerned, all this is deeply troubling, and there is a tendency to repress these fissures and tensions.

If it is the case that the third *Critique* neatly rounds off Kant's 'system' as the bourgeois scholars like to think, why does the third *Critique* open with a devastating admission of 'an immense gulf' (Kant 1987: 14) between the faculties of the understanding and of reason, between cognitive judgments according to the visible nature of things and moral judgments according to the supersensible principles of 'the good'? The problem for Kant is that his philosophy is painfully divided between two halves, which do not, as Adorno would say, add up. The objects of theoretical philosophy mapped out in *Critique of Pure Reason* are the '*concepts of nature*' (Kant 1987: 9), which generate theoretical cognition governed by a priori principles immune to experience and the individual experiencing subject. Practical philosophy, which formed the basis of *Critique of Practical Reason*, by contrast, is governed by the concept of freedom which negates the given determinateness implied by concepts of nature and 'gives rise to expansive principles for the determination of the will' (Kant 1987: 10). Practical philosophy is thus the domain of moral philosophy, because it is only when we can make choices, that is act independently from mechanically deterministic causes, that free will becomes a possibility and that the reflection on the moral principles for our practices becomes relevant.

Now, as Kant notes, this division between theoretical and practical philosophy had led to some confusion, because we might think, according to it, that *all* practical activity was governed by the principle of free will. But this is not so, because much (indeed most) of our practical activity is in fact governed by the a priori conceptual principles of nature. So Kant makes a further distinction within practical activity between the *technically practical* and the *morally practical* (Kant 1987: 10). The technically practical comes under the domain of theoretical philosophy (essentially natural science). And it becomes clear which of the two practical parts of philosophy (technical and moral) dominates life in practical terms.

> All technically practical rules (i.e., those of art and of skill in general, or for that matter prudence, i.e., skill influencing people's volition), insofar as their

principles rest on concepts, must be included only in theoretical philosophy, as corollaries. For they concern nothing but the possibility of things according to concepts of nature; and this includes not only the means we find in nature for producing them, but even the will (as power of desire and hence as a natural power), as far as it can be determined, in conformity with the mentioned rules, by natural incentives... domestic, agricultural, or political economy, the art of social relations, the precepts of hygiene, or even the general theory [Lehre] of [how to attain] happiness, indeed not even – with that goal in mind – the taming of our inclinations and the subjugation of our affects... all of these arts contain only rules of skill, which are therefore only technically practical, for producing an affect that is possible according to concepts of nature about causes and effects...

Kant (1987: 11)

The cultivation of techniques and skills across a range of social practices is associated with instrumentality insofar as it is designed to achieve a purpose that, it is implied, advances individual interests. The ability of such skills to be effective in their instrumental pursuits is in turn dependent on techniques obeying nature or 'the possibility of things according to concepts of nature'. There is more than a kernel of materialism here. The wealth of techniques developed in the economy of agriculture rests on the nature of nature to which those techniques have adapted themselves in the pursuit of agricultural production. The difficulty comes when the active side of the process, the one which signals our intervention into nature as creative beings consciously choosing within a determinate range of possibilities, is closed down. Thus, as Kant implies, the techniques of political economy (that is to say market transactions) also rest solely on the concepts of nature. Kant even suggests that techniques developed to subdue our natural inclinations towards self-interested goals are themselves instrumental goals cultivated on the basis of 'concepts of nature about causes and effects'. The circle appears to be closed. The subject is surrounded by a reified nature, which they can do little to change.

Thus the realm of morally practical action is hugely diminished and circumscribed on all sides by the realm of the technically practical. Morally practical activity is governed by reason, that is the exercise of free will. But reason appears to have little to do; it has little scope for 'legislation' when it comes to the domain of the technically practical. All it can do, as Kant puts it:

... with regard to theoretical cognition (of nature) ... (given the familiarity with the laws that it has attained by means of the understanding) is to use given laws to infer consequences from them, which however remain always with nature.

Kant (1987: 13)

Here the shrunken scope of Kant's moral reason stands exposed with courageous honesty and it is this that constitutes the central problem that the *Critique of Judgment* seeks to address, via the aesthetic. If reason can only 'infer consequences' from the laws of nature then it is barely the exercise of moral reason at all and is instead the splitting off of reason from its moral powers and the subordination of it to the understanding. This is the transformation of reason into mere rationality. Kant's distinction between the technically practical and the morally practical anticipates Herbert Marcuse's critique of technological rationality. At the point of production and consumption, the 'efficient individual is the one whose performance is an action only insofar as it is the proper reaction to the objective requirements of the apparatus' (Marcuse 1982: 142). The Kantian motif of the scope for individual reason shrinking in the face of an objective world of imperatives seemingly resistant to a moral realm of 'oughts' is powerfully evoked here. One hundred and fifty years after Kant, the tension which he describes between the technically practical and the morally practical is, under the force of this technological rationality, encouraging a self-denying impatience with the very *notion* of freedom and critical autonomous thinking. Commenting on the fate of the subject under advanced capitalism, Marcuse, in a strong echo and lament for the loss of the Kantian moral subject, notes:

> His matter-of-factness, his distrust of all values which transcend the facts of observations, his resentment against all 'quasi-personal' and metaphysical interpretations, his suspicion of all standards which relate the observable order of things, the rationality of the apparatus, to the rationality of freedom – this whole attitude serves all too well those who are interested in perpetuating the prevailing form of matters of fact.
>
> Marcuse (1982: 145)

Yet this profound division which Kant's philosophy prophetically anticipates is too frequently passed over in silence by Kantian scholars or managed away by other means. For Paul Guyer, it is not 'immediately apparent what gulf Kant has in mind' in his opening remarks of the third *Critique* (Guyer 1992: 21). Acknowledging, though, that some emerging problem between determination and freedom is evidently troubling Kant, Guyer resolves the issue by arguing that since the determinateness of our rationally constructed grid for mapping appearances of causality in nature is grounded in the transcendental subject, it is not incompatible with the principle of moral reason, which, similarly, we ourselves bring to bear on human nature. So Guyer retains the 'unity' of the three critiques by absorbing the incipient but deterministic materialism of theoretical philosophy, the moral questions posed by practical philosophy and the aesthetic into the idealist transcendental subject. These are merely in the end different components of a unified transcendental subject, not symptoms of problems in the real world.

Within bourgeois scholarship, the idea of a *break* between the first and third *Critique* has been resisted, but the more the third *Critique* is recovered from the traditional hierarchy which usually treats it as a minor footnote, the more it seems to call into question the basis of the first two *Critiques*. Rudolf Makkreel's important book *Imagination and Interpretation in Kant* (1990), for example, identifies how the third *Critique* lays the philosophical basis for developing our interpretative, decoding and imaginative capacities that the first *Critique* largely shuts down. Makkreel conceives the third *Critique* as making an 'important redefinition and expansion of the imagination's tasks' (1990: 45) on the first *Critique* but without challenging its foundations. Nor does Makkreel show any interest in exploring the political implications of the new powers of interpretation and imaginative reconstruction that Kant lays out in the third *Critique*.

In 'The Idea of Genesis in Kant's Aesthetics' (originally published in 1963), the early Deleuze noted that the faculty of reason has an interest that is *metaphorical* in the beauty of nature, that is it detects in the forms of nature analogies for rational ideas (2000: 65). This is a kind of play outside the usual commands of moral judgments, and indeed cognitive judgment, and while it is also (for Deleuze) outside aesthetic judgment strictly speaking it gives us a model of what the aesthetic is doing – playing with nature for the presentation of ideas. This is significant because it shows how in the third *Critique* Kant was thinking about how the aesthetic could overcome the divisions between the faculties that the previous *Critiques* had revealed. As Deleuze notes, in the third *Critique* 'Kant has never been closer to a dialectical conception of the faculties' (Deleuze 2000: 63). However, Deleuze in his early engagement with Kant is as committed to explicating the supposed systematic unity of Kant's thought and disavowing contradiction as any mainstream Kantian scholar. Deleuze certainly inverts the usual bourgeois hierarchy between the three *Critiques*. For him the *Critique of Judgment* provides the *ground* for the other two *Critiques*. The ability of the faculties of the understanding and reason to alternate according to their different tasks (cognition or moral judgment) presupposes a certain freedom, namely a freedom to choose, a freedom to bring intuition, imagination, concepts and moral-political ideas into particular configurations according to the *modus operandi* of the two faculties (understanding and reason). Thus, *freedom* underpins the obligations that both faculties impose in the giving of their judgments and it is in the aesthetic that the genesis of this freedom, Deleuze argues, is to be grounded. As Deleuze puts it, 'every determinate proportion of the faculties presupposes the possibility of this [the aesthetic's] free and spontaneous harmony' (Deleuze 2000: 68). This is an important idea, but it will need a much more substantive social and materialist grounding in the course of this book than Deleuze is interested in offering. In formulating the third *Critique* as the ground for the first two *Critiques*, Deleuze also smoothes out the contradictions and internal tensions of Kant's work. If the third *Critique* is the ground for the first two *Critiques*, it is also a rupture with them and indeed has its own internal ruptures. For example, in the (second) introduction we have seen that Kant includes 'art' in the craft sense and 'skill' under the category of the technically practical, and yet he is a bit more equivocal in the first introduction, situating a craft skill such as surveying as a scholia or sub-branch of the natural science of geometry which opens up some distance with the technically practical (Kant 1987: 388). Further shifts that open up a space for thinking of (craft) practice as having some substantive differentiation from theoretical philosophy and the technically practical are abundant in the text, as we shall see.

Kant's historical and philosophical context

For historical materialists, the twists and turns of a text or an *oeuvre* especially one produced by a philosopher as great as Kant should be decoded as signs of historically emerging social contradictions. Adorno remarked that from 'a certain point of view, the fissures and flaws in a philosophy are more essential to it than the continuity of its meaning' (Adorno 1991a: 160). In *The German Ideology*, Marx slams Kant's *Critique of Practical Reason* and sees in him a 'whitewashing spokesman' for the German bourgeoisie (Marx and Engels 1989: 99). The paralysis of moral practice and freedom, for example, in Kant's philosophy 'fully corresponds to the impotence, depression and wretchedness of the German burghers' (Marx and Engels 1989: 97) when compared to the commercial activity of the English bourgeoisie or the political activity of the French bourgeoisie. This is akin to the Marx of *The Communist Manifesto*, praising the heroic phase of the bourgeoisie for tearing away the remnants of feudalism and seeing in the development of the cash nexus a laying bare of the new more clearly defined class relations of capitalism (Marx and Engels 1985: 82). Later, however, with his theory of commodity fetishism in *Capital*, Marx would fundamentally rethink the cash nexus and see in it new powers of mystification.

In terms of Kant's historical situation, Adorno puts things more dialectically than Marx on this score:

> Kant stands precisely on the threshold, the historical threshold, at which the potential, the destructive potential of heteronomy, that is, the passive acceptance of what is merely the case, has appeared menacingly on the horizon, just as on the other side of the horizon the shadows of the old dogmatism are about to be dissipated and to disappear. I believe that the dialectical image, the historical juncture which enables us to understand Kant is precisely the moment in which these two conflicting historical tendencies arrive at a kind of stalemate, a point at which each balances the other and enters into a highly complex configuration within his philosophy.
>
> Adorno (2001a: 121)

The old dogmatism shadowing the Enlightenment modernity of Kant's philosophy is still in evidence where Kant associates moral reason with categories derived from theology, such as the soul and God. Unlike Marx, however, in *The German Ideology*, Adorno does not associate the paralysis of reason with the *backwardness* of the German bourgeoisie. More tellingly, the advancing threat of heteronomy, which 'has appeared menacingly on the horizon', is not to be traced to the dissipating dogmatism of feudalism, but in fact is *internal* to the very development of bourgeois economic relations that are the future horizon. The classic articulation of this theory comes of course from Lukács and the collection of essays published in 1923 as *History and Class Consciousness*. There Lukács built on Marx's critique of commodity fetishism in *Capital*, where the relations between commodities in the market – for example, their rising and falling prices, their availability or scarcity, their embrace of the masses or their exclusivity – acquire the appearance (not an illusion but an institutional reality within the ontologically stratified real) of an autonomous dynamic between commodities themselves and their universal means of exchange, money. The result is that the moral and political dimensions of our social being atrophy, becoming increasingly *contemplative* (Lukács 1971: 89). When the commodity structure becomes universalized throughout society (once labour-power has become a universal commodity) its dominance, Lukács argued, pushes the fetishism inherent in it, throughout all institutional arrangements and conscious life. This generalization of fetishism Lukács called *reification*. As is well known, this generalization was grasped by Lukács through his reading and appropriation of Max Weber's distinction between formal and substantive rationality. But this distinction in turn derives, as we have seen, from Kant's distinction between the technically and the morally practical.

Lucien Goldmann (2011: 38–49) suggests that it was the very economic underdevelopment of Germany (the 'wretchedness of the German burghers', according to Marx) and its fractured condition as a political unity that forced Kant into a decisive confrontation with David Hume's empiricism, in order to refashion the central philosophical resources of the European bourgeoisie: rationalism (which dominated French thought) and empiricism (which dominated English and Scottish thought). The challenge of empiricism was that it perfectly suited the conditions of the English bourgeoisie, as Perry Anderson argued (1964: 40), but as such it was a philosophy that could only weaken the struggle against the power of the aristocracy in the rest of Europe. For only in England (and a now subordinated Scotland) had the bourgeoisie already acquired economic and political power (thanks to the mid-seventeenth century revolution) to which the aristocracy had accommodated themselves. Empiricism, with its affirmation of the *actually existing*, provided little in the way of radical intellectual resources for the coming struggle in the rest of Europe where nearly 150 years after the English revolution, the aristocracy still dominated. Hume's accentuation of the scepticism which empiricism has towards any structures which predetermine sensuous experience of reality certainly fits with a consolidated market economy already happily reproducing itself day in and day out. But for Kant, to have given up on the prospect that a post-aristocratic world would have its own built-in unity and harmony based on reason, before the bourgeoisie has fully acquired power, would have been to have lost a powerful cultural, intellectual and philosophical weapon. At the same time, it was clear that empirical sense-experience as mapped out by Locke and Hume had to be incorporated into a new philosophical configuration with rationalism. The confident, even dogmatic rationalism of an ascending bourgeois class in France, about to overthrow the old order as Kant wrote the third *Critique*, could not be taken up unproblematically in Germany, whose wretched political underdevelopment had to be confronted as an empirical fact if it was to be overcome.

If rationalism orientated Kant's thinking towards objective structures (even if only of the mind) that hinted at social determinateness, and the empirical tradition attuned Kant's thinking towards sensuous apprehension and the activity of the flesh-and-blood individual in making sense of the world, the aesthetic turn added something to the mix that helped Kant begin to overcome the aporias in his philosophical architecture. What Kant's philosophy utilizes from the aesthetic, and what constitutes a methodological break between the first two *Critiques* and the third, is in fact *metaphor*. We have seen that for Deleuze, Kant's faculty of reason in the third *Critique* has a metaphorical interest in nature as material forms for reason's ideas. It is this feature of Kant's philosophical architecture that will be developed in the course of this book. It is through metaphor that Kant pushes past the dichotomy between material nature and its subjective reordering. I do not see metaphor as merely a device of the aesthetic, a literary technique for example. Rather, metaphor represents a species-being capacity we have to remake the world, a remaking in which the imagination plays a crucial role. Praxis, where theory or ideas or intellectual formulations combine with sense-based experiential practice in an often tension-filled way, makes human labour possible and our productive activity historical and social in nature. Metaphor is an activity of imaginative reshaping that feeds and is simultaneously made possible by what Marx and Engels called the '[t]he first historical act … the production of the means to satisfy … needs, the production of material life itself' (Marx and Engels 1989: 48).

Kantian-Marxism

After the death of Marx in 1883, a version of Marxism came to dominate the international Marxist movement with extraordinary completeness that bore the mark of a historical reification. Orthodox Marxism was unconsciously in tune with the revival of interest in Kant (especially the neo-Kantianism of the Marburg School) insofar as its 'concepts of nature' were extended without modification to the laws of society. What were taken to be invariant regularities found in the scientific observation of nature were transferred to society where similarly invariant relations were said to produce social laws. Marxist theory discovers these laws and distinguishes them from the otherwise bewildering profusion of events, causes and forces that make up history. Amongst all these observable phenomena, economic causes and class interests are the key conditioning forces that explain the other phenomena in history. These economic forces have a uniformity and necessity of effects just as natural laws do. This model of Marxism, which became the orthodoxy after Marx's death, underpinned the thinking of most Marxists in this period, despite various political differences. There are strong continuities on this score between the Second International Marxism of Plekhanov, Kautsky and Bernstein, and the Third International Marxism of the Bolsheviks, despite the space which Lenin and Trotsky also kept open for political intervention that could modify historical 'laws'. For example, the Bolshevik Nicolai Bukharin unashamedly conflated the cause-effect laws of nature with social processes in an exceptionally crude way (Bukharin 1978) as Lenin himself noted.

The shared philosophical framework of orthodox Marxism and the neo-Kantian revival set the terms for the emergence of Kantian-Marxism and its limitations. Kant's first *Critique* explored the transcendental subject as a universal system of consciousness that makes objective cognitions of the world possible. For the Austrian-Marxist Max Adler, Kant's transcendental subject is thus read as providing the philosophical foundations for understanding the social construction of individual consciousness. The kernel of materialism that could be found in Kant's synthesis of rationalism and empiricism in the first *Critique* is that it insists that consciousness is a determinate and structured affair, something which empiricism on its own could not sustain. Unfortunately, in uncritically sliding from the transcendental subject to the social, from nature to culture, Adler committed himself to the nascent reification inscribed into Kant's philosophical argument which neo-Kantianism then reinforced by 'tidying' Kant up and downplaying or eliminating as mystical his crucial category of the noumena, which acts as an internal critique of Kant's universalization of empirical reality under logical structures.

This failure to be adequately critical of the deterministic tendencies, abstract universalism and empiricism of the first *Critique* is typical of Kantian-Marxism, and it also compromised the interest of the Kantian-Marxists of this period in the second *Critique*. For Adler and the German Kantian-Marxist Karl Vorländer, Kant's second *Critique* mapped out moral principles that were congruent with Marxism but which Marxism itself seemed reluctant to articulate. Kant's categorical moral imperative that every human being should be treated as an end in themselves and not merely as a means for some end that is extrinsic to them seemed to provide a moral dimension to the critique of the commodification of labour. Goldmann rejects the view that Kant's categorical imperative is merely formal. If its content cannot be realized then that points to the problems of bourgeois society and its atomistic economic structure, not Kant's moral law (Goldmann 2011: 168). For the Kantian-Marxists, the moral arguments of the second *Critique* could be *added* to the now dominant positivist Marxism in order to explain not only why socialism was inevitable, but also why socialism would be morally desirable (Kolakowski 1978: 247).

The problem with Goldmann's attempt to find bourgeois society wanting because it does not substantively live up to Kant's moral law is that it has little to say concerning the relationship between abstract moral injunctions and the fact that in its phenomenal appearances, capitalism does indeed seem to live up to such moral principles. Thus abstract moral principles provide ideological cover for decontextualized empirical action where force and violence has been disguised. If every human being should be treated as an end in themselves, then there is a problem when the dominant socio-historical form of being an end is for the capitalist to assert their private property rights as owners of the means of production. Since this consigns the majority to being means for that end we have here an irresolvable contradiction, 'an antinomy, right against right' as Marx put it (1983: 225). And yet the abstract capitalist principle that everyone has a right to property, if only their own labour-power, gives the appearance that freedom has been universalized and that relations are based on the right to enter into contractual relations based on what you have that you want to exchange.

Despite this, Goldmann's argument that Kant's moral law constitutes a critique of the content of bourgeois life at some level does carry some weight. In the second *Critique*, Kant repeatedly cites examples to show that the maximization of self-interest, now the dominant principle of life, could never become a universal law without annihilating itself (Kant 2002: 41). But in recoiling in horror from bourgeois life as it is lived, Kant is forced to make the moral law as abstract and formal as possible, because the actual content of social life is so antithetical to the formulation of a genuinely universal moral law. Yet while Kant's abstract formalism rescues the moral law from a society unable to generate up any moral principle from its actual conduct, other than a subjective maxim to advance at the expense of everyone else if necessary, the stigmata of bourgeois society inscribes itself in the Kantian moral law nonetheless. For its very abstractness, which can then only be heroically put into action by an abstract monadic subject, implies that moral principles require no alternative *social relations* and *institutions* in order to be realized consistently. This leaves the actually existing social relations of capitalism that systematically violates the right to be an end for oneself again and again, untouched. Mere empirical identification of such abuses likewise lack the resources to analyse the pattern of systematic infringements and the causal forces responsible for that pattern. This is why the combination of abstract reason and decontextualized empiricism which structures the first *Critique* is problematic and why the moral law of the second *Critique* cannot simply be added to it, but is itself, in its abstractness, the symptom of a problem that has been individualized at a transcendental level.

What though of the concept of 'purposiveness' that is so central to the third *Critique*? Perhaps this concept could be *added* to the first *Critique* and correct its determinism by reintroducing human consciousness back into the equation? However, the introduction of purposiveness by Kantian-Marxism into a natural science view of social forces only challenges the orthodox Marxist extension of natural law to social analysis, if the purposes are registered as more than the passing of natural laws across the screen of consciousness. If purposiveness is to generate new forms of causal relations it must signify how human consciousness, via practice, interposes itself into natural laws and produces new kinds of connections that break with mechanical cause-effect relations.

The importance of the third *Critique* in this regard was at once both recognized and bungled by Kantian-Marxists. A representative figure here is the Kantian-influenced Marxist and Italian philosopher Lucio Colletti. He notes how the late-nineteenth-century Marxists, both Kantian-inspired reformists such as Bernstein and orthodox Marxists such as Plekhanov, remained committed to 'a vulgar and naïve conception of the "economy"' (Colletti 1972: 63). This conception separated the 'economy' from the social relations in which it is embedded and eradicated the essential notion of *production* as the making of men and women, of ideas and of the social relations themselves as a historical process. It thus reduced the economy to technology and techniques determining everything else. So far, so promising. As Colletti puts it,

> Traditional materialism, which sees men as products of their environment, forgets, according to Marx that men in turn change their circumstances and that 'it is essential to educate the educator himself'. It forgets that it is not enough to consider practical-material circumstances as the *cause* and man as their *effect* – the inverse must also be taken into account.
>
> Colletti (1972: 66)

Colletti identifies Kant's comments on cause and effect in *Critique of Judgment*, correctly in my view, as establishing the philosophical basis for a break with the mechanistic and naturalistic view of social phenomena that more or less eradicates reflexive consciousness. In *Critique of Judgment*, Kant discusses how the interposition of conscious aims into the cause-effect process transforms the relations of cause and effect given by nature. Instead the effect desired rounds on and transforms causal chains as a result of conscious, intentional goals (Kant 1987: 251). This, as Colletti notes, is the basis of Marx's concept of production as an imaginative projection of goals through material forces that differentiates our species from purely instinctual activity. This teleological orientation Kant called final cause, but in the act of labour, Colletti points out, it is coupled with the efficient causes that govern natural relations.

> On the other hand, insofar as it is necessary for the *realization* of the idea or the labour project that it takes into account the specific nature of the materials employed, the labour process reveals as well as finalism, *efficient causation*.
>
> Colletti (1972: 67)

Colletti seeks to *combine* the teleological viewpoint (final causes) with those 'concepts of nature' that governed Kant's *Critique of Pure Reason* (efficient causes). With the teleological orientation implied by the final cause, a subjective *concept* or idea becomes a causal force within natural relations. As we shall see, it is no accident that Kant manages to formulate a concept close to the Marxist notion of praxis via his consideration of the aesthetic. Yet Colletti does not draw the conclusion of a *break* in Kant's methodology. Instead, he evidently sees the third *Critique* in much the same way as bourgeois scholars do, as 'completing' Kant's system. And so Colletti, despite his critique of the positivism of the Second International, reproduces his own commitments to positivism. For Colletti, the lesson of the third *Critique* is that it must be added to the lessons of the first *Critique*, which he does not read against the grain. Thus the idea of praxis, which he wins from Kant, is immediately eviscerated by reducing it to the notion of the 'idea' or theory that lies behind *observation and hypothesis in empirical scientific experiment* (Colletti 1972: 68). This, however, is not a theory of praxis, since natural scientific experiment only engineers a laboratory situation in order to reveal natural causal relations which act *outside* the laboratory *independent* of the activity of human beings. Thus to reduce Kant's concept of purposiveness to natural scientific observation and deductive hypothesis is to carelessly throw away the insight into praxis that he wins from the third *Critique*. As we shall see in due course, Kant's concept of purposiveness in the third *Critique* and its related concepts, such as reflective judgment, formal purposiveness and even the more problematic concept of purposiveness without purpose, represent a break with the first *Critique*. They are not analogous to the framework of deduction which structures the first *Critique*. Rather something new is added to the philosophical architecture which turns the third *Critique* into a critique of the first *Critique* and its reified structures.

Colletti's failure to draw the right conclusions from his insight into the third *Critique* can only be put down to a powerful anti-Hegelian animus which typically motivates an attraction (Marxist or otherwise) to Kant. For Colletti, Hegelian-Marxism remains trapped in an abstract schema of dialectical patterns removed from real history, in which the Idea dominates reality, and indeed seeks to smash reality in a romantic rage against the facts of nature. His gloss on Hegel and its dire impact on Marxism is outlined in his book *Marxism and Hegel*:

'Real' are not those things external to thought, but those things penetrated by thought ('pensate'): i.e. those things which are *no longer things* but simple 'logical objects' or ideal moments. The negation, the 'annihilation' of matter is precisely in this passage from 'outside' to 'within'.

Colletti (1979: 16)

We can immediately detect how limited Colletti's vision of the power of consciousness to interpose itself into the cause-effect relations of nature must be if he denounces the idea of 'thought' penetrating things. Instead for Colletti, thought, the idea, and theory is restricted to scientific deductions as it moves from the empirical to the universal. But such deductions merely formulate as axioms what already exists in nature. The dialectic, by contrast, is a methodology that allows us to think reflexively about consciousness as at once grounded in being while also transforming matter and being in social practices that include our metabolic exchange with nature. If Kantian-Marxism had not been so quick to follow the neo-Kantian elimination of Kant's distinction between phenomena and noumena, then this fundamental mistake of equating the deductive-empirical terrain of natural science with the real (the dynamic totality of relations) might have been more easily avoided. Thus, Colletti did not advance much further than the first wave of Kantian-Marxists, and his hostility to the dialectic is very largely the cause of this theoretical stagnation.

For Colletti, Hegel represents an unacceptable romantic-Promethian destruction of reality under the power of consciousness. Reality for Colletti, again in positivistic vein, consists of:

all those determinate propositions and statements founded on the principle of non-contradiction, to which thought remains bound as long as it considers itself tied to and constricted by the existence of factual data.

Colletti (1979: 69)

The extension of this framework to social analysis was to eventually prove devastating for Colletti's Marxism. His floundering in trying to reconcile the principle of non-contradiction with the centrality of contradiction in Marx's analysis of *social* relations is painfully evident in an interview with Perry Anderson (Colletti 1974: 19). Along with his commitment to non-contradiction in social reality goes the logical positivist's commitment to the separation of things, which is the basis of market economics. His hostility to Hegel's *destruction of the finite* is a peculiarly literal reading of Hegel's philosophy. For Colletti, in his essay 'From Hegel to Marcuse' Hegel's idealism can be found in his desire to annihilate the finite as an independently existing thing in favour of the 'infinite', which Colletti reads as God. He fails to see how crucial a philosophical move this is as a strategy of de-reification that reconnects what appears to be independent and separate (the finite, Marx's phenomenal forms, etc.) to its deeper, concealed conditions of existence (the totality). He also appears to believe that Hegel's insistence on the contradictory character of everything that exists promotes an anti-materialist 'ephemerality and nullity' that facilitates the destruction of matter by consciousness or God (Colletti 1972: 123). Such philosophical commitments no doubt played their part in Colletti's political trajectory, which involved not only leaving Marxism behind, but eventually joining the political camp of Silvio Berlucsoni. That is not a happy omen but it would be absurd to think that the road to reaction or even reformism is the only path one can take from Kant.

Now, while the Hegelian-Marxist tradition from Lukács onwards generally regards Kant's philosophy as hopelessly paralyzed by a series of dualities, this is not true of Lucien Goldmann, who, despite his philosophical closeness to Lukács, unusually situates Kant as a precursor to and in the tradition of Hegel, Marx and Lukács. He sees Kant as laying the 'philosophical foundations for a most penetrating critique of bourgeois individualist society' (Goldmann 2011:110) by seeding the philosophical development of the category of totality (epistemology) and community (politics/ethics). Goldmann's great strength is teasing out the social and historical origins and implications of what appear to bourgeois scholars, exclusively philosophical issues. We have already noted his argument about how Kant's philosophical reworking of empiricism and rationalism was shaped by German political and economic backwardness. Reading Goldmann on Kant, it is clear that Kant's method was a proto-dialectical one in many ways, as he proceeded by forcing a confrontation between these two great philosophical traditions. Kant critiques empiricism for its inability to conceive of pre-structuring conditions that make individual experience possible. And from this Kantian-Marxism sees in the first *Critique* a model of the subject as socially conditioned (Goldmann 2011: 156–157). Conversely, Kant critiques rationalism for its haughty distance from and lack of engagement with empirical experience. However, in line with Kantian-Marxism generally, Goldmann is insufficiently critical of the limited extent to which Kant's intimations of totality in the first *Critique* remain trapped within an abstract and monadic framework of rationalism. He tends to treat the three *Critiques* as having an overall coherence, thus failing to identify a break between the first two *Critiques* and the third or identify how crucial the aesthetic is in achieving that break (through) that connects Kant to Marxism. In relation to the first *Critique*, Goldmann writes,

> the function of combining the material of sensible impressions into universal experience was fulfilled by form. Between form and matter there was no contradiction. The two being, as it were, complimentary, neither could have an autonomous existence; together however, they constituted human thought as it is encountered in everyday life and in the empirical sciences.
>
> Goldmann (2011: 168)

As we shall see, however, the immense gulf already discussed between theoretical philosophy and practical philosophy derives directly from the division between form and content in the first *Critique*. The intimations in that work for overcoming that dichotomy cannot leave Kant's conceptions of form and content, rationalism and individual sense-perception, unreconstructed. The model of 'combining the material of sensible impressions into universal experience' is, as we shall see in the next chapter, fundamentally contradictory in the first *Critique*. As with Colletti, Goldmann is insufficiently critical of the overextension of the natural empirical sciences as a model for understanding 'everyday life' in its social and historical dimension.

Nevertheless, that Kant has a critical procedure that is rather more than simply collapsing into the static dualisms that Lukács found in Kant has been more recently affirmed by Kojin Karatani in his influential book *Transcritique: Kant and Marx*. For Karatani, transcritique involves a 'critical oscillation' between the terms of an antinomy and between opposing discourses or positions. In the oscillation, critical thought becomes aware of the partial truths of each term and the incommensurable division between them, which in turn alludes to a transcendental or objective situation which encompasses the opposed terms but which neither side can grasp on its own, but which we can only allude to in the oscillation itself. This critical movement is a 'parallax', a constant shuttling between perspectives that *cannot* be synthesized (Karatani 2005: 47–50). So here we have a kind of parallax between two critical procedures: the Kantian parallax and the Hegelian dialectic. In the latter, it is the element of negation internal to a position or thing which causes it to stir, to move, to change. But the philosophically undesirable elimination of non-identity is the constant temptation of the dialectic as it presses forward into new syntheses. It was for this reason that Adorno was attracted to Kant's work, for it seemed a way to sustain the negativity of the dialectic beyond the moment of synthesis. Adorno wrote not of a parallax but of the 'vibration' in Kant's work between opposing propositions (Adorno 2001b: 110). Adorno is that rare Marxist who wanted to use Kant to revivify the dialectic, not to bury it.

There is a good reason why we should neither want to bury the dialectic nor maintain an absolute dichotomy between Kant and Hegel. From the perspective of the dialectic, the parallax as a critical procedure threatens to remain trapped within the antinomy and give up on transforming its fundamental conditions of existence. Yet, if, as Fredric Jameson argues, the dialectic actually has the binary opposition as its germinating ground (Jameson 2010) then the opposition between the parallax and the dialectic is only a partial truth, as Adorno sensed when he claimed with regard to the *Critique of Pure Reason* that 'the transition to dialectics is a necessary consequence of the objective shape of Kantian philosophy' (Adorno 2001a: 88). This is most explicitly the case where Kant advances his arguments by hurling the antithetical positions arising from his investigations into a 'dialectical combat arena' (Kant 1996: 455) as he puts it in the first *Critique*. The antithesis between nature and freedom comes to a decisive conclusion in the section entitled 'On the Dialectical Inferences of Pure Reason' in the first *Critique*, while the antithesis between the apparent objectivity and subjectivity of the aesthetic judgment again comes to a decisive reformulation in the chapter entitled 'Dialectic of Aesthetic Judgment' in the third *Critique*. If, on the one hand, the architecture of Kant's philosophy is characterized by a compartmentalization effect between his concepts, there is, on the other hand, an internal pressure observably building up within the first *Critique* that seeks to find points of mediation between the antinomies of his thought. The trajectory of his thought from the first to the third *Critique* is one in which an internal momentum within his philosophy to overcome these antinomies achieves a breakthrough via Kant's aesthetic turn – for the aesthetic may be thought of as the dialectical combat arena *par excellence*.

***

Both bourgeois and Kantian-Marxist traditions have tended to view Kant's work as a systematic unity, with the *Critiques* mapping out respectively the domains of objective knowledge, moral action and aesthetic taste in a neat division of intellectual labour for the transcendental subject. Even where bourgeois interpretations of Kant recognize that the third *Critique* is either opening up hermeneutic capacities occluded by the first *Critique* (Makkreel) or even that it provides the foundation of the first two *Critiques* (Deleuze) there is a marked reluctance to read Kant's work as a site of contradictions or link those contradictions to historical circumstances. Even the Kantian-Marxist tradition, trapped within the gravitational force field of orthodox Marxism and neo-Kantianism, has operated within this framework that each of the *Critiques* can be added together in a complimentary filling in of absences. Kantian-Marxism thus tried to add Kant's moral law to fill in the normative basis of Marxism without critiquing Kant's abstract formulations. This satisfaction with Kant's moral law derives from an insufficiently critical engagement with Kant's reworking of rationalism and empiricism in the first *Critique*. This reworking did not resolve the abstract determinism of rationalism or the limits of decontextualized phenomenal forms in the empirical tradition. Kantian-Marxists such as Adler, Colletti and Goldman were unable to perceive that the contradictions and limitations of the first *Critique* motivated Kant's aesthetic turn in which a partial but significant break was achieved from his hitherto existing philosophical architecture. Even when, as with Colletti, Kant's proto-dialectical concept of purposiveness is recognized, this is merely uncritically integrated into the reified objectivity of the first *Critique*. Thus, together with the bourgeois tradition, Kantian-Marxism has effaced what Lukács thought was Kant's greatness as a philosopher, namely that:

> he made no attempt to conceal the intractability of the problem by means of an arbitrary dogmatic resolution of any sort, but that he bluntly elaborated the contradiction and presented it in an undiluted form.
>
> Lukács (1971: 134)

While the Kantian and Kantian-Marxist tradition downplay Kant's internal contradictions, the orthodox-Marxist interpretation of Kant freezes Kant's contradictions into a static structure that trapped his thought completely. What is missing is a sense of an internal dynamic and momentum in Kant's thought, a sense of development and mutation that at least partially pushes past and reconfigures these contradictions in the third *Critique*. To really understand that a break occurs in the third *Critique*, we have to take seriously Kant's investigation into the aesthetic and its role in mediating between the dichotomies of nature and moral-political reason or freedom. To understand the problems Kant encountered in his parallax operation of bringing rationalism and empiricism into a new relationship, to understand how, despite the unresolved issues, Kant also began to lay the basis for going beyond the aporias of the first *Critique* and to appreciate how and to what extent Kant's aesthetic turn constituted a break in his philosophical structure, we need to turn now and assess the first *Critique* in more detail.

2

Kant's First *Critique* and the Problem of Reification

Like the third *Critique, The Critique of Pure Reason* has something of the quality of a work in progress. It exists in two versions (the A and B versions), which Kant published in 1781 and 1787, respectively. The task in this chapter is to map out the broad outlines of Kant's philosophical architecture and indicate which problems Kant will attempt to resolve by his aesthetic turn and which concepts he uses in the first *Critique* that he will return to or modify in the third *Critique* to think his way past the aporias of his philosophical position.

In the first *Critique*, Kant maps out what we might call, with very deliberate Newtonian connotations, a conceptual and perceptual machinery of consciousness. This was Kant's attempt to synthesize the two contesting philosophical traditions of rationalism, based on logic, and empiricism, based on sense-perception, into a single unified system. The conceptual and the perceptual/sensual mark the frontier not only between these two systems of thought but other antinomies as well, such as form and content, the social and the individual, the universal/necessary and the contingent and beyond Kant himself, in the twentieth century, logical positivism and phenomenology, as well as that wider debate within the social sciences concerning structure and agency or in linguistics between langue and parole. However, in trying to yoke the logical-rational to the empirical, Kant found himself caught between conflicting imperatives. In order to escape the tautology of rationalist logic, the conceptual apparatus of the machinery of consciousness needs the empirical to open it up to material that lies outside pure thought that unfolds its own logical relations. But in order to preserve the necessity and universality that logical principles guarantee, conceptuality must be firmly protected from any contamination by the empirical.

> No experience whatever can give us necessity. Experience can indeed teach us that something else usually follows. But it cannot teach us that something else must follow.
>
> Kant (1996: 162/A112)

This 'must' Kant will ground not in the real – which is flattened to the empirically observable – but in the transcendental subject, that is to say in the logical-rational principles of the mind that make intelligible experience possible in the first place. For Kant, the conceptual and the perceptual are dependent on each other; they must be *added* to each other but they are not to be thought of as *interdependent*. Instead for Kant they have a merely external relationship to one another and a deeply hierarchical relationship, with the conceptual lording it over the empirical and the experiential in order to preserve the universality and necessity of thought. However, this hierarchical relationship is qualified by Kant's 'parallax' methodology. The parallax alternation between conceptual and perceptual ordering gives Kant's philosophical architecture a latent dialectical quality but at the same time Kant strives to resist the tendential momentum within the first *Critique* to break down the absolute wall between concepts and the experiential categories of individual perception. This is one of the central dramas of the first *Critique*.

The contradictions between the conceptual and the perceptual in Kant's philosophical architecture are central to my exposition and critique of Kant's first *Critique* because the aesthetic is centrally concerned with their reconfiguration into a kind of perceptual thinking. At the deepest historical level, the split between conceptuality and percepts is grounded in that momentous historical rupture when intellectual labour in the form of the first priests emerged as a power over manual labour, at the dawn of class societies (Marx and Engels 1989: 52–53). But the particular relationship between conceptuality and percepts in Kant's philosophy speaks to a very modern and more historically specific problem. It concerns an emerging capitalist society that is shaking the foundations of the old. Here both conceptual power (tied to the sciences and technological innovation) and experiential categories (of scientific observation and social change) are acquiring new importance and centrality. On the other hand, the relationship between conceptuality and perception in Kant's philosophical architecture speaks to that emerging problem of reification, which I discussed in the previous chapter. For the separation of the conceptual from the perceptual, logical form from sensuous content, is precisely what rigidifies understanding, turning the properly determinate into something quite different, the deterministic. It is for this reason that I term Kant's faculty of understanding a 'machinery of consciousness' despite the emphasis that Kant also gives to the self-activity of the subject who must synthesize sensation into meaningful patterns of cognition. The problems which the first *Critique* poses in terms of its entrapment in a proto-positivistic and reified framework, which it is itself also undermining, provide the motive force for Kant's aesthetic turn in the third *Critique*.

The division between conceptuality and percepts is inextricably connected to and helps generate that division or antinomy between the faculty of the understanding, which governs cognition of the world, and the faculty of reason, which is supposed to govern our moral-political responses to the world cognized. The division between understanding and reason becomes one of the chief sources by which rationality, perversely, becomes separated from reason, appropriated as it were to the understanding, to begin its long march through the bourgeois centuries, combining advanced technology and planning with the most brutal and inhuman of projects. The split between understanding and reason is reproduced as the division between conceptuality and perception within the faculty of the understanding. This division protects conceptuality not only from the experiential life of the individual subject, which will become nothing more than a quantitative calculation under the capitalist *Ratio* as Kracauer called it (Kracauer 1995), but also from the historical and the social which the empirical registers, if only partially or symptomatically.

If the *Critique of Pure Reason* is fissured by the antinomy between the faculty of the understanding and the faculty of reason, where moral-political judgments are supposed to be exercised, then the other dichotomy which structures Kant's philosophical architecture in the first *Critique* is that between the phenomenal world of appearances and the noumenal realm which lies beyond empirical sense-perception. If the logico-rational is on the one hand divided off from the empirical, they are also added together on the basis that the a priori concepts of the understanding provide the logical rules by which we can process empirical phenomena. Yet this very *identity* between the logical and the empirical raises the prospect of a limit to this mode of knowledge acquisition. The first *Critique* insists on the virtues of the limits of empirically based knowledge as the basis of objective knowledge governed by logical relations while also being haunted by the limitations (especially to moral-political reasoning) when we can only know the world according to these logico-empirical relations. Phenomena for Kant are, by definition, appearances that we can process according to our conceptual and perceptual machinery of consciousness. But Kant is no Bishop Berkley; such phenomena he knows are generated by forces that have an existence that is independent of our apprehension of them (Kant 1996: 102/B71). It is just that for Kant these forces are absolutely and by definition beyond our capacity to register in the realm of the senses. This absolute division between phenomena and noumena will be one of the key modifications Kant will make to his philosophy with the third *Critique*. There, the aesthetic will be able to register something of what Kant calls the supersensible world. And this in turn seeds the development of critical philosophy and social science. For the noumena gestures towards a model of the real as a stratified ontology of appearances and essences that Marx would later develop.

The identity between the logico-empirical and the non-identity between the understanding and reason and between phenomena and noumena constitute one of the richest seams for philosophical discussion of Kant's work, for someone like Adorno. His masterful exposition of the first *Critique* in his lectures is still among the best available. On the question of identity and non-identity in the first *Critique*, Adorno famously wrote,

> To give a stark description we might say that the book contains an identity philosophy – that is, a philosophy that attempts to ground being in the subject – and also a non-identity philosophy – one that attempts to restrict that claim to identity by insisting on the obstacles, the *block*, encountered by the subject in its search for knowledge.
>
> Adorno (2001a: 66)

This notion of identity and non-identity fissuring Kant's philosophical architecture is crucial. Non-identity is not to be simply championed against identity in fact. For the negative side of non-identity is that it is closely connected to Kant's dichotomous philosophical structure. Conversely, the positive side of identity is that lying suppressed and unarticulated within it is the buried concept of mediation. We shall see that there is an internal momentum within Kant's philosophical architecture propelling him towards the sort of non-identical mediation that Adorno was searching for. This is why Kant's first *Critique* was so important for him:

> the profundity of a philosophy ... is not a matter of its capacity for resolving contradictions, but rather of its ability to bring to the surface contradictions that are deeply embedded in the subject under investigation, to raise such contradictions to the level of consciousness, and at the same time, to understand the necessity for them; that is, to understand their meaning.
>
> Adorno (2001a: 82).

The transcendental aesthetic

We should start, broadly as Kant did, with the perceptual machinery of consciousness that he called the transcendental aesthetic. The conceptual and perceptual machinery of consciousness that makes cognition possible has both empirical and transcendental dimensions. The transcendental dimension provides the a priori basis (independent of experience) for handling the empirical material in an intelligible way. Both the understanding (the conceptual machinery) and the aesthetic (the perceptual machinery) have transcendental a priori operations that govern their work. Both also have empirical dimensions (the 'content' of experience) which the a priori governs.

The perceptual dimension deals with specific sense data coming to the subject from outside. But this sense data is governed by an a priori but *non-conceptual* ability built into our perceptual apparatus which demands that we order sense data according to their spatial and temporal principles. As Kant puts it, 'the subject's receptivity for being affected by objects precedes necessarily all intuitions of these objects' (Kant 1996: 81/B42). That receptivity is transcendental or 'pure' intuition that is independent of and a condition for having the particular experiences which the individual 'processes'.

That our perceptual apparatus has an a priori basis that is non-discursive is significant because it acknowledges, within an overall abstract and idealist philosophy, the presence of the empirical body: 'All our intuitions, as sensible, rest on our being affected' (1996: 121B/93) notes Kant and of course this question of affect will become hugely significant in the third *Critique* in his discussion of the beautiful and the sublime, where something *felt* may stir thought beyond the reified mapping of the world by the understanding. In the first *Critique*, however, the contradiction between the 'social' dimension of the transcendental subject as an abstract and formal condition of experience and the empirical individual who does the experiencing is immediately evident where Kant argues that the pure intuition of space (and time) does not include anything empirical that can 'become objects of the senses for us'. Taste and colours, for example, are 'added effects of the special character of our organs' that are based on sensation and feeling, such as pleasure and displeasure (Kant 1996: 83/A29). Kant's aesthetic turn will try and address the question whether certain pleasures and displeasures, such as the beautiful and the sublime, can be considered as having an a priori dimension. He will argue in the third *Critique* that 'it is not the pleasure, but *the universal validity of this pleasure*' that is a priori (Kant 1987: 154) and this will open up the whole domain of intersubjectivity and communication, since pleasure is no longer conceived merely a private or inconsequential response to empirical things.

In the first *Critique*, the focus is by contrast on the relationship between the transcendental subject and the individual empirical subject in which the transcendental machinery of consciousness is operating. Accordingly, the empirical is raw data to be processed by the transcendental subject and Kant characterizes sensation as a *passive* reception of what has arrived to our senses from outside us. He contrasts this passivity of the senses with the active formation of concepts in the conceptual machinery of consciousness – which he describes as a *spontaneous* process of construction (Kant 1996: 171/A126). The nature of that spontaneity, however, will turn out to be deeply ambivalent and evacuated of that element of freedom that we would usually associate with spontaneity. By contrast, that part of the imagination that deals with sense-perception, what Kant calls the reproductive imagination, and which is supposed to therefore be determined by the necessities of putting together the temporal and spatial coordinates of phenomena, often seems to be an organizing, self-active power embodied in the individual subject and more authentically spontaneous. It is this dimension of the aesthetic that Kant will expand in the third *Critique*, and significantly uncouple from its subservient role in the first *Critique* of providing the faculty of the understanding and its concepts, the content with which to form cognitions.

The transcendental aesthetic, then, is the a priori organization of sense data according to our built-in principles of spatial and temporal mapping. Space is not derived from concepts but rather 'only through the presentation of space is … outer experience possible in the first place' (Kant 1996: 77/B38). Despite the importance accorded to the concepts of the faculty of the understanding, and which will later seed the development of formal logic, Kant's methodology accords great importance to the transcendental aesthetic for the development of concepts:

> … no geometric principles – e.g., the principle that in a triangle two sides together are greater than the third – are ever derived from universal concepts of *line* and *triangle*; rather, they are all derived from intuition, and are derived from it moreover a priori.
>
> Kant (1996: 79/B40)

Line and triangle are concepts of the understanding, but it is pure intuition of spatial relations that allows us to combine such concepts as 'line', 'length' and 'angle' into geometric principles. Thus, some form of figuration becomes essential for the understanding to *combine* concepts and generate knowledge of principles, and this lays one of the bases for overcoming the otherwise sharp division Kant establishes between the transcendental aesthetic and the understanding and further, between the pure transcendental conditions of experience and its particular (socially and historically determinate) 'contents'.

For Kant, space is at once objective, insofar as it is a condition of experience, and subjective, insofar as it is a condition imposed by the transcendental dimensions of subjectivity. Like space, time is a non-discursive (non-conceptual) a priori dimension of the transcendental aesthetic. 'Time is not a discursive or, as it is called, universal concept; rather, it is a pure form of sensible intuition' (Kant 1996: 86/A32). As with spatial relations, time is both objective insofar as it is a condition of experience that we order sense data coming to us according to temporal principles and it is also subjective insofar as it is the transcendental dimension of the subject that imposes such conditions as an a priori condition of experience, not the nature of the universe imposing time as a condition of cognition on the subject: 'time attaches not to objects themselves, but merely to the subject intuiting them' (Kant 1996: 91/A38). As with space, so time plays a crucial role in us being able to develop our understanding and use of concepts of the understanding, so many of which depend on a temporal intuition. The concept of change presupposes something changing *in time* according to the two key principles of time: successive ordering and simultaneous ordering which the individual empirical subject performs on sense data. Again, as we shall see later, this allows Kant to open up the tautological subject of rationalism to the principles of figuration, the ability to picture, to imagine figures in space and time that make concepts of the understanding actually intelligible. At the same time, Kant is careful to stress that the transcendental aesthetic is, like the understanding, a priori, in order to protect his system from the contingency of the empirical. The principles of time and space 'hold as rules under which alone experiences are possible at all: and they instruct us prior to experience, not through it' (Kant 1996: 86/B47). Thus Kant's system both admits experience into it and limits the extent to which experience can change what is regarded as given.

In the first *Critique*, the perceptual is cast firmly in its place. Initially it is conceived by Kant as a very lowly faculty indeed compared to the activity of concept formation. Concepts, he tells us, 'are based on the spontaneity of thought, where as sensible intuitions are based on the receptivity for impressions' (1996: 121/B93). Summarizing the joint work of the perceptual and the conceptual, Kant states,

The first [thing] that we must be given a priori in order to cognize any object is the *manifold* of pure intuition. The second [thing] is the *synthesis* of this manifold by the imagination. But this synthesis does not yet yield cognition. The third [thing we need] in order to cognize an object we encounter is the concepts, which give unity *to this pure synthesis and which consist solely in the presentation of this necessary synthetic unity.*

Kant (1996: 131/A79)

By the manifold of pure intuition, Kant refers to the transcendental capacity to organize sense data in temporal and spatial terms. The concept of the 'manifold' is suggestive of both 'manifest' and the 'folds' or multiple elements out of which appearances are composed. These folds and their temporal and spatial dimensions have to be synthesized. The manifold must 'be gone through and gathered together' (Kant 1996: 153/A99) in a process that Kant calls *synthesis* and Kant awards this job to the imagination, or what he calls at the level of mere perceptual data, the reproductive imagination.

If each singular presentation were entirely foreign to – isolated from, as it were – every other presentation and separated from it, then there would never arise anything like cognition; for cognition is a whole consisting of compared and connected presentations.

Kant (1996: 152/A97)

The reproductive imagination retains a memory of a sequence of impressions, linked by contact or proximity and therefore temporal (linear) and spatial (part-whole) unity. Kant's model of consciousness is not unlike Hollywood continuity editing, where we move from a long shot to a medium shot while retaining in our minds the wider context which the second shot has eclipsed but which we still use to orientate us spatially and temporally. The model is a mathematical one building up our apprehension of the manifold through addition, not of numerical units but objects and their relations in time and space. If we take these relations as not only the necessary but also the sufficient basis for thinking about consciousness, then we occlude a whole range of relationships that lie outside *immediate* sense-perception and which are important for thinking about socially arranged relationships whose temporal-spatial dynamics escape sensuous immediacy. This larger scale, this intimation of a temporal and spatial totality is precisely what Kant largely rules out (represses) in the first *Critique* by posing a very sharp and absolute division between appearances of the phenomenal world and the noumena. As we have seen, time and space for Kant 'apply to objects merely insofar as these are regarded as appearances, but do not exhibit things in themselves' (Kant 1996: 92/B56). Sometimes Kant seems to be saying something less absolute, that noumena refers to the impossibility of knowing forces without factoring in the mediating role of the transcendental subject, 'without regard to the way in which it [the object] is intuited' (Kant 1996: 91/B55). More generally, however, there is an absolute division so that 'however deeply we explore ... objects, we deal with nothing whatever but appearances' (Kant 1996: 97/B63). One of the consequences of this division is that the object can never impress itself onto the subject because by definition, as soon as it does so it enters the realm of appearances and becomes assimilated to the subject's own processing of sense data. As we shall see, this absolute division forces Kant back into a tautological model of the subject.

For Kant the realm of appearances is characterized by a particular model of unity, linearity and part–whole relations that constrain consciousness within bourgeois social relations. In terms of unity, Kant's machinery of consciousness is grounded in the self-consciousness of the *I*, what Kant calls *apperception*. For 'this *one* consciousness is what unites in one presentation what is manifold, intuited little by little, and then reproduced' (Kant 1996: 156/A103). Only if the different parts in the chain of synthesis are understood as being processed by the same 'one self-consciousness' (Kant 1996: 180/B137) can any unity of the manifold be achieved. The only unity which Kant can conceive in the first *Critique* is the unity of the monad (not the totality), which takes the form at the empirical level of the single percept which in turn needs to be joined into a linear unity and this in turn is presupposed by the unity of the single transcendental consciousness, the *I* of apperception which can add things together. But because this active consciousness is also an isolated consciousness, it finds itself thrown against the massive indifference of a deterministic nature. As Andrew Bowie argues, this *I* grounds self-consciousness in the capacity to *synthesize* and be present as a consciousness throughout the synthesizing activity. It is self-causing and the ground of freedom and yet what the *I* synthesizes appears to be merely deterministic nature which offers little ground for freedom (Bowie 2003: 21).

The shift to the aesthetic in the third *Critique* will open up this bourgeois monadic subject to intersubjectivity at the point of reception while the aesthetic will become a subtle register of the social realm absent or repressed in the first *Critique*. The third *Critique* opens up a whole new vista of possibilities through the non-contiguous comparison and connection of sense-percepts (the play of forms). In the first *Critique*, the role of the imagination is too tied to ordering percepts according to the principles of empirical time and space to acquire anything other than a reproductive quality to it, which has the effect of imprisoning consciousness within a mechanically conceived consciousness: 'the synthesis of the reproductive imagination is subject solely to empirical laws, viz., to the laws of association' (Kant 1996: 192/B152). It will be different laws of association that Kant will bring to bear on sensuousness in the third *Critique*, but in the first *Critique* freedom is essentially associated with the non-empirical, either the noumena or the production of 'pure' concepts, which if not an act of freedom is at least a productive act.

Kant terms the active arrangement of concepts independent of any empirical trace within the first *Critique* as the power 'to exhibit', and this power is awarded to what he calls the *productive* imagination. To 'exhibit', then, refers to our a priori powers to determine, not to how we have been affected by the sensuous. With Kant's aesthetic turn, some reconciliation will be achieved whereby the power to exhibit in an original way can be thought through and in relation with sense-impressions, thus connecting Kant with the subsequent German philosophical critique of the inadequacies of empirical *vorstellung* (representation) and inquiry into how we can produce sensuous *darstellung* (Helfer 1996). In the Marxist German philosophy of the aesthetic, this debate revolves around such notions as mimesis and the dialectical image.

The productive imagination, then, is that formative power to exhibit, and Kant will suggest that it is a capacity that operates across both the faculty of the understanding and the transcendental aesthetic or pure intuition of space and time. '[I]nsofar as the imagination is spontaneity, I sometimes also call it the *productive* imagination' (Kant 1996: 191/B152), states Kant. It marks a determining power to *form* independently of specific content and clearly this is the basis for any powers we have to enlarge our understanding of the determinate conditions of the empirical and experiential. We have seen that this ability to develop the concepts of the understanding is also dependent on the aesthetic, but this is the transcendental aesthetic which is a priori the actual sensuous data the empirical individual encounters. One way, then, of thinking about Kant's system is that both the transcendental aesthetic and the pure concepts of the understanding stress the *form* that appearances must take in order for them to be intelligible, over the contents of particular appearances. As Adorno notes,

> ...since this content is something accidental and contingent, something changeable, which therefore does not belong in philosophy as Kant understands it, it follows that the whole of philosophy cannot really be anything other than the *analysis of form*.
>
> Adorno (2001a: 44)

Although there are dangers here of formalism, which Kant himself commits, Kant's sense that *form* and the power to form is crucial bears the trace not of an escape from the social but an intimation of how thoroughly social we have become. Form's relative mobility across different content (and not being beholden to a particular content) is a key feature of the aesthetic imagination, as well as our technical, cultural and scientific progress. Central to our creative activity is the ability to find resemblances *between forms* that have on the face of it different content (the power of analogy). As we shall see in Chapter 6, the concept of the productive imagination links the aesthetic to human labour and its prodigious productive capacities.

Kant's attempt to establish an identity between the logico-rational and the empirical and protect the former from the latter constantly pushes him to develop straddling concepts that simultaneously resist mediation. The elusive concept of the *schema*, which is a function of the imagination, is one such example of this pressure towards and resistance against the need for mediation between the conceptual and the perceptual. The term refers to an act of the reproductive imagination whereby *thought* matches a concept with an empirical image, an example of the concept *in concreto*. The schema is the universal and necessary procedure of the imagination, a rule in fact, that provides a concept with the abstract outline or shape that prepares it for application to the empirical – for example, a circle for a plate or a 'four footed animal' for a dog. At the same time, the schema is not 'limited to any single and particular shape offered to me by experience, or even to all possible images that I can exhibit *in concreto*' (Kant 1996: 213–214/A141). Later, in the third *Critique*, Kant will uncouple sensuous form-determination from its rigid conceptual 'stamping' by the logical operation of the schema in the name of objective cognitions. Instead in the third *Critique*, 'the imagination's freedom consists precisely in its schematizing without a concept' (Kant 1987: 151). Yet even before Kant famously modifies the concept of the schema to stress the possibility of a play with form, the concept of the schema brings Kant's philosophy perilously close to confronting the possibility that the *trace of the image*, the outline shape of the schema, suggests that concepts may emerge scandalously from percepts (or sensuous practice). As Ernst Fisher notes, in his materialist anthropology on the origins of language, concepts are abstractions that emerge to name the prototype that is embodied in a tool, such as an axe, once it becomes imitated (reproduced) again and again (Fisher 2010: 38).

This implicit undermining of the very dichotomy between concepts and images that Kant sets up is developed further in a wonderful book called *Visual*

Thinking, by the Gestalt psychologist and art theorist Rudolf Arnheim. There he tried to break down what he suggested was a 'pathological' separation between the conceptual and the perceptual in contemporary society (Arnheim 1972: 151). Arnheim relates how he set his students the task of giving visual representation to such abstract concepts as past, present and future, or democracy, good and bad marriage and youth. They accomplished the task with a series of non-mimetic shapes and lines that articulated ideas and institutions using dynamic patterns or squiggles. These experiments help break down the dichotomy between concepts and images by showing how non-empirical concepts are meaningful precisely because they have for us implicit imagistic dimensions to them (Kant's schemata). Concepts and percepts, then, while differentiated, also retain their common roots in one another. In the *perception of form* lies the 'beginnings of concept formation' (Arnheim 1972: 27) and conversely, in the most abstract concept there resides the trace of perceptual form.

Kant's transcendental subject, however, can only survive if this dialectic between conceptual knowledge and sensuousness is suppressed even as his whole architecture pushes irresistibly towards such a conclusion. What the aesthetic will do in the third *Critique* and beyond is give us the opportunity to rethink both sides of cognition – concept and percept. Concept becomes rather different from an abstraction that empties out content in the name of achieving generality. Instead, as Arnheim notes, abstraction is best thought of as *the practice of grasping the salient structural features of the environment*, not stripping all particulars away and leaving a contentless word/world (Arnheim 1972: 194–195). What the aesthetic does is tie this sifting and sharpening of thought to the sensuous perception of form. Conversely, perception is also rethought in the aesthetic mode so that the empirical limits of sense-perception (and the body that occupies a specific point in time and space which sense-perception is necessarily tied to) are overcome by some new mode of form-making from which arises a new kind of de-reified thinking or concept formation that contextualizes the sense-percept along an axis of (social) consciousness that Kant's atomistic, linear and additive model of the first *Critique* cannot traverse.

Transcendental logic

We have seen that the synthesis of perception that makes intelligible experience possible is governed by the principles of the transcendental aesthetic that are a priori as well as the reproductive imagination. They in turn work in conjunction with the transcendental logic of the understanding. Without such principles, experience would be 'a rhapsody of perceptions', a startlingly *aesthetic* phrase.

> Such a rhapsody of perceptions, would not fit together in any context conforming to rules of a thoroughly connected (possible) consciousness, and hence would also not fit together to agree with the transcendental and necessary unity of apperception.
>
> Kant (1996: 227/A156)

Having affirmed the importance of the pure forms of intuition that makes intelligible experience possible when dealing with the perceptual side of consciousness, Kant turns to the transcendental logic and penetrates more deeply into the a priori conceptual principles for synthetic judgments. But he still maintains that without the empirical, the transcendental logic 'would have no content' (Kant 1996: 129/A77); it would be a mere play with abstract presentations. While the conceptual machinery of consciousness is ultimately grounded by Kant in the transcendental logic of the understanding, the problem with rationalism grounded in logic is that it is tautological. In the analytic philosophical tradition which underpins rationalism, the subject and the predicate are universally and necessarily related, intrinsically connected if the subject is to be what we understand it to be. Thus all causes have effects, all bachelors are unmarried and all triangles are three-sided closed figures made up of straight lines with three angles. The strict universality of the rule that links the predicates to these subjects in each case is a priori independent of any empirical instance of a given triangle, a given cause and a given bachelor.

Yet such lawfulness comes at the price of being unable to offer a philosophical account of how *new* knowledge might be achieved. The entirety of Kant's project is unintelligible without seeing it as a philosophical response to the expanding field of the natural sciences, which were beginning to make such massive breakthroughs as Newton's theory of gravity. Here was a science that used empirical observation but which, at least after a long history of trial and error, could aim to formulate axiomatic deductions that were a priori universal and necessary. Insofar as those laws of natural science could be discovered they must have some *affinity* with the logical laws beloved of rationalism governing the conceptual machinery of consciousness. Insofar as the 'strict universality of the rule is indeed no property what ever of empirical rules' (Kant 1996: 146/A92) natural science must make some kind of 'leap' from its a posteriori evidence base to a priori deductions of the laws governing particular natural science phenomena. Clearly this methodology inspires Kant's own search for the a priori laws governing the possibility of empirical experience as such:

> all appearances stand in a thoroughgoing connection according to necessary laws, and hence stand in a *transcendental affinity* of which the *empirical* affinity is the mere consequence.
>
> Kant (1996: 163/A114)

Here Kant stresses that affinity means an identity between the logical and the empirical. But what is the basis of this affinity between the logical and the empirical? When Kant speaks of the gathering together of the manifold, he presupposes, if there is to be an a priori ground for the empirical, an a priori mode of judging that likewise *combines* concepts and does not merely, as the analytic judgment does, unfold what is already implicit within the subject–predicate relations of a concept. This Kant will call the a priori synthetic judgment, and it is the basis for expanding knowledge of the empirical world and for providing a philosophy that can map the everyday empirical world according to a priori laws.

> In an analytic judgment I keep to the given concept, in order to establish something about it.... In synthetic judgments, however, I am to go outside the given concept, in order to consider, in relation with this concept, something quite different from what was thought in it.
>
> Kant (1996: 225/B194)

To bring out the implicit social implications of Kant's transcendental subject that Kantian-Marxists correctly identified in his philosophy, we can use examples that are somewhat different to the logical ones beloved of analytic philosophy. 'Capital is accumulation' is an analytic judgment since the predicate of accumulation is already essential to what the subject, capital is. 'Capital accumulates by buying labour power' is a synthetic judgment, combining the concept of capital as accumulation with another concept that identifies the source of capital's self-expansion. In fact it is an *a priori* synthetic judgment, since there can be no particular case of capital accumulating without some connection, somewhere, with the buying of labour-power. Of course it is not a *logical* a priori synthetic judgment, but a judgment made about and arising from particular social and historical relations. It is worth noting how the combination of capital as accumulation with buying labour-power brings out something that was hidden within the analytic judgment that links subject and predicate necessarily: the crucial dimension of time. Accumulation and buying and the establishment of a relationship between capital and labour presuppose

Kant's transcendental aesthetic (time and space) as the means by which an a priori synthetic judgment can be made. That accords a very significant role to the aesthetic, making figuration in space and time a presupposition for intelligibility. As with the relationship between concepts and percepts, Kant fights tooth and nail to rigidly keep the transcendental basis of his system, the pure aesthetic separated from empirical content, pure form from things that take place *in* time and *in* space.

Kant's own example of an a priori synthetic judgment still grounded in logic is 'every change has a cause'. Here the cause-effect relation, which is an analytic judgment, is now combined with the concept of change which once again presupposes the a priori of time, the pure intuition of the transcendental aesthetic. The transcendental aesthetic makes it possible to combine concepts to generate new concepts. At the same time, Kant argues that the

> transcendental aesthetic, cannot include among its a priori data the concept of change. For time itself does not change; rather, what changes is something that is in time. Therefore the concept of change requires the perception of some existent and of the succession of its determinations; hence it requires experience.
>
> Kant (1996: 94/B58)

Although time and space are transcendental, motion *in* space and change *in* time both require experiential data, both require a 'content' to fill the empty intuitive form of space and time. Once again, Kant is trying to bring the empirical into his philosophy without sacrificing the a priori conditions of the transcendental. Once again, form and content are rigidly divided according to a Newtonian concept of time as absolute ('time itself does not change') which we now know, after Einstein, is untenable: mass (content) does effect or warp the space–time continuum.

The a priori synthetic judgment was Kant's great innovation and attempted to mediate between pure logic and the empirical. It maintained the universality and necessity which logic craves but at the same time opened judgment up to the empirical. It thus seemed to be neatly compatible with the natural sciences, which could also combine a priori deductions out of a series of empirical intuitions. Kant's philosophy is constantly on a knife-edge between the a priori and the empirical, constantly inventing mediating concepts between them and still wanting to retain the logical form's independence from the empirical. We have seen this in relation to the productive and reproductive imagination and the schema. Now the same thing happens in relation to the a priori synthetic judgment and the transcendental aesthetic. Cause and effect cannot in fact be combined with change unless we can figure concepts as having a temporal dimension. This affirms the necessity of the perceptual and at the same time safe-guards the a priori from the empirical because although 'change requires the perception of some existent' (Kant 1996: 94/B58), temporality itself is a transcendental if non-discursive given of our subjectivity. Time and space as the a priori condition of sense-perception brings Kant once more, as with the concept of the schema, close to thinking about abstract figuration as an essential part of understanding and comprehension.

> For change is a combination of contradictorily opposed determination in the existence of one and the same thing. Now, how it is possible that from a given state there should follow an opposite state of the same thing – not only can no reason make this comprehensible to itself without an example, but it cannot make this understandable to itself without intuition even. And this intuition is that of the motion of a point in space; solely the point's existence in different locations (as a succession of opposite determinations) is what first makes change intuitive.
>
> Kant (1996: 300/B292)

Here we have the proto-dialectical argument that conceptuality must be joined with temporal and spatial figuration for grasping a 'contradictorily opposed determination in the existence of one and the same thing'. And although motion and change were not accorded the status of the a priori of space and time in the transcendental aesthetic, Kant is here conceding how crucial these concepts are to intuition. Thus the divide between form and content *within* the transcendental aesthetic is under pressure. But further, in terms of the relationship between the aesthetic and the understanding, not only does Kant say that time and space are the essential coordinates by which we can connect concepts such as cause-effect and change in a priori synthetic judgments, he also argues that they even make any intelligible mental use of an analytic judgment possible. To think an analytic judgment such as cause and effect in any usable way requires temporality. For although we can analytically deduce that cause and effect go together necessarily, without time we would not even begin to be able to distinguish what was cause and what was effect, since temporality is required to sequence the two states. The same is true with other fundamental concepts such as magnitude:

> No one can explicate the concept of magnitude as such, except perhaps by saying that it is that determination of a thing whereby we can think how many times a unit is posited in it. Yet this how-many times is based on successive repetition, and hence on time and the synthesis (of the homogenous) in time.
>
> Kant (1996: 308/A242)

So the mathematical concept of magnitude is based on the successive repetition of a unit and repetition implies or rather requires temporality, just as capital accumulation does (which no doubt provides one of the material conditions for Kant's emphasis on the importance of time). The importance of temporality in assembling a cognitive map of our environment, and indeed the importance of retaining a sense of a continuous self that can remember what has been previously mentally assembled, opens up the whole prospect of a philosophy attuned to history. Thus, the implicit dialectic between the transcendental logic and transcendental aesthetic gestures towards the possibility of a dialectical relationship between the transcendental (understood now as the structural conditions for a thing's possibility) and the empirical. But it is hard to read a passage such as the one above and not believe that these were the lines scanned by Walter Benjamin which led him to critique, in his 'Theses on the Philosophy of History', that bourgeois version of history (which abolishes history) as mere repetition and addition of homogenous time, from which it is absolutely impossible to think the concept of revolution (Benjamin 1999a). Here, as elsewhere, Kant's words only need to be accented in a critical direction for a description of reification to be turned into its unmasking and for the prospect of the radically and authentically *new* to be admitted into the world.

We have seen that transcendental time and space make it possible to think connections between concepts which allow the a priori synthetic judgment to govern the mapping of temporal and spatial relationships at the empirical level. The a priori synthetic judgments mediate not only with the transcendental aesthetic but also what Kant called the 'pure categories' of the understanding. Drawing on Aristotle's thinking, Kant identifies four main pure categories (or fundamental concepts) some of which we have already been using: Quantity, Quality, Modality and Relation. For nothing can be thought that does not have some Quantity, some Quality, some Relation (to itself and to other things) and some Modality (the most important for Kant being whether something has objective grounding in a combination of the laws of logic and empirical intuitions, or whether something is thought merely subjectively, which Kant will later associate with the aesthetic experience of taste).

Each of the four pure categories has three subsections which need not detain us but it is worth just pausing and considering two of the subsections of the pure category of Relation, namely causality and community. We have seen that Kant can only really conceive of causality in the linear terms of proximity and contact that became the dominant interpretation of Newton's concept of classical mechanics. This notion of causality is in some tension with conceiving

of relations associated with community or wholes that are more than the
sum of their parts, insofar as the relationships between the parts constitute a
mutually determining structure on the whole. When briefly considering the
pure category of community, Kant writes of the *coordination* of concepts rather
than the subordination of concepts in a hierarchy (pure categories, empirical
concepts, transcendental aesthetic, empirical sense-percepts). For Makkreel,
this is a crucial difference which the third *Critique* will open up in ways that
the first *Critique* cannot. 'Where as subordination is a logical mode of form,
coordination is an aesthetic mode of form ...' (Makkreel 1990: 12). The search
for a mode of form determination that is genuinely (i.e. freely) social marks
Kant's trajectory from the first *Critique* to the third. Kant associates community
with reciprocity rather than the unidirectional determination that dominates
the first *Critique*. But Kant is unable to activate the pure category of community
in the first *Critique* in any substantive way since it is subordinate to the logical
form. Reciprocity between form and content, concept and percept, would
destroy the basis of his idealist and dichotomous philosophy in the first *Critique*.
When Kant returns later on in the first *Critique* to the concept of community
it is striking how he cannot conceive of it in the proto-dialectical terms above,
but instead collapses it into the *serial* concept of causality he distinguished it
from earlier:

> Without community every perception (of appearance in space) would be severed
> from any other; the chain of empirical presentations – i.e., experience – would
> begin entirely a new with each new object and the previous chain could not in
> the least cohere with it or stand to it in a time relation.
>
> Kant (1996: 279/B261)

We have seen that the linearity of Kant's model of consciousness works both
at a horizontal level within the manifold of appearance that must be gathered
together and vertically as it were between conceptuality and perception.

> Whenever an object is subsumed under a concept, the presentation of the object
> must be *homogeneous* with the concept; i.e., the concept must contain what is
> presented in the object that is to be subsumed under it.
>
> Kant (1996: 209/B176)

Here is a passage crackling with tensions and contradictions. Only the keywords
'the presentation of the object' keep the real at bay and ensure that whatever
empirical phenomena are affecting the subject is being absorbed into the
subject's *own* processing machinery. The empirical thus does not represent

something outside the subject but only what outside the subject the subject can itself process and present. This maintains Kant's idealist position of a subject radically cut off from the object, but at the cost really of driving the subject back into the tautological position which Kant had tried to break from by introducing the a priori synthetic judgment which could combine concepts so that the subject can map the empirical without sacrificing universality and necessity. Kant wants to open up the subject to the empirical in order for the subject to be able to have thoughts (objective cognitions) that are more than simply an extension of the subject's own tautological analytical processes. But on the other hand Kant must absorb all empirical matter into the subject's machinery of consciousness to preserve the necessity and universality of the transcendental subject. This is why Kant conceives the relationship or affinity between conceptuality and perception as identity, or here as the homogeneity of the object with the concept.

The transcoding of the structure of the Kantian problematic on reification into terms congruent with a Marxist framework 'simply' brings what is already symptomatically outlined to a point of critical consciousness. For Adorno, the critical enterprise must be dedicated (in combat against logical positivism) to fracturing the concept's assumed self-identity with the thing to which it refers (or subsumes under it). The task of philosophy is to rescue what philosophy has traditionally dismissed as unimportant: the non-conceptual (that which escapes abstraction), individuality, particularity and the experiential. These are all *concepts* that refer to dimensions of life that the aesthetic is particularly strong in representing and provides a clue as to the aesthetic's importance for both Kant and Adorno. The conceptual–perceptual synthesis of experience under conceptuality denotes for Adorno not objective knowledge as it did for Kant, but the exercise of power and domination. However, Adorno is not advocating abandoning conceptual thought – which would be absurd. Adorno rejects entirely philosophies such as Bergson, a 'hater of the rigid general concept' who collapsed into a 'cult of irrational immediacy' (Adorno 1973: 8). Our conceptual life cannot be cast off anymore than our social and mediated relations can. For concepts are the accumulated heritage of our social relations and are immense resources which we cannot do without. But what also accumulates inside those concepts is the coercive history of our social relationships, which under capitalism is concealed by the apparent identity between concept and thing or abstract referent. The task for Adorno is to give the concept a 'turn toward non-identity' and this is the 'hinge of negative dialectics' (Adorno 1973: 12). As Adorno argues,

Insight into the constitutive character of the nonconceptual in the concept
would end the compulsive identification which the concept brings unless halted
by such reflection.

Adorno (1973: 12)

Adorno's mode of reflection, negative dialectics, becomes a liberating critical
practice unleashed against *capitalist* conceptuality. Today concepts like
freedom, democracy, civilization, choice, equality, rights, and so forth, which
are central to bourgeois society, are non-identical to the actual real conditions
they refer to. If there is freedom, it is primarily freedom to buy and sell and
since even freedom can be bought and sold (daily in the labour market) then
this contradicts the concept of freedom; if there is democracy, it is only political
democracy which contradicts the meaning of the Greek origins of the word
as participation of the majority in all spheres of life; if there is civilization, it
is coupled with a barbarism that contradicts civilization; if there is choice, it
is determined by the ability to pay which denies choice; if there is equality
within a legal framework, the boss and the worker meet on very unequal terms;
if there are rights, these evade the crucial distinctions that give some people
far more rights than others (e.g. the right to private ownership of the means
of production empowers capitalists over non-capitalist property owners and
negates the right to collective or public ownership). These are all contradictions
that are non-identical to the concept, which is as necessarily indifferent to those
contradictions as exchange value under capitalism (and not exchange value
throughout history as Adorno suggested) is indifferent to the particularities of
use value. As Fredric Jameson points out, identity thinking is 'something like
occluded system, totality forgotten or repressed' (Jameson 2007: 27).

For Adorno and Horkheimer, writing in *Dialectic of Enlightenment*, logical
positivism exactly captured the ideology of the subject whose outlines can be
detected in Kant's first *Critique*. On the one hand, this ideology means that
reality is assimilated to the subject and feeds the subject's fantasy of power over
reality. On the other hand, the ideology of the subject is really the ideology of the
system (Kant's transcendental subject) *over* the individual subject and to which
the subject must bow down to:

What appears to be the triumph of subjective rationality, the subjection of all
reality to logical formalism, is paid for by the obedient subjection of reason
to what is directly given. What is abandoned is the whole claim and approach
of knowledge: to comprehend the given as such; not merely to determine the
abstract spatio-temporal relations of the facts which allow them just to be

grasped, but on the contrary to conceive them as the superficies, as mediated conceptual moments which come to fulfillment only in the development of their social, historical and human significance. The task of cognition does not consist in mere apprehension, classification, and calculation, but in the determinate negation of each immediacy.

Adorno and Horkheimer (1997: 26–27)

For Kant, judgment is essentially a question of matching concepts to percepts and determining the latter according to synthetic principles. The process of synthesis, on the one hand, requires an individual subject to engage in 'an act of the subject's self-activity' (Kant 1996: 176/B130). Paradoxically – but crucially, for Kant's later trajectory – this occurs strongest at the level of the transcendental aesthetic and the imagination. But as this activity is subsumed under the higher conceptual operations of the understanding, so this self-activity becomes imprisoned within an increasingly reified system. Since the transcendental logic is either right or erroneous there does not seem to be much scope for the independent exercise of judgment. Hence the understanding 'is an island, and is enclosed by nature itself within unchangeable bounds' (Kant 1996: 303/B295). The 'spontaneous' quality, then, of concept formation acquires the unfortunate connotations in the first *Critique* not so much of autonomy in evaluating things, but as the imposition of the transcendental subject on the individual subject. Spontaneous really means, ultimately for Kant in the first *Critique*, the automaticity of reified natural givens rather than something like freedom. Adorno identifies this selfsame contradiction in the first *Critique*:

> If the transcendental, or rather the transcendental subject, that is to say, the most general point of reference that is supposed to guarantee the possibility of universally valid and necessary knowledge, is really no more than a merely logical unity, we could not imagine how spontaneity or activity could be ascribed to it. How something that is not in any sense individuated in time and space ... is able to generate representations, remains completely obscure.

Adorno (2001a: 213)

This reification of the transcendental subject makes Karatani's stimulating reading of the first *Critique* odd in one respect. He argues that Kant's transcendental subject in the first *Critique* is not founded on a priori logical laws and that the transcendental subject in *Critique of Pure Reason* refers to just one transcendental subject among others (Karatani 2005: 37). This is certainly unorthodox but the evidence for this reading comes largely by transposing the third *Critique* onto his reading of the first. The third *Critique* does indeed broach the question of not only plural subjects, as Karatani rightly argues, but also historical subjects. Yet, and this is typical of the Kantian-Marxist tradition, which has been insufficiently critical of the positivism of the first *Critique*, there is a peculiar reluctance to admit that between the first *Critique* and the third, there is some sort of productive break. 'For Kant, who was also a scientist, it was self evident that an a priori synthetic judgment is not easily attained' (Karatani 2003: 43). Yet Kant is not interested in the content of natural science in the first *Critique*. He is only interested in the formal laws under which experience becomes possible, and he demonstrates that synthetic judgments are made routinely by non-scientists as part of our conceptual–perceptual machinery of consciousness and these are in turn made possible by the a priori rules of synthesis and connection. His philosophy is not at all about what scientists do even though it was stimulated by natural science methodologies. Instead the first *Critique* is about the subject, where a priori synthetic judgments vis-à-vis empirical intuitions are the routine requirements for a possible experience. The particular laws of natural science are certainly not easily attained, but insofar as they can be known at all, they *must* conform with the conceptual–perceptual machinery of consciousness:

> Particular laws, because they concern appearances that are determined empirically, are *not derivable completely* from those laws [the pure categories], although the particular laws are one and all subject to the categories. Experience must be added in order for us to become acquainted with particular laws *at all*; but the a priori laws alone give us information about experience as such.
>
> Kant (1996: 200–201/B164)

The scientific accuracy of the particular laws of natural science cannot be guaranteed because they are congruent with the a priori laws of logic, but it is a minimal condition of us knowing nature at all that they are congruent with those laws when they have gone through the long and difficult process of scientific experimentation and debate. It will be the gap between the uniformity of the pure laws of the a priori categories and the plurality of the laws of empirical nature that have yet to be discovered, which will be one of Kant's starting points in the third *Critique*. Once more, with the sun of the Enlightenment rising over his shoulders, Kant asks how we can discover something new in the world, but as he extends this question beyond natural science into the aesthetic, the 'new' in question lies outside the reified objectivity of the understanding as mapped out in the first *Critique*.

Noumena

Categories, Kant argues,

> are concepts that prescribe laws a priori to appearances, and hence to
> nature.... Since the categories are not derived from nature and do not conform
> to it as their model (for then they would be merely empirical), how are we to
> comprehend the fact that nature must conform to the categories, i.e., how can
> the categories determine a priori the combination of nature's manifold without
> gleaning that combination from nature?
>
> Kant (1996: 199/B163)

Kant's answer is that the understanding can only operate in relation to
appearances and appearances are, tautologically, only what the subject can
assimilate from the object into its own structures of cognition. Appearances,
however, come from somewhere and thus are always made up of 'two sides'.
On the one side is the conceptual and perceptual form of apprehension which
belongs to 'the subject to whom the object appears.' On the other side is the
object 'in itself', the origin of the sense data from outside the subject (Kant
1996: 91–92/B55). Yet the object 'in itself' 'apart from all this receptivity of our
sensibility remains to us entirely unknown. All we know is the way in which we
perceive them' (Kant 1996: 94/A42). The object is thus denoted as an unknown
'X', and since we can know nothing of it, it is literally 'nothing for us' (Kant 1996:
157/A105).

This, then, is Kant's famous noumenon, the 'thing in itself' which is distinct
from the phenomena of appearances. The greatness of Kant's philosophy is
that he pushes on into this territory of the noumena even though its explicit
articulation generates further questions and problems, which again provide
an internal propulsion within Kant's philosophy for his aesthetic turn. In
the first *Critique*, Kant needs the concept of the noumena in order to mark
the objective limits of sensible cognition. For he wants to specify the limits of the
understanding in order to secure what it can know with confidence. Kant argues
that the transcendental subject of the understanding is grounded in principles
that are both independent of empirical experience and can only be used for a
possible empirical experience. A concept should not be used for anything but
appearances, otherwise it overreaches itself and strays into areas beyond its
remit for making objective judgments.

> The categories are not, as regards their origin, based on sensibility, as are the
> *forms of intuition*, space and time: they therefore seem to admit of an application

expanded beyond all objects of the senses. Yet they themselves are in turn
nothing but *forms of thought* that contain the logical ability to unite a priori in
one consciousness the manifold given in intuition.

Kant (1996: 313–316/B305–306)

It is because Kant reduces what we can know of the world to the empirical that
he is forced to drive a wedge between the conceptual and the empirical. For only
by doing so can he retain the universality and necessity of the transcendental
subject which is the condition for the possibility of meaningful experience
but which experience itself cannot ground. If any trace of the perceptual or
experiential is left over from the formative processing of the faculty of the
understanding, then its universality and necessity is compromised. The
concept of the noumena, however, gestures symptomatically to the possibility
that the determinative structuring of experience may also lie on the *other*
side of the empirical, in its origins in the object. For Kant's Transcendental
Idealism, what determines empirical phenomena are *rules of logic* derived
from the machinery of consciousness. For Marx and for the materialist
philosophy of Critical Realism developed by Bhaskar, Archer and others,
empirical phenomena are to be understood as an indicator, not of *rules* lodged
in consciousness, but of underlying causal forces at work within material and
social nature itself. Like Kant's Transcendental Idealism, these causal forces
are non-reducible to the empirically observable phenomena in which they
can, sometimes, be observed. But unlike Transcendental Idealism, these
causal forces reside at the level of Being, independent of consciousness and
perception alone. Both Critical Realism and Marxism view material and
social reality as a stratified ontology in which causal forces are at work that
may reveal themselves in certain often *symptomatic* forms, but, equally, they
may not, or whether they can be said to reveal themselves, is itself an act of
critical interpretation that requires certain historical conditions as much as
critical procedures. Deep structure causal forces, Bhaskar argues, can remain
active or potentially active, exercised but unrealized due to contrary forces
and realized with or without registration by empirical consciousness (Archer
et al. 1998: 77). The subject, with its conceptual and perceptual abilities,
has a formative way of processing the world it encounters and makes, but
that form-making must emerge in an active relationship with an objectively
structured world (natural and social). The subject is made in an active but
non-identical relationship with the object world and this non-identity both
preserves the independence of the real from the subject (the basis of any real

materialist philosophy) and allows for the relative autonomy of the subject vis-à-vis objective structures, without which we cannot account for something new, historically and socially, to come into the world (the basis for any *non-mechanical* materialist philosophy).

As Adorno argued, in Kant's philosophy the non-identical and the identical vie with each other. Insofar as the empirical subject that does the sensing of appearances in time and space is subordinate to replicating the transcendental subject that guarantees universality and necessity, Kant's philosophy is based on an identity philosophy. This, as we have seen, involves the empirical subject internalizing the rules of the system and amplifying to a fantasy degree their own agency within that system (of exchange) which fundamentally condemns them to reproducing their own subordination. This is one of the secret meanings of Kant's tautological philosophical structure, for capital of course, with its abstract demand for accumulation, is just one giant tautology, as Marx's formula for the circulation of capital (M-C-M^+, money-commodity-more money) demonstrates. Kant wants to account for how new knowledge can be produced, but he does so within the horizons of capital. Capitalism, as I have suggested elsewhere, creates subjectless subjects, that is subjects who in a doomed attempt to win back the very agency they have given up internalize the objectifying logic of the social relationships that foreclose a priori on their activity according to the imperatives of capital (Wayne 2003: 192–193). Its emblematic image is the subject in the marketplace, carrying, as Marx puts it, their social relationship in their pocket, in the form of money, which gives them an agency completely on the terms that ensure their subordination to the system that hollows out any more authentic (collective) agency.

But the concept of the noumena opens up the prospect that the identity between logic (transcendental subject of the understanding) and experience (empirical subject) is fissured by a non-identity, that the thing in itself may not be identical with and may indeed directly contradict phenomenal appearances. Despite the fact that Kant associates the noumena with that which is outside time and space, it is clear that it is a precursor to Marx's distinction between phenomenal forms of appearance and real essences.

> In present bourgeois society as a whole, this positing of prices and their circulation etc., appears as the surface process, beneath which, however, in the depths, entirely different processes go on, in which this apparent individual equality and liberty disappears.
>
> Marx (1993: 247)

Viewed from this angle, that is the need for a *theoretical* reconstruction of the conditions for the possibility of experience, the empirical has an extremely restricted cognitive reach. But viewed from another angle, that is the need to ground the conditions for the possibility of experience *in* experience, the empirical and the experiential fracture the kinds of abstract conceptualizations that Kant's faculty of the understanding (as well as bourgeois moral reasoning) offers. Marx's social science solution to this problem is something like a dialectical phenomenology (Bologh 1979). Here, the conditions of possible experience are reconstructed by starting with sensuous experience itself (of the commodity, for example) and working up a complex of conceptual mediations. Deriving concepts from percepts was resisted by Kant, as we have seen, but for Marx the objectivity of the concepts is grounded in the real world independent of consciousness which the conceptual network tries to catch. Since the empirical and the real are non-identical, Marx's concepts are not abstractions of atomistically conceived empirical phenomena, but are instead the paradox we might term 'concrete abstractions', constellations of concepts that are adequate to the empirical conceived as the site of a rich intersection of many (potentially contradictory) deep structure forces.

Kant's concept of the noumena lays the foundations for just this sort of breakthrough. '[T]he range outside the sphere of appearances is (for us) empty' (Kant 1996: 319/A255) – and it was this empty space that Marxism and psychoanalysis would subsequently theorize as the unconscious (social and individual, respectively). The X that Kant argues lies beyond our scope of objective knowledge really denotes some other notion of the pure category of Relation, some other way of conceiving causality, that lies outside the atomistic, linear and additive non-contradictory unity of intuitions in time and space which the faculty of the understanding deals with.

It is little exaggeration to say that with the noumena Kant begins to ground philosophically the whole function for the aesthetic as well as a future critical social science – namely to represent that which cannot be fully represented merely at the empirical level, or alternatively to use the empirical as a sign of some determinate set of non-empirical relations or forces. Kant argues that we can know the noumena only in a negative sense – as that which we cannot know as a *'boundary concept'* (Kant 1996: 319/B311) serving to limit the pretensions of knowledge (for Kant, equivalent to sensibility). Even once we transform the concept of the noumena in a more critical social science direction, we would not want to lose this sense of the noumena as a boundary concept, forever inscribing provisionality into our methods.

For Kant, to know noumena in a more positive sense would be to acquire capacities, which the Kant of the first *Critique* suggests we do not have. He defines a noumenon as a flat paradox, an '*object of a nonsensible intuition*' (Kant 1996: 317/B307). An intuition is a way of presenting in time and space. We have seen that there are two types of intuition. A pure intuition is 'sensible' only in the most abstract sense, a figuring within time and space (e.g. geometry) that does not derive from external sources. Its origin derives from the productive imagination uncontaminated by the empirical. An empirical intuition, by contrast, is one in which a sense impression from outside the subject is mapped and constructed by our a priori synthetic judgments (when, for example, we apply the concepts of cause and change to a concrete empirical thing). In both cases, temporal and spatial apprehension inevitably involves an intuition (abstract or empirical). So the idea of a 'non-sensible intuition' is a paradox by which Kant expresses the notion that cognition might articulate something beyond the empirical but through it. Kant also described the domain of the noumena as corresponding to an 'intellectual intuition'. Again the faculty of the understanding does not deal with 'ideas' (these are the province of reason) but with concepts, whether pure or empirical, that can only be usefully applied to the observable world. So the concept of an intuition that somehow occupies a point in time and space but also has its origins in something comparable to the ideas of reason is also a paradox for Kant. Now, the non-sensible or intellectual intuition is essentially a precursor to Marx's concrete abstractions on the one hand and Kant's own aesthetic turn on the other: it provides the fork in the road which leads to critical social science and the aesthetic.

***

Kant's concept of the synthetic a priori may be viewed as his attempt to reconcile structural determination with the possibility of accounting for something new (such as knowledge) emerging in the world in response to empirical phenomena. The a priori synthetic allowed the pure categories which establish the conditions of a possible experience to interact with the empirically observable world which the tautological analytic concepts of pure rationalism had been unable to do. Insofar as outlining a philosophy that could account for new knowledge of the world that was nevertheless determinate rather than purely contingent, Kant's philosophical architecture was deeply problematic. The division between form and content, concept and sense, phenomena and noumena ultimately led Kant to a reified structure that cancelled the possibility of the genuinely new ever emerging, at least insofar as social and moral-political knowledge is concerned.

In its combination of an abstract universalism unmediated by the sensuous and the empirical unmediated by degrees of abstraction that can map the social, Kant's first *Critique* outlines in embryonic form a future logical positivism. At the same time, we have seen that there are all sorts of various internal conceptual pressures within the architecture of the first *Critique* that are sowing the seeds for a future development in another direction altogether. The tendency towards compartmentalization is coupled with the pressure for mediation between form and content, concept and sense, the cognitive processes outlined in the transcendental logic and the sensuous reception of empirical reality by the transcendental aesthetic. Crucially the transcendental aesthetic is shown to be a presupposition to and an aid for thinking and it will be the role of the aesthetic, uncoupled from its subservient position vis-à-vis the reified concepts of the understanding, that will be substantively developed in the third *Critique*. What Adorno described as the 'transition to dialectics' (Adorno 2001a: 88) in the first *Critique* is well under way and not only between the conceptual and the sensuous, form and content. The noumena, for example, represents an X outside the machinery of consciousness calling for a new architectural configuration in which concepts must derive ultimately from social life. As social life becomes ever more complex, so merely empirical concepts cannot be expected to exhaust or be adequate to that life in its complexity and determinateness. In the first *Critique*, Kant holds to an absolute dichotomy between phenomena and noumena. But with the aesthetic play of sensuous forms, he begins to be able to think that there may be a way for noumena to find some register in the phenomenal.

Kant's aesthetic turn will enable him to go beyond the limits of the first *Critique* and explore the possibilities of what appears to be an unfathomable paradox: the intellectual intuition. The intellectual intuition becomes a way of overcoming the impotence of reason (and the subject) vis-à-vis the logical-empirical world of the understanding. The dichotomies between concept and sense-perception as embodied by the individual subject, noumena and reason constitute the four points that the later German philosophical tradition of Adorno, Kracauer, Benjamin and others would seek to coordinate into the basis of a liberation from capital at the level of critical philosophy. The aesthetic would be as crucial to them in trying to achieve that new coordination of concept, sense-perception, noumena and (critical) reason as it would be for Kant. But if this reading of Kant's trajectory is plausible, then it must be that the dominant reading of the third *Critique*, as advocating a conceptless experience in the aesthetic, is inadequate. For if that is the case, then there is no methodological break between the first *Critique* and the third. Instead the third *Critique* would merely valorize what it partially downgrades in the first *Critique* (the sensuous, the subjective) but without overcoming the dichotomous architecture that is causing all the problems. The next chapter, then, will need to take on this issue of the aesthetic and its relationship (or non-relationship) to conceptuality and cognition.

3

The Aesthetic, the Beautiful and Praxis

There are two apparently different starting points or motivations for Kant's aesthetic turn suggested in the introduction of the third *Critique*. We have seen that it was the paralysis of moral reason (freedom) in the face of a reified society that provoked Kant into writing a book that would address the 'immense gulf' (1987: 14) between freedom and cognition. For Kant would like to believe that 'it must be possible to think of nature as being such that the lawfulness in its form will harmonize with at least the possibility of [achieving] the purposes that we are to achieve in nature according to the laws of freedom' (Kant 1987: 15). This is a perhaps surprisingly materialist ambition, namely to posit as central to our relationship with nature, that despite its determinate qualities there is scope for its creative reworking. Marx will later call this our metabolic exchange with nature. Unfortunately, as we have seen, the lawfulness of nature's form, in Kant's first *Critique*, absolutely ruled out achieving any purposes governed by freedom. As Kant noted in the first *Critique*, 'in the question concerning nature and freedom we ... encounter the difficulty as to whether freedom is even possible at all ...' (Kant 1996: 537). In order to keep open that possibility, and given that we can at least think it as a idea it seems necessary to do so, Kant restricted determination to the realm of the sensible, to phenomena where time and a linear cause-effect series reigns supreme. For 'if appearances are things in themselves, then freedom cannot be saved' (Kant 1996: 538). In order to save freedom, the noumena must be posited as that dimension of every empirical thing that lies outside appearance, outside determinative nature. Thus Kant can posit causes by reference to the 'thing in itself' that are other to, and free from, the causal determinations mapped out in the transcendental subject. Phenomena and noumena are connected as symptom is to (non-empirical) cause, but there is no real way of reconstructing those (types of) 'free causes' and so ultimately phenomena and noumena are dichotomously opposed:

> The appearances must be capable of being explained by pursuing, as the supreme basis of explanation, their merely empirical character, and by entirely bypassing as unknown the intelligible character that is the empirical character's

transcendental cause – except insofar as this intelligible character is indicated by
the empirical character as the intelligible character's sensible sign.

                                                              Kant (1996: 544)

The empirical is the 'sign' of that which we cannot know. All we can know of
noumena is a general concept of it, which includes the idea that it would be
free of the kinds of 'unfree' determinations we know from empirical experience.
The 'thing in itself' dimension of every empirical thing 'would to this extent be
independent and free in its actions from all natural necessity, which is found
only in the world of sense' (Kant 1996: 541). If the noumena saves freedom
for the supersensible world that is external to us, it must therefore, *by analogy*,
confirm at least the possibility of supersensible freedom within us as well (the
faculty of reason).

Evidently dissatisfied with the tenuousness of this 'solution', Kant's aesthetic
turn attempts to seed the concept of praxis that will produce what Kant calls
a 'transition' or point of mediation between nature and freedom, between
the sensible, the conceptual and cognitive framework of the faculty of the
understanding and the ideas of moral reason which guide how we *ought* to
respond to what the cognitive machinery of consciousness encounters.

If the antinomy between necessity and freedom forms one starting point
for Kant in the third *Critique*, an apparently rather different consideration also
quickly moves into view. This is the gap between the transcendental laws of the
understanding, which form the conditions of cognition and experience in the
first *Critique*, and the problem of diverse empirical laws, both known and, more
importantly, yet to be discovered. Kant's transcendental arguments regarding
a priori synthetic judgments open the individual subject up to empirical
experience and therefore the possibility of generating new knowledge without
sacrificing universality.

But there remains a troubling gap between Kant's transcendental laws of
the understanding and the actual diversity of empirical laws. The problem is
that the 'empirical laws might be so *infinitely diverse* and *the forms* of nature
which pertain to particular experience so *very heterogeneous*' (Kant 1987:
392) that there is no prima facie reason why these empirical laws might be
subsumed under more general empirical laws and constitute a connected unity
of lawful relations as presupposed by the transcendental subject. For Kant
the rationalist that is troubling because 'for particular experience to cohere
thoroughly in terms of fixed principles, it must have this systematic coherence'
otherwise the whole process of subsuming the particular under more universal

laws or even classifications, as in taxonomy, would be impossible. 'For unless this [systematic coherence of empirical laws] is presupposed, particular experiences cannot have thoroughly lawful coherence' (Kant 1987: 392–393) and worse, experience would ultimately amount to 'a crude chaotic aggregate without the slightest trace of...a system' (Kant 1987: 398). In other words, Kant's transcendental subject may break apart under the pressure of the diversity of empirical laws, leading to the triumph of David Hume's sceptical empirical philosophy where custom and habit, and not universal laws, pattern empirical phenomena.

Now on the face of it these two concerns with which the third *Critique* opens, that of the division between the faculty of the understanding and the faculty of reason and the division between Kant's transcendental laws of the understanding and the empirical investigations of natural science, do not seem to be connected. But they are connected as manifestations of the problem of form and content, the universal and the particular, deduction and induction. The transcendental form of the faculty of the understanding resists any grounding in the empirical content of life and this must raise questions about how methodologically Kant's philosophical system can be reconciled with natural science investigation into empirical phenomena. At the same time, as we have seen, the transcendental form of the understanding leaves little basis to ground freedom in the empirical domain. As a result of that form determination, moral reason can only be preserved by shielding it absolutely from the reification of empirical cognition, but then the moral good can only be preserved in a form of impotence as well as abstract formalism. The noumena functions as that non-sensible idea of freedom (within us) that has been expunged from empirical reality. Kant's aesthetic turn essentially seeks to overcome the absolute division between empirical sign and noumena in order to make the idea of freedom palpable or sensuous. This move will transform his philosophical architecture.

Lukács, very much following Hegel's critique of Kant, saw Kant as exemplifying the dualism of bourgeois consciousness in which an abstract formal rationalism must view the content of life, experience and the material substratum, as irrational, because even in the qualified rationalism of Kant, only form (separated from the messy historical contingency of content) could be truly lawful (Lukács 1971). Against this:

> ...praxis can only be really established as a philosophical principle if, at the same time, a conception of form can be found whose basis and validity no longer rest on that pure rationality and that freedom from every definition of content.

> In so far as the principle of praxis is the prescription for changing reality, it must
> be tailored to the concrete material substratum of action if it is to impinge upon
> it to any effect.
>
> Lukács (1971: 126)

In Kant's *Critique of Practical Reason*, ethical practical activity is locked up in the private individual subject, self-generated, inwardly orientated and uncoupled from 'external' institutional practices that must obey the a priori laws of nature mapped out in the *Critique of Pure Reason*. Thus the ethical act 'collapses as soon as the first concrete content is to be created' (Lukács 1971: 125). If Lukács is right about the first two *Critiques* (and broadly I think he is, although he is blind to the internal contradictions pushing Kant beyond those dichotomies in the first *Critique*), he has very little to say about the *Critique of Judgment* in *History and Class Consciousness* and seems not to register (as Hegel, at least partially did) how the third *Critique* marks a methodological break in some significant ways. Let us now take a look at how Kant poses this methodological break and how it addresses the problem of the form–content dichotomy. It emerges initially largely around the question of the relationship between the abstraction of transcendental laws and the concrete content of empirical natural science.

Natural science and the aesthetic

Judgment, Kant argues in the first introduction, is the power to subsume the particular under universal principles, of either cognition or reason. It is a special cognitive power that has the 'ability to subsume under concepts given from elsewhere' (Kant 1987: 392), which means that it cannot generate up its *own* concepts or moral ideas, at least not as *objective* concepts or ideas. In terms of cognition, judgment is the power to unify the manifold and match perception with empirical concepts (to schematize) under universal principles or categories. It also, of course, is supposed to make sense of empirical experience in terms of the principles of moral good and freedom but as we have seen it is here confronted with the massive indifference of nature to freedom. Judgment thus already plays or is meant to play a mediating role within Kant's philosophical architecture but this means it has no independence from the faculty of the understanding or reason, but must instead assist each in their operations. It gives up freedom when assisting the faculty of the understanding and it gives up the sensuous empirical realization of the moral idea when it assists the faculty of reason. In terms of the faculty of the understanding and the process of cognition, judgment takes a determinative and *subsumptive* form. This mode of judging is spectacularly indifferent to the particularity of a thing, and this has implications for natural science as much as it does for freedom. For the transcendental laws of the understanding, a particular thing 'is marked out a priori' (Kant 1987: 19) and this means that the particularity of the particular and the empirical laws which govern it are of little concern for determinative judgment, which is then ill-designed to produce detailed or *new* natural scientific knowledge.

The *Critique of Judgment*, then, attempts to address this by freeing the power of judgment from its subordinate role vis-à-vis understanding and reason and allowing it to cleave more closely to the sensuous particular. However, the only a priori principle which judgment can have once it asserts a certain independence from the other faculties is a *subjective* principle: 'it provides no basis for a theoretical cognition of nature, nor for a practical principle of freedom' (Kant 1987: 393) states Kant emphatically, although as we shall see, this belies the contradictory dynamics of his philosophical architecture. This subjective principle turns out to be of a particular kind, what we can call the *as if* principle. By treating nature *as if* it were made for our purposes, Kant lays the basis for potentially overcoming the immense gulf within his philosophical architecture. In terms of the problem of natural science, we may treat nature *as if* it were a work of art, which is to say that we treat nature as if it were creatively arranged by a purpose to conform to our powers of cognition.

> Hence the concept that arises originally from judgment, as its own concept, is the concept of nature as *art*; in other words, it is the concept of the *technic of nature* regarding its *particular* [*besonder*] laws.
>
> Kant (1987: 393)

When natural science is confronted by 'such diverse forms of nature', and 'so many modifications as it were of the universal transcendental concepts of nature' (Kant 1987: 19), it must presuppose that there is nevertheless a unity of empirical laws in nature 'since otherwise our empirical cognition could not thoroughly cohere to [form] a whole of experience' (Kant 1987: 23). It is the presupposition that empirical nature will cohere under determinate laws (as if it had been creatively arranged) that makes scientific enquiry a rational activity. And without this presupposition there would be no affinity between the lawfulness of the empirical world discovered by natural science and Kant's transcendental system. The transcendental subject also has a presupposition (the entire apparatus of the faculty of understanding) but because it is only concerned with 'the conditions under which experience as such is possible as far as its form is concerned' (Kant 1987: 398), it is not one that can adequately engage with the multiplicity of the empirical. Kant thus supplements this transcendental system and presupposition with another one, but one that is subjective and takes as its starting point the empirical. To get science under way and for the existential stability of everyday cognition,

> it is subjectively necessary [for us to make the] transcendental *presupposition* that nature [as experience possible for us] does not have this disturbing boundless heterogeneity [*Ungleichartigkeit*] of empirical laws.
>
> Kant (1987: 398)

What is quite extraordinary about Kant's move here is that he has discovered at the heart of the objective natural sciences, whose purpose is to enquire not into the formal laws of the understanding which he mapped out in the first *Critique*, but the actual laws of empirical nature that make up the content of experience, a crucial subjective methodological trick 'where we merely *judge* [certain] objects of nature *as if* they were made possible through art' (Kant 1987: 390), that is as if it were the product of a willed purpose that gives it its unity. At the same time, this subjective principle also seems to open up the prospect of thinking about freedom in a new way, and this takes Kant's thought far beyond simply the question of natural science. In the third *Critique*, the objective and deterministic model of nature that is the object of cognition for the faculty of the understanding is replaced with a model of nature in which we are allegorically present and involved in (nature as art places us *imaginatively* as makers of nature).

Kant calls his presupposed lawfulness, this *as if* strategy necessary to get scientific activity under way, *formal purposiveness*. It is formal in a number of important senses. Firstly, it is something that the subject constructs in order to achieve a particular effect on its own mental powers (the *as if* function of the aesthetic). Secondly, then, formal purposiveness has no objective content in and of itself, for it 'provides no basis for a theoretical cognition of nature' (Kant 1987: 393). This, however, does not rule out that *through* this heuristic device, knowledge of a certain objective kind cannot be acquired. Here Kant is talking about knowledge of empirical laws in natural science investigations. Kant calls such knowledge, which formal purposiveness may lead to, knowledge of *natural purposes*. He has thus established, and against the thrust of his argument elsewhere, that the aesthetic procedure of analogy may have a connection with knowledge production. Thirdly, formal purposiveness is formal in the sense that despite its subjective nature (i.e. orientated towards the subject rather than the object of cognition) it is a transcendental a priori assumption not drawn from any basis *in* experience, but is instead the basis *of* (coherent) experience. In other words, Kant is not abandoning his critique of empirical scepticism and collapsing into induction. Finally, we may say that it is *formal* in that it involves an *arrangement* of things open to sense-perception, an aesthetic *technic*. This reconnects the idea that the aesthetic involves a relationship to our own mental powers, with the aesthetic as sense-perception/ arrangement from the first *Critique*. However, this capacity to now *(re)arrange* sense-perception is very different in quality to the automaticity of organizing the manifold of sense-perception in the first *Critique*. And this difference, I suggest, also includes a break with the positivism of sense-perception that dominates the first *Critique*.

If the first *Critique* to some extent tried to synthesize rationalism and empiricism on terms that favoured the former, it left both philosophical systems very much intact, if bolted together in some contradiction with each other. As Lucien Goldmann has argued, Kant tried to rescue the concept of totality from Hume's sceptical empiricism. For Humean scepticism, there

> ... is no *theoretical* totality, because human knowledge is restricted to *factual* connections resulting from habit and the association of ideas. There is no *practical* totality, because we have no right to argue from what is to the possibility of a better or higher existence, the empirical given being the only true and legitimate source of knowledge.
>
> Goldmann (2011: 104–105)

It is interesting that Goldmann associates totality with the ought-utopian imperative of reason, but he is insufficiently critical of the positivistic cast of the cognitive totality formulated in the first *Critique* and the contradiction between the two types of totality. Insensitive to the contradiction between the cognitive and moral totalities, Goldmann does not identify that there is any *break* going on in the third *Critique* that might bypass this antinomy in Kant's philosophical architecture. As we have seen, the form determination of the first *Critique* is dichotomously opposed to the content, to the particularities of empirical phenomena. The latter is sacrificed in the name of positing a priori transcendental principles that account for the possibility of experience as such. Conversely, a purely inductive approach that starts with particulars struggles to articulate the deep causal relations that shape the particulars but instead tends to satisfy itself with the observation of regularities. Kant's solution to this in the third *Critique* is to combine induction (starting with the empirical) and deduction (making the subjective a priori and transcendental) with *analogy*.

As Kant notes, scientific knowledge (and indeed everyday reason) can proceed by way of analogy. We often 'use the principles by which we explain and understand one product in order to explain and grasp [*begreifen*] another as well, thereby making coherent experience out of material ...' (Kant 1987: 25). This is an important source of pleasure in everyday cognition in fact. It is well established in the philosophy of science that scientists use analogy when they draw connections between one part of nature which they know about to another part of nature which they are seeking to formulate hypotheses about (Archer, Bhaskar et al. 1998: 55–65, McMullin 2001).

A classic example of the role of analogy in the natural sciences can be found in Darwin. While Darwin's method is widely taken to be of the hypothetical-deductive kind it has also been argued that however he presented his findings, he also made significant use of analogous comparisons between particulars to develop the key planks of his theory (Darden 1982, Evans 1984). Darwin compared inherited variations of plants and animals artificially introduced through horticulture and agriculture for advantage by humans with inherited variations developed by organisms in the wild to demonstrate that hereditary variations that are useful for the species tend to be reproduced over those that are less useful for survival. The analogy between natural selection and domesticated selection allowed Darwin to formulate a *general principle* by close observation of *particulars* within the domesticated production of plants and animals (where favourable selection was artificially controlled).

Effectively such a procedure requires particulars from non-contiguous 'domains' of reality (in Darwin's case, nature and cultivated nature) to be placed by the subject (here the scientist) into a communicative relationship that makes them speak to each other for the benefit of knowledge production. To the extent that they do 'communicate' across the differences between these different parts of nature, then some higher principles of nature that unites the particulars may be hypothesized while still retaining a sensitivity to the particularities of the particulars. We have in this operation of analogy some of the key features of the aesthetic proper. The inscription of difference between sensuously apprehended particulars cuts to the core of its peculiar mode of form determination, although one that also reconfigures our understanding of the 'universal'.

All this requires a mode of judgment different from the determinative judgment of the first *Critique*. The third *Critique's* significance pivots on a new mode of judgment that Kant calls *reflective*. In the first edition introduction of the third *Critique*, Kant describes reflective judgment as involving the '*specification* of the diverse under a given concept' (Kant 1987: 402), which is quite different from the usual process of abstraction that involves stripping particulars of their particularities in order to achieve an empty general truth. With reflective judgment, the universal concept is unpacked as it were: 'we *make the universal concept specific* by indicating the diverse [that falls] under it' (Kant 1987: 403).

In the second edition introduction of the third *Critique*, Kant goes further than saying that the universal finds its specification in the diverse. In the act of determinative cognition as performed by the understanding, 'the universal (the rule, principle, law) is given' and so the particular is subsumed under it. 'But if only the particular is given and judgment has to find the universal for it, then this power is ... *reflective*' (Kant 1987: 19). This is a more radical position than arguing that the universal must specify itself. Now the process is seen from the point of view of the specification itself – not as the realization of the universal, but as the sign of a suspended or problematic universal, or one that at best might be provisionally glimpsed via a particular arrangement of particulars. This is a universal that is simultaneously presupposed by a heuristic device that also marks its absence. Is this not quite close to Marx's position? The universal, social peace and economic equilibrium, is not given, and yet at the same time, the very conceptual totality which explains why it is not given (the presence of class divisions) and is indeed impossible within the given order presupposes not only the cognitive conceptual totality that contests abstract bourgeois universality, but also the ought-utopian possibility (no more than that) of a real universality to come. The aesthetic correlation to that critical social scientific project might, for example, be Benjamin's concept of the constellation or dialectics at a standstill. This implies a transitory glimpse of a real potential universal and critiques the actually existing false universal. The constellation is a paradoxical snapshot that is simultaneously totalizing but necessarily contingent, this side of the historical conditions that could actually realize true universality. As such, its provisional quality was also Benjamin's riposte to comforting reformist dialectical schemas that progress beyond capitalism was a universal given.

Kant's 'not given' is a huge blow to the reified philosophical architecture of the first *Critique* and in order to contain its implications Kant must insist on the purely subjective nature of reflective judgment. Everything Kant is now developing in terms of praxis, dialectical thinking and a new mode of form determination must be classified as merely subjective, if his system is to retain some appearance of coherence. Yet at so many points, Kant himself is undermining the rigid division he seeks to hold onto. We have seen this before, in the first *Critique*, with Kant developing and resisting concepts of mediation between form and content. In the third *Critique*, Kant simultaneously places the objective and subjective in close proximity with one another and then baulks at the implications for his system of building such bridges. Yet he has built them, not least in placing the *technic* of the aesthetic at the heart of natural science and making it possible for formal purposiveness to connect with knowledge about natural purposes. This in turn suggests that formal purposiveness might connect with another type of objectively given complex, namely socially constructed nature.

Hegel argued that in the third *Critique* Kant went beyond the dichotomous oppositions that structured Kant's philosophy in the first two *Critiques*. However,

> even here he stopped again at the opposition of the subjective to objectivity, so that while he does affirm the abstract dissolution of the opposition between concept and reality, universal and particular, understanding and sense, and therefore the Idea, he makes this dissolution and reconciliation into a purely *subjective* one.
>
> Hegel (1988: 57)

Although Kant suggests that the transcendental principle of reflective judgment 'merely reflects upon but does not determine objects' (Kant 1987: 35), which is to say it is merely subjective, elsewhere, in the first edition introduction to the *Critique of Judgment*, he gives an example that suggests how through an act of labour, this exercise of the imagination is transformed into a production of *new* nature that does imply precisely an objective (practical) determination of objects.

> For example, if we say that the crystal lens in the eye has the *purpose* of bringing about by means of a second refraction of light rays [the result] that the light rays emanating from one point will be reunited in one point of the retina of the eye, all we are saying is that our thought of the causality nature [exercised] in producing an eye includes the thought of the presentation of a purpose, because such an idea serves us as a principle by which we can guide our investigation of

the eye as far as its lens is concerned, and also because thinking the presentation of a purpose here might [help] us devise means to further that effect [if the natural lens does not do so adequately].

Kant (1987: 425)

By the principle of formal purposiveness, we satisfy our need to subjectively regulate our relationship to empirical diversity and apparent contingency (why does the lens of the eye have the qualities it does?) by means of an assumption of a unity of purposes. In this example, formal purposiveness in fact has a dynamic relationship with practical purposes flowing into it and transforming itself from a merely subjective a priori maxim to guide the discovery of knowledge into a *real objective force*. As Kant says, the presentation of a 'purpose' to the eye not only guides investigation but it also guides further technological *adaptation* of nature by humankind. Hence the presentation of a purpose enables us to 'devise means' to adapt nature (the production of artificial lenses, such as for glasses or magnifying instruments which Kant must have had in mind, but further down the historical line, the production of cameras for example). In such adaptations, a 'universal' comes into existence in the act of labour. A concept or assemblage of concepts, such as those that allow us to master the network of empirical laws that govern the human eye, determines the production of material nature (a magnifying glass or instrument for projecting images, for example). This ensemble of concepts underpinned by determinative judgments are only *provisionally universal* and only provisionally determinative (even in the natural sciences) and are constantly, through the historical process, being reworked in the course of modifying our practical and social relationships to nature. Such modifications require the creative act of reflective judgment, which is the basis of bringing *something genuinely new into the world*, something which ruptures the chain of determinative judgments *previously* set and creates a new set of such judgments. What brings Kant to the cusp of this materialist and even dialectical conception of the relationship between nature and culture, knowledge and productive forces, determinative and reflective judgment, is the role analogy plays in comparing and contrasting nature's 'organized bodies' with our own cognitive powers (formal purposiveness) and material productions (practical purposiveness).

> To *reflect* (or consider [*überlegen*]) is to hold given presentations up to, and compare them with, either other presentations or one's cognitive power [itself], in reference to a concept that this [comparison] makes possible.
>
> Kant (1987: 400)

This is the crucial passage, clearly defining Kant's own methodology in the third *Critique*, which is structured around comparisons between nature and art and between both of these and our own cognitive powers, and more implicitly, between art, nature and society. Here we have very clearly the origins of what would later be called negative dialectics, that is subjective, aesthetically tinged, 'poetic' juxtapositions that illuminate specific materialist truths of an epoch. Here we have the rationale for a critical procedure (analogy or metaphor) that makes it possible to *think* a concept through perception that it was difficult or not possible to think without that sensible operation. And here we have a rejection of the static positivist identity concept of affinity that dominated the first *Critique*. The whole question of the relationship or rather non-relationship between Kant's aesthetic and conceptuality is central to the dominant interpretation and conflicting evaluations of his aesthetic philosophy. As the above quote suggests, however, Kant's aesthetic is not antithetical to conceptuality, but instead it is an attempt to generate a *different* kind or modality of conceptuality than that which dominated the first *Critique*. This has not been widely recognized.

The beautiful

We have thus far been focusing on Kant's two introductions, mapping out the methodological break he achieves in the third *Critique* in anticipation of rescuing the 'Analytic of the Beautiful' from its entombment as a bourgeois philosophy of the aesthetic. Again, we must approach this section with an eye for the contrary impulses at work in Kant's text and with a sense that this is a project that is still very much unfinished and hence what we have here with Kant's final words is a snapshot of thought in process. This is especially the case when we come to consider the relationship of the aesthetic to conceptual thought. For there is a dominant interpretation that Kant's aesthetic is essentially *non-conceptual*. Differences then emerge about how to evaluate that – but there seems to be a remarkably widespread agreement that however it is evaluated, the Kantian aesthetic is non-conceptual.

We have already had cause to raise questions about this interpretation of the Kantian aesthetic by noting some aspects of the architecture of Kant's philosophy – such as placing an essentially aesthetic operation at the root of natural science, or noting his statements where he explicitly links the aesthetic to some notion of conceptuality or the possibility he opens up for formal purposiveness to pass into practical purposiveness. But perhaps the connotations of the word 'beauty' in Kant's aesthetic overwhelm these indications that the dominant interpretation is not quite as safe as it is assumed to be? The adherents or defenders of beauty derived from a reading of Kant may be split into two camps: the conservative and liberal bourgeois critics want to recover a classical version of art as disinterested contemplation of formal harmony and unity usually in the visual field which triggers feelings within the viewing subject that in turn articulates in a non-conceptual way something vaguely universal about the human condition (our appreciation of beauty). This discourse can be found alive and well in, for example, pretty much any issue of *The British Journal of Aesthetics*. It is a discourse that is empirical, intuitive (about individual feeling) and psychological (not psychoanalytic), and it exists in a kind of time warp, as if the major critical movements (the hermeneutic revolutions) of the twentieth century never happened. There is certainly enough in the way of arguments in Kant's third *Critique* to make him the foundation for this aesthetic and its disavowed political project. But there is also the radical wing of the bourgeois intelligentsia, who have gone through Marxism, post-structuralism, psychoanalysis, and so forth, and for whom a language of affect and feeling marks a point of resistance to the tyranny of conceptual language which these various theoretical paradigms have elucidated in their different ways, but offered, for these theorists, unsatisfactory solutions. They return to a quite traditional reading of Kant via the hermeneutic revolutions of the post–Second World War period in order to find intensities of affect that disrupt traditional hierarchies. Gilles Deleuze and his Anglophone interpreter Steven Shaviro come to mind and to some extent (as we shall see in the next chapter) Jacques Rancière.

Then there are those (in the orbit of Marxism) for whom Kant still remains very largely the inexhaustible source of a bourgeois ideology of the aesthetic, which is to be opposed by a discourse focusing on politics, contradiction and history. Obviously this is my direction of travel too, but in my reading Kant is a fellow traveller, not an obstacle to this journey. For many writers in the anti-Kant camp, the very word 'aesthetic' is a problem and is taken to be virtually synonymous with ideology. Against the aesthetic they champion the various forms of the avant-garde as a kind of anti-aesthetic (although this is a self-contradictory gesture as the anti-aesthetic is only an aesthetic attack on a specific institutionalized form of the aesthetic). One of the distinguishing features of this anti-aesthetic is its self-consciousness of its own theoretical presuppositions – a self-consciousness that is the necessary precondition for it to be able to attack the dominant institutions of art and institutionalized art itself. This latent awareness of its own conceptuality makes the anti-aesthetic a natural ally to Theory with a capital 'T', that is all those hermeneutic revolutions that have assaulted the bourgeois naturalization of methodology and practice across the disciplines, including, of course, art criticism. Thus the anti-aesthetic seems resolutely anti-Kant.

In one version of this position Peter Osborne has criticized Kant's conflation of aesthetics with art. In Kant, argues Osborne, aesthetics is defined as a general capacity to make judgments, but not in terms of specific judgments on the objects that provoke this capacity in the first place. In other words, Kant is read (quite plausibly) as founding a discourse on aesthetics that cannot engage with the specificity of art itself or its conditions of existence (Osborne 2004: 660). According to Osborne, in Kant there is a reduction or assimilation of the art*work* to the internal operations of the faculties which produce the power to judge in general, or, as Osborne puts it, 'the infinite reflexivity of a self positing subject' (Osborne 2004: 661). The self-positing subject feeling *themselves* exercise their powers is a Kantian-inspired discourse on art that is strangely indifferent to the formal and contextual specificity of the artwork (its conditions).

Central to this argument is an acceptance of the traditional reading of the Kantian aesthetic as grounded in a non-conceptual modality. Again, certainly Kant says this often enough to make this reading not only plausible but apparently indisputable to most commentators. This non-conceptuality resists a conceptual language that recognizes the conceptual, cognitive dimensions of the artwork and in turn the historical and political conditions which shape conceptuality in art. In Osborne's reading, the Kantian aesthetic is a combination of the first *Critique*, where it is a positivist sensuous presentation, and the third *Critique*, where sense-perception triggers a different kind of aesthetic, an internal reflection on the general capacities for this kind of subjective judgment. Both versions of the aesthetic are problematic in and of themselves, leading to naturalism in the first case and an inward-looking bourgeois subjectivity in the second case. Nevertheless, some sense of the aesthetic as sensuous and as provoking a subjective response are, Osborne admits, 'ineliminable' but also crucially '*radically insufficient*' (Osborne 2004: 664). Osborne notes that the anti-aesthetic attack on aesthetics by conceptual art proved, by its failure to eradicate pictorialism, the ineliminable aspect of aesthetics. But nevertheless, it also demonstrated that 'aesthetics' as defined on this reading of Kant was in itself inadequate. A sensuousness that is naturalistic and a abstract, formalist, transcendental capacity on the part of the subject to make judgments of taste cannot get to the historical specificity of the artwork and is therefore a poor basis for developing a criticism of art practices. Osborne both ascribes to Kant a division between sensuousness and conceptuality, which I think is far from unchallengeable, and he accepts that division, by the formulation that aesthetics in both its senses is ineliminable but radically insufficient. This acceptance, rather than working towards a more dialectical interpenetration of the sensuous and the conceptual, perhaps bears the residual trace of the influence of Althusser and Lacan, with their critique of the Imaginary (the sensuous and the unified subject) and at least in Althusser's case, the affirmation of theory as the basis of scientific knowledge. Thus Osborne notes that Kant seems to endorse a subjectivist, anti-theoretical mode of enquiry in the aesthetic by twice explicitly rejecting the idea that there can be a 'science' of the beautiful (Osborne 2004: 658). In such circumstances, then, it seems perverse to think that a Marxist theory of the aesthetic could owe anything to Kant, for whom, as we shall see, conceptuality appears to be antithetical to the aesthetic.

There are many instances where Kant makes the argument that the aesthetic judgment of taste is a purely subjective judgment, where pleasure and displeasure 'designates nothing whatsoever in the object, but here the subject feels himself [namely] how he is affected by the presentation' (Kant 1987: 44). And again a little later Kant ties the aesthetic to an internal subjective play of the powers we have to present objects. 'This power does not contribute anything to cognition, but merely compares the given presentation in the subject with the entire presentational power, of which the mind becomes conscious when it feels its own state' (Kant 1987: 44). So a given presentation is compared with our presentational powers in general and it is the feeling for these powers that the aesthetic initiates. Other signifiers of a bourgeois mode of reception are also to be found – for example, the serene passivity of an inward auto-referential 'contemplation' of intuition or reflection.

> A judgment of taste … is merely *contemplative*, i.e., it is a judgment that is indifferent to the existence of the object: it [considers] the character of the object only by holding it up to our feeling of pleasure and displeasure.
>
> Kant (1987: 51)

Here Kant dematerializes the aesthetic object, even though in the first introduction of the third *Critique* it is the formal arrangement of reflective judgment that makes it possible to produce a new concept or perhaps better a new kind of concept. So it would be absurd to deny that there is plenty of textual evidence to support a bourgeois reading of Kant. My argument is only that it is possible to construct a reading of Kant that is *at least* as plausible as the bourgeois interpretation (right or left) on the basis that Kant's text does not present a coherent unified project and that this reading while only aspiring to be at least as plausible is also *more* productive than the bourgeois and standard Marxist interpretations for our current needs (to think the relationship between the aesthetic and the social in the depths of the permanent crisis of bourgeois society).

Kant's zigzagging discussion of the role of pleasure–displeasure is a good example of the contradictory currents at work within his text. Pleasure is linked to the attainment of an aim and aims always have something to do with the discovery of a unity of principles, laws, rules, ideas, and so forth, that make experience coherent.

> it is a fact that when we discover that two or more heterogeneous empirical laws of nature can be unified under one principle that comprises them both, the discovery does give rise to a quite noticeable pleasure ...
>
> Kant (1987: 27)

A certain pleasure in the discovery of how nature (and we may add, social nature) *works* is, Kant adds, a part of 'even the commonest experience [which] would be impossible without it' (Kant 1987: 27). Now *that* is a very crucial and interesting point. For if the feeling of pleasure lies at the root of our everyday discovery of the world, then the strong dichotomy between a purely subjective feeling of pleasure and objective cognition is undermined. Here, Kant suggests that in part the aesthetic may be connected with the recovery of that worldly pleasure of childhood in finding out how things work which has been lost, forgotten or repressed in the process of conformism otherwise known as maturation. But this linking of pleasure to everyday cognition is also just as quickly repudiated by Kant when he declares that objective cognitive determination in the understanding (the subject of the first *Critique*) 'has nothing to do with a feeling of pleasure in things but rather with the understanding in our judging of them' (Kant 1987: 32–33). A little earlier he had already driven a wedge between pleasure and cognition when he states that in the aesthetic 'the presentation of the object is not an empirical concept but a feeling of pleasure (hence no concept at all)' (Kant 1987: 31). Yet it is not hard to find counterstatements that seem to lead in another direction altogether.

> A liking [*Wohlgefallen*] for the beautiful must depend on the reflection, regarding
> an object, that leads to some concept or other (but it is indeterminate which
> concept this is).
>
> Kant (1987: 49)

Here conceptuality is reintroduced but it is indeterminate *which* concept the
aesthetic might lead to. That is very different from saying that it involves no
concept whatsoever – and this is one of many examples of textual evidence we
can produce which suggests not that Kant could not make up his mind, but
that his thought is in the process of development. He wants to get to a position
where he can articulate something that is not purely subjective but neither is it
like the deterministic (reified) conceptuality involved in the cognitive process
mapped out in the first *Critique*. In short, he wants to use the aesthetic, not to
propose a non-conceptual mode of consciousness, but *a new and different type
of relationship between sensuousness and conceptuality*, which would later come
to be known within Marxism as praxis.

There are various aspects in the architecture of Kant's philosophical system,
that is in the relationships he constructs between concepts, which add weight to
the argument that there is a powerful internal dynamic pushing Kant decisively
away from his explicit statements regarding the non-conceptuality of the aesthetic
and aesthetic pleasure. The relationship between the understanding and the
imagination in the aesthetic mode is a case in point. Kant argues that in the
aesthetic, the relationship between the understanding and the imagination is
quite different from the relationship that obtains when making logical judgments.
As discussed in the previous chapter, the empirical or reproductive imagination
is in a subordinate position vis-à-vis the understanding and its imperatives (the
imperatives of the pure categories and the empirical concepts they organize
in order to have intelligible experience). In the aesthetic something different
happens:

> the cognitive powers brought into play by this presentation are in free play,
> because no determinate concept restricts them to a particular rule of cognition.
> Hence the mental state in this presentation must be a feeling, accompanying
> the given presentation, of a free play of the presentational powers directed to
> cognition in general.
>
> Kant (1987: 62)

Here as elsewhere, there is a tendency in Kant towards dematerializing the object
which makes the presentation possible (Osborne's complaint) and reducing the

'mental state' which the presentation engenders to a transcendental a priori abstraction (which subsequent bourgeois criticism has often reduced to the merely psychological). Nevertheless, with that caveat duly acknowledged, Kant here identifies the aesthetic as emerging in a *free play* between the presentational powers. That is significant in identifying the relative autonomy of the aesthetic. It is relative and it is not purely subjective, because the imagination is still in some kind of relationship with the understanding and its (bourgeois) materialism (i.e. a materialism of physical and logical relations). As Makkreel puts it:

> Although self-activating, the aesthetic imagination is not autonomous, that is, it does not establish its own laws. It conforms to laws that are still the laws of the understanding. The 'free conformity' of the aesthetic imagination to the laws of the understanding means that the imagination may not violate the categorical framework of the understanding, although it may explicate possibilities left open by that framework.
>
> Makreel (1990: 46–47)

I would phrase things a little differently. It is precisely because the framework of the understanding left open very little in the way of any possibilities associated with freedom that Kant turns to the aesthetic where the sensuous, the conceptual and the idea can be combined. In his later discussion of aesthetic production Kant returns to the question of the relationship between the understanding and the imagination, and it is, I think, clear that his thinking has definitely evolved in the direction I am suggesting. Now the aesthetic is defined as:

> the ability to exhibit *aesthetic ideas*; and by an aesthetic idea I mean a presentation of the imagination which prompts much thought, but to which no determinate thought whatsoever, i.e., no [determinate] *concept*, can be adequate, so that no language can express it completely and allow us to grasp it. It is easy to see that an aesthetic idea is the counterpart (pendant) of a *rational idea*, which is, conversely, a concept to which no *intuition* (presentation of the imagination) can be adequate.
>
> Kant (1987: 182)

The new and different type of concept that Kant is moving towards is here articulated as the aesthetic idea. The aesthetic idea is different from a *determinate* concept, but not necessarily to all conceptuality. It is in fact a counterpart to the rational idea which works with concepts but, in the case of moral reason, bends them, or *ought* to bend them, to its free affirmation of the good. However, unlike the rational idea, the aesthetic idea is grounded in intuition, in sensuousness, but unlike the sensuousness which is governed by determinate conceptuality, the tendency towards reification, where determinateness becomes a priori determinism, is checked, and this is articulated by the concept of the indeterminate that Kant uses elsewhere. Here the meaning is slightly different from the use of the indeterminate discussed previously. It is not that which concept we are led to is indeterminate, but rather that the quality of the concept (whatever it may be) itself is indeterminate. We may take both senses of indeterminate to be useful: aesthetic pleasure may be led in numerous unplanned directions and to relatively (relative to determinative judgments) more clusters of meaning and possibility than can be subjected to the subject's responses. Kant now writes of how the 'presentation aesthetically expands the concept itself in an unlimited way' (Kant 1987: 183) or how the aesthetic imagination is characterized by a relative freedom which develops 'material for the understanding which the latter disregarded in its concept' (Kant 1987: 185). That is very suggestive of the kind of space the aesthetic opens up, but it also implies a feedback loop between the aesthetic judgment and the understanding which again undercuts Kant's insistence on the 'merely subjective' nature of the aesthetic judgment. For if it is developing 'material for the understanding' which the understanding neglected because of the reified universe of concepts, then the aesthetic is clearly not *merely* subjective. In his final word on the subject, in the solution to the antinomy of taste, his thought seems to have moved decisively and fairly unequivocally beyond the earlier definitions of the aesthetic which the bourgeois and indeed Marxist interpreters have made so much of:

> A judgment of taste is not based on determinate concepts.... A judgment of taste is indeed based on a concept, but on an *indeterminate* one (namely, that of the supersensible substrate of appearances).
>
> Kant (1987: 213)

If the aesthetic is to behave aesthetically, *determinate* concepts and *determinate* cognitions should not form the basis of its special formal operations. That is why there can be no 'science' of the aesthetic, since science here means the science of logical determinative judgments. There can of course be a critique of the aesthetic – a theoretical account of its transcendental conditions of existence which Kant does elsewhere (if we are that hung up on the word) also call a *science* (Kant: 1987: 150). Working according to its own principles, what should be possible within the aesthetic are the development of *critical* concepts and *critical* cognitions (but in the sensuous-imaginative mode of the aesthetic). The indeterminate concept is one which can go beyond the limitations of the merely empirical and touch on the supersensible substrate of appearances while still basing itself in appearances. It does so because it is grounded in the reflective judgment, which arranges the empirical according to a formal relation. The supersensible substrate of appearances is precisely the invisible space between the empirically observable and the relations that have been organized according to principles that have to be conceived rather than directly observed. Conversely, when determinate concepts and cognitions *do* enter the formal structure of the aesthetic, then it becomes yoked to stereotypes and rigid ideological value-formations. If for Kant the aesthetic activates a mode of individual judging very different from the schema of the *Critique of Pure Reason*, where transcendental rules match concepts with sense-impressions, then when the aesthetic imitates the operations of the schema, there its provisional, critical and exploratory possibilities are vitiated. This indeed was Adorno's judgment on the culture industry, that it is a kind of folding back of the aesthetic into the *Critique of Pure Reason*, now understood as institutionalized industrial monopoly capitalism: 'The sensuous moment of art transforms itself under the eyes of mass culture into the measurement, comparison and assessment of physical phenomena' (Adorno 1991b: 75).

The absence of any dialogic dimension to our relationship with nature in the first *Critique* means that the aesthetic idea is conversely closely connected with the notion of the communicability of the aesthetic experience. Kant argues that the communicability of the aesthetic involves a certain *as if* quality, just as the principle and the methodology of the reflective judgment does. The *as if* character of the aesthetic in terms of communicability manifests itself because on the one hand the judgment opens up the possibility of individual responses to sensuous apprehension and on the other this response feels as if it were an objective property of the thing that is called beautiful. This is why we feel that an aesthetic judgment is one that can be shared, that is it can be communicated with others and even that we feel others should agree with us that this is beautiful. Disagreement may and usually does follow but the claim to agreement presupposes that it is worth having a discussion about the claim in the first place. The subjective dimension which the aesthetic opens up here does not mean that which pertains only to the individual – since that contradicts the communicability of the judgment. Subjective here refers to a mode of form determination in play that has scope for a plasticity of response and feeling different from determinate judgments. On the other hand, it has this shared, intersubjective basis as well, as if it were an objective judgment, and yet it has none of the deterministic qualities which characterize such logical judgments.

Now within the traditional bourgeois reception of Kant, the tension we may read into Kant's work between the individual response to the given presentation of an aesthetic object and its social conditions, implied by the communicability of the mental state, has been resolved decisively in favour of the individual as well as the non-conceptual. If the orthodox Marxist response to Kant is a certain suspicion of the aesthetic, understood as sensuousness, and a championing of rigorous theoretical conceptual 'science', the bourgeois response is the mirror opposite: suspicion of the conceptual and a championing of the sensuous, of feeling and the apparently non-conceptual. The left-wing Deleuzian version of this reception and interpretation, however, offers a critique of the bourgeois individual subject in which these values are usually invested. For Shaviro, the non-conceptuality of the beautiful is accepted. Aesthetic judgments are purely 'affective, rather than cognitive' (Shaviro 2009: 3). This provides the basis for an affective intensity of response that circumvents 'hierarchical conceptual relations' (Shaviro 2002: 13). Affect is conceived as a transpersonal energy or force that like labour-power can be commodified for the business of exchange (Shaviro 2010: 5). Despite this it is always in some kind of excess or surplus to such fixings. It is flow and process, so can never be definitively 'owned'; it courses through objects, individuals and institutions which capture it according to various classifying systems, but can never corral it completely. Affect relativizes stable and essential distinctions suggesting that criteria are always situational rather than universal (Shaviro 2009: 23). This amounts to a poetics of resistance, evoking some sort of vague collectivity and materialist emphasis on flux in opposition to the old-fashioned static bourgeois individualism.

The potential for the aesthetic to act as a site of resistance to or circumnavigation of reification is of course central to my argument. But I am unwilling to sever the aesthetic from conceptuality, and so, I would argue, is Kant. The supposed non-conceptuality of intuitive feeling has implications for the communicability of the aesthetic experience and the aesthetic experience as a mode of communication:

> Kant's very demand for the universal communicability of aesthetic judgment thus presupposes its own conceptual impossibility. The actual pleasure or sensation of beauty cannot be communicated.
>
> Shaviro (2002: 14)

Shaviro pushes Kant's aesthetic to the point where it rows back from the possibility of non-instrumental communication (and relations) that Kant himself was moving towards. Shaviro's position rests on a strongly dualist division between affect, feeling and sensuousness, on the one hand, and thought, consciousness and conceptualization, on the other. Kant himself was very clear that *communicability* comes first and that 'pleasure in the object must be its consequence' (Kant 1987: 61). That seems to me to be a fairly unequivocal statement that the pleasure of aesthetic response is forged in a social, intersubjective relation with others, no matter how intense the pleasurable and affective dimension of the response is for the individual concerned. This inner feeling always traces its origins to a relation with others, indeed, as we shall see in the next chapter, beauty is in fact an encounter with difference. The contemporary bourgeois reception of Kant regresses on Kant's own position, either locating feeling as the property of the solitary already formed individual or tracing feeling and subjectivity as emerging out of radically discontinuous, multiple encounters that are so contingent that they resist any form of naming (Shaviro 2009: 20). In either case, the social nature of the aesthetic is unfathomable.

Closely linked with the possibility for reading Kant's emphasis on affect as a source of resistance to classification is the concept of singularity. In the Deleuzian-inspired interpretation of Kant, singularity refers to a radically contingent, random or unpredictable break with conceptual classifications. But if we can imagine that singularity might not be non-conceptual but just differentially cognitive, then we can read it in more social terms without robbing it of its critical character. In the aesthetic there is no 'rule' that can persuade us that something is beautiful prior to its presentation to us, for 'we want to submit the object to our own eyes, just as if our liking of it depended on that sensation' (Kant 1987: 59). This insistence that judgment is grounded in the direct relationship between the experiencing subject and the object of judgment is quite contrary to so much of our reified public sphere under late capitalism, where political, economic and military discourses circulate meanings that we are asked to assent to but which are uncoupled from the real experiences which those discourses imply or initiate. This uncoupling facilitates assent precisely because the human cost is not really embodied in the 'knowledge' produced by these discourses. In the aesthetic mode, by contrast, judgment remains embodied in the sensuous experience itself. The nature of the unexpected discovery of meaning within the aesthetic may well include the discovery of what we 'know' but have not had the opportunity to admit into our knowledge *as sensuous experience*. The widespread phenomenon of disavowal in consumer capitalism depends on the separation of sensuous experience from knowing. The subsumption of sense-impressions under concepts in the faculty of the understanding opens up a rift between concepts and experience that reflects the division of society into those whose elite experiences are unjustifiably universalized and therefore dominate those whose mass experiences are prevented from achieving universal conceptual recognition. When minority class experiences are the basis for conceptualizing the world universally, then those concepts are typically emptied of sensuous content in order to masquerade as universal. Hence the tendency of bourgeois thought towards abstract formalism, composed of hollowed-out concepts that can preserve their unity and non-contradictory status only on condition that they shield themselves from engaging with the real sensuous content of life. Conversely, the real sensuous content of life struggles to find adequate expression, recognition and self-recognition in a conceptual universe alien to it.

Eagleton and the ideology of the aesthetic

Perhaps, though, the aesthetic is not our friend in this struggle against the fetishism of sensuousness cut off from the capacity to reflect on its conditions of existence and the fetishism of concepts cut off from the real experiential content they allude to but must bracket off? Perhaps instead the aesthetic is the ally of the dominant social order? This essentially is the argument put forward by Terry Eagleton and it will be useful to clarify what is at stake and how my argument differs from the standard Marxist reading of Kant by concluding this chapter with some remarks on Eagleton's reading of the Kantian aesthetic. Eagleton's broader critique of the ideology of the aesthetic is to cast what I have been presenting as a bottom-up sensuous exploration of 'laws', as a hegemonic project in which the concepts of the ruling order fashion a discourse which can make sense of the terrain of 'passion and perception' (Eagleton 1997: 14). This is the whole affective life of the subject which the ruling order needs to be able to speak to and orchestrate if a successful shift in the modality of domination, from the coercion of absolutism to consent, is to be made. Although Eagleton acknowledges in places that the aesthetic is 'a dangerous, ambiguous affair' (Eagleton 1997: 28), the thrust of his argument stresses its successful hegemonic function (perhaps because he is focusing on critical discourses of the aesthetic more than aesthetic cultural production). This emphasis closes off a more productive Marxist engagement with Kant's aesthetic philosophy.

   I want to focus on two aspects of the aesthetic that loom large in Kant's discussion of the beautiful: the question of the relationship between subjectivity and objectivity, and the relationship between sensuousness and conceptual abstraction. Eagleton comes perilously close in both of these aspects to suggesting that to establish some sort of reciprocal relationship between the paired terms in each case is quintessentially an ideological move. I would suggest that because capitalism is characterized by the dualistic rupture between subject and object, sensuous particular and the abstract, that Marxists ought be extremely interested in theoretical and practical efforts to establish more productive relations between these terms.

In terms of a philosophy of praxis, if we transpose Kant's discussion of the aesthetic as a way of thinking about the constituent parts of our species being, namely that we are of nature, part of nature and immersed in the natural world and *yet* differentiated from nature by dint of *our* nature as social beings equipped with tremendous creative capacities, then Kant's discussion of the aesthetic, contradictory as it is, begins to look like he is prefiguring Marx in some important respects. We can see a proto-materialist formulation in parts of Kant's aesthetic not unlike Marx's discussion of our 'metabolic' relation to nature in *Capital*. Eagleton, by contrast, sees Kant's aesthetic almost wholly as a form of ideological consolation. The extent to which it can be seen as a register in which subject–object relations different to the dualities of the *Critique of Pure Reason* can be gropingly formulated is underplayed and cast as bourgeois wish fulfilment:

> …in the aesthetic sphere, objects are uncovered which seem at once real yet wholly given for the subject, veritable bits of material Nature which are nevertheless delightfully pliant to the mind.
>
> Eagleton (1997: 78)

Eagleton, however, tends to blur – through style – the distinction between ontological categories such as subject and object, essential really to any philosophy of praxis, and ideological renditions of those categories. I would dispute Eagleton's characterization that the Kantian aesthetic gives the object 'wholly' over to the subject, because the 'play' *between* the imagination and the understanding expressly contradicts this. But perhaps the reader's hesitation here over 'wholly' is swept aside by that strategic use of 'delightfully', which in the fashion of Bakhtin's dialogical class struggle appropriates a key and recognizable word from the enemy (middle-class taste) and inserts it here to rhetorically ramp up the critique of a bourgeois idealist overinflation of subjectivity at the expense of the obdurate qualities of the object world. In so doing, it is not clear whether Eagleton is critiquing Kant's specific formulation of the aesthetic, or whether he sees any productive relationship between subject and object as essentially an ideological discourse.

That Eagleton's stylistic strategies obfuscate such distinctions are compounded by his conceptual underpinnings that are hard to square with the

Marxist tradition. Kant's aesthetic, he argues, offers a consoling account of a centred human subject 'in an imaginary relation to a pliable, purposive reality, thereby granting it a delightful sense of its own inner coherence and confirming its status as an ethical agent' (1997: 98). According to Eagleton, the notion of the human subject having a purposive relation to a relatively ordered external reality such that it can make some aspects of it 'pliable', which in turn raises ethical questions over the choices we make, is thoroughly ideological (note the word 'delightful' again). Yet some version of this model – discredited as it is within the Althusserian/Lacanian discourse Eagleton here invokes to critique the 'centred' subject – is necessary if we are to have any rational discussion about history and society. If Eagleton believes that it is merely a consoling fantasy that the material world might be regarded as recoverable as the product of the active subject (collective and individual), then the trajectory of the argument is clearly outside the orbit of Marxism. Further, it is not even clear that the middle-class taste formation that he has in mind is an accurate barometer of what Kant actually argues.

> Aesthetic judgment is then a kind of pleasurable free-wheeling of our faculties, a kind of parody of conceptual understanding, a non-referential pseudo-cognition which does not nail down the object to an identifiable thing, and so is agreeably free of a certain material constraint.
>
> Eagleton (1997: 85)

Now, there are sections of Kant's argument where this is a more than plausible reading. But it cannot encompass everything that Kant says and, I would argue, cannot even account for the main thrust of Kant's discussion. What Kant calls the 'attunement of the cognitive powers' (Kant 1987: 88), that interplay between the understanding and the imagination in the aesthetic mode, is necessary for both cognitive and aesthetic judgment. But in the latter case, it is an attunement 'in which this inner relation is most conducive to the (mutual) quickening of the two mental powers with a view to cognition (of given objects) in general' (Kant 1987: 88). Here at least, if not everywhere, to assess the Kantian aesthetic as a parody of cognitive judgment seems wide of the mark. Developing the thrust of Kant's point, Deleuze argues that:

> The faculties would never enter into an accord that was determined or fixed by one of them if they were not in the first place, by themselves and spontaneously, capable of an indeterminate accord, a free harmony, a harmony without fixed proportions.
>
> Deleuze (2000: 60)

For the understanding to legislate in the sphere of cognition, reason must freely submit to it in the form of limiting itself to merely rational judgments; for reason to legislate, the understanding must relinquish its hold and allow moral judgments to dominate. These 'accords' depend in turn on the free harmony of the aesthetic mode. Far from being a parody, the aesthetic is indicative of capacities and powers that are the basis of cognitive judgment. For the early Deleuze, these accords between the faculties also register that they have a certain amount of discord between them, insofar as they exercise judgments that seem to operate according to conflicting principles. Thus instead of the aesthetic being a parody of cognitive judgment, reified cognitive judgment revokes the principles which form its basis (a degree of freedom) and it is this basis that is exemplified by and preserved in the aesthetic. Note that Eagleton accepts unquestioningly the idea that Kant's aesthetic is without conceptual and therefore without cognitive content or implications. We have already seen that at the level of Kant's overall philosophical architecture, explicit statements or the general trend of his argument, this is far from being an unchallengeable argument, even if it has remained remarkably widespread.

Elsewhere Eagleton describes the aesthetic not as a parody of conceptual thought but as 'concrete thought or sensuous analogue of the concept' (Eagleton 1988: 328). But this he sees as dangerously close to the essence of bourgeois ideology and its hegemonic project. For Eagleton, the aesthetic is a rather more effective means of winning the battle of ideas than either civil society – which is too competitive, egotistical and materialistic – or the state – which is too obviously about coercion and power. The aesthetic provides a means whereby abstract doctrines and ideologies can interpellate subjects in ways that hit their guts, so to speak, combining a powerful affective dimension to those abstract doctrines that avoids the need for reflexive rationalization ('that's just the way I feel') while providing such feelings with a universal righteousness that transcends mere subjective whim and particularity. This is a perfect combination for hegemonic communication.

> In ideology and the aesthetic we stay with the thing itself, which is preserved in all its concrete materiality rather than dissolved to its abstract conditions; yet this very materiality, this uniquely unrepeatable form or body, comes mysteriously to assume all the compelling logic of a global decree.
>
> Eagleton (1997: 95)

Eagleton brilliantly articulates the manner in which the ideological stirs people up while insulating them from really reflecting on the assumptions behind their deeply felt concerns. But is this in fact *also* a description of the aesthetic? To say that the aesthetic can be a vehicle or a predicate for ideology goes without saying, but to say that the aesthetic is inherently ideological because it unites abstraction with the perceptible/sensual, as Eagleton does, really closes off an important resource for the left. Indeed, given the way capitalism's tendency towards abstraction massively increases the disjunctive relations between concept world and experience, then the aesthetic is a crucial pedagogic resource. This ability to relativize concepts and make abstractions from experience, as well as the ability to see alterations in the physical appearance of things as a register of social relations (through a close-up or editing, for example, in film), has been central to what has attracted generations of Marxist cultural theorists and practitioners (from Eisenstein to Jameson) to the aesthetic mode (and film in particular). Unlike Kant's reason, the aesthetic combines free (but not autonomous) deliberation with a sensuous manifestation thus overcoming the divide between the sensible and the supersensible.

Where abstract doctrines such as sexism and racism acquire a felt, lived power through aesthetics, ideology is *hijacking* the aesthetic and negating some of the characteristics that make the aesthetic, aesthetic. Engagement with the particularity of lived experience, for example, becomes highly selective and narrow. From Gaye Tuchman's 'symbolic annihilation' of women in the mass media (1978) to Edward Said's critique of orientalism (1995), the narrow social basis on which representation is founded reveals itself in the aesthetic as a pseudo-engagement with the particular and is the pseudo-sensuous counterpart to the emptying out of discursive language of any real substantive content in favour of formalism. A film like *The Mummy* (1999) conforms to the racial Othering which Said analysed in *Orientalism*. The white British and American characters are presented as daring, adventurous, brave, ingenious and resourceful, exactly the sort of people in whose hands the treasures they seek and find should belong, while *their* presence in Egypt is only ever cast in terms of the threat which others (the natives) pose to them, not what threat they pose to the native. The native, by contrast, when they come out of the background of the mise-en-scène, are sneaky, cunning, cowardly, threatening and power hungry, exactly the sort of people who need to be kept in line by civilized and knowledgeable white westerners. The film was a Universal Pictures production and as well as film sequels, video games on PlayStation and other platforms were released off the back of its success. Universal Pictures is a subsidiary of General Electric, the energy corporation that signed a $3 billion contract with the Iraqi government to provide power generation equipment and services in 2009. Needless to say, GE did not have a market in Iraq before the 2003 invasion by the United States and the United Kingdom. Clearly, then, the yoking of the aesthetic to ideology involves us in economic, political and military power that must win consent to the exercise of those powers or at least passive tolerance to its goals and methods if it is not to court political danger. Yet the occlusion of the real Arab subject is a sure sign that *The Mummy* is a vehicle for ideology rather than an example of the inherently ideological nature of the aesthetic. In violation of the working up of 'universals' from the particular, here we have the precise opposite, where the a priori determinative judgment ('we whites are superior') masquerades as an inductive process. This in no way correlates with Kant's reflective judgment. Instead it is motivated by a pre-existing and rigidly a priori value system closed to experiential learning (including *mediated* experiential learning). It is very far from the 'indeterminate' quality Kant finds characteristic of the aesthetic. Eagleton interprets Kant's concept of the 'indeterminate' as a complacent middle-class refusal to engage with the real world and as symptomatic of a resistance to theoretical and conceptual language that cognitively 'determines' the nature of things. But again, Eagleton has missed the precise sense and meaning by which Kant is contrasting 'determinate' judgments with critical and provisional 'indeterminate' ones, and therefore missing the de-reifying potential of the indeterminate, the potential to reveal the relations that are invisible in the determinative judgment.

In the determinative judgment, the universal remains disjunctive with the particular or simply assimilates it and in either case refuses to allow the particular to impact on and shape the universal. In short contact with the Arab other is not going to lead to a reassessment of white western preconceptions in a film like *The Mummy*. The relationship between particular and universal, the experiential and the abstract, is radically different in the two kinds of judgment. Eagleton, however, does not distinguish between the two. For him, the 'universal voice' that the subject finds in the aesthetic is one that is analogous to the way 'gut feelings' are given the status of universal and incontrovertible truth so typical of ideology. Yet the analogy is inexact in crucial ways. For what Kant is suggesting is that the 'universal voice' with which we speak is precisely our capacity for discussion, precisely our capacity *not* to just accept what is given (those a priori judgments), precisely a universal that retains its material ground and is therefore always provisional, precisely the capacity for us to *imagine* nature and social relations differently from the way they have been constituted for us previously and by historical conditions.

***

We began this chapter by noting that the dichotomy between Kant's transcendental laws and empirical laws and the dichotomy between nature and freedom were subsets of the division between form and content in his philosophical architecture. Central to my argument is that the third *Critique* represents a methodological break from the first (and second) *Critique* and its form–content dichotomy. One reason why Kant's interpreters can argue that the three *Critiques* have a systematic unity is that superficially, many of the same concepts and lines of thought appear to connect them. Thus in the appendix to the *Critique of Pure Reason*, where he is discussing reason's use of regulative ideas, Kant seems already to have anticipated his discussion of reflective judgment. In the first *Critique* he notes that when 'the universal is assumed only *problematically*' (Kant 1996: 621), then the idea of systematic unity 'is nothing more than a *projected* unity' (Kant 1996: 622), that is a hypothetical use of reason to enable it to work (in relation to empirical discovery) in the absence of the objective unity of empirical laws which it must presuppose. Does this suggest that there is in fact no methodological break between the first *Critique* and the third?

Well, no. In the first *Critique* it is only reason's more empirical rational capacities that are in operation when problematizing universality. It is reason subordinating itself to the *lawfulness* of nature and aiding the understanding in its search for rational unity in empirical laws. In the third *Critique*, the power of judgment borrows the concept of unity and freedom from *moral* reason and opens it up to a qualitatively different interpretation (that of formal purposiveness) by stressing the subjective dimension of judgment. Crucially, there is nothing in the first *Critique* comparable to the third in terms of comparing nature to art. While in the appendix of the first *Critique* Kant develops his concept of affinity to now include *difference* as well as homogeneity, this is all conceived within the framework of a natural science graduated mapping of empirical nature (Kant 1996: 630–631). Concepts like the circular, the elliptical and the parabolic that were used to analyse gravity and the planets by astronomers have a 'step-wise increase of difference' and permit the elucidation of differences of empirical phenomena in terms of the kinds of sense intuitions they describe. What will happen in the third *Critique*, however, is that affinity becomes more strongly connected with ideas and disputes (moral reason). This allows the resemblances and differences of form to make connections that go beyond mapping empirical similarities and differences. It opens up the whole domain of creative metaphor.

A relationship to nature that seeds the concept of praxis is to be found in the *as if* principle of formal purposiveness, that subjective arrangement and manipulation of nature to achieve a particular mental effect and concept or idea generation. The *as if* principle operates in the space between the reified what is (known) and what is unknown or unacknowledged and through the formal procedure of analogy posits a relationship between *creative* reason and nature, between the subjective act of a purposive arrangement in the *form* of things, natural purposes and practical purposes (the making of social nature).

Through analogy or reflective judgment Kant began to overcome the compartmentalization of his thought, including the divisions between the subjective and the objective, the individual and society. Lyotard rightly sees the shift from the first *Critique* to the third in terms of a move from the tautological to the heuristic that is grounded in reflective judgment:

> ... reflection is the (subjective) laboratory of all objectivities. In its heuristic aspect reflection thus seems to be the nerve of critical thought as such.
>
> Lyotard (1994: 26)

Kant's concept of reflective judgment was designed to address a tension or contradiction within the first *Critique* that Lyotard identified. A transcendental critique requires elaborating the conditions of possibility for knowledge, but this elaboration ('deduction') itself requires the discriminating powers of knowledge to work on those 'conditions' and reveal them. Thus critique 'must have the enigmatic capacity to judge the proper conditions of judgment "before" being able to make use of, before having the right to make use of these conditions' (Lyotard 1994: 31). The concept of reflective judgment is Kant's attempt to think about how thought can round upon its own conditions of possibility – which bears more than a passing resemblance to the project of historical materialism.

Eclipsing the materialist implications of reflective judgment, bourgeois critics celebrate Kant's supposedly non-conceptual aesthetic – either valorizing it in the name of a traditional model of subjectivity and naturalistic representation or as a radical model of subjectivity seeking to subvert traditional bourgeois classifications. For Marxist critics, the Kantian aesthetic and its apparent grounding in the non-conceptual is synonymous with ideology. I have suggested that in many ways this dominant assessment of the relationship between the Kantian aesthetic and conceptuality is questionable. There is the overall architecture of Kant's thought in the third *Critique*, such as the relationships between formal purposiveness and natural science or the play between the imagination and the understanding. There are plenty of explicit counterstatements that link the aesthetic to a new relationship with or new kinds of concepts. There is also the overall direction of his thought, such as his unequivocal stress that pleasure rests on and is the consequence of the communicability of the aesthetic experience. Finally, Kant's thought culminates, at the end of part one of the third *Critique*, in the definition of the aesthetic idea. This suggests that the aesthetic, when it is working aesthetically (i.e. not hijacked by ideology) works up its sensuous content according to the principles of reflective judgment that de-reify the determinate concepts impregnated within the sensuous experience of everyday life. The Kantian aesthetic is similar to the critical social science of Marx's project, except aesthetic form determination has much greater scope, much greater 'play' in relation to the categorical framework of the understanding than Marx's critical social science project or the natural sciences. This is what makes it imaginative rather than scientific.

4

The Aesthetic and Class Interests

Perhaps the most difficult aspect of Kant's philosophy for a Marxist reconstruction of it that would release Kant from his entombment as a bourgeois philosopher is his claim that a pure aesthetic judgment is not only non-conceptual, but also, because of that independence from instrumental cognition, 'disinterested'. 'Everyone has to admit', Kant claims, 'that if a judgment about beauty is mingled with the least interest then it is very partial and not a pure judgment of taste' (Kant 1987: 46). Yet Kant's claim – even if we take it as meaning what everyone seems to take it as meaning – still poses a problem that cannot be easily dismissed: how to do justice to the *specificity* of the aesthetic while situating it in some relation to socially interested practices, especially class practices. How can we think this relationship to class-interested practices that does not reduce the aesthetic to a *mere expression* of a given set of class interests and practices? This is the task that Kant sets us and it is a task that Marxist responses to Kant have been trying to answer ever since. We have, as Karatani would argue, a parallax, a constant shuttling between two poles: aesthetic judgments are (class) interested, and aesthetic judgments are not (class) interested. I am going to argue that a non-reductive philosophy of the aesthetic and its relations with social interests, especially class interests, can be inspired by Kant's third *Critique*. This must sound paradoxical, but a different reading of Kant may emerge once we reinterpret what he means by 'interests' and 'disinterest'. The concept of reflective judgment meanwhile continues to help us, now aiding our ability to think of the aesthetic as a reflection *of* and a reflection *on* its material conditions of existence and it does so precisely at that point where classes become *aware* of each other, not just at the level of content, but above all at the level of aesthetic form. The beautiful, by which we mean an object that has a special kind of purposive form, turns out to be an encounter with otherness, not wholeness, but difference spliced with inequality. In order to develop this alternative reading of Kant and illuminate what is at stake for contemporary debates around aesthetics and class, I want to discuss two key figures that have been, in very different ways, influenced by Kant: Pierre Bourdieu from an anti-Kantian position and the recent work of Jacques Rancière from a more 'pro' Kantian position. At stake in this parallax between Bourdieu and Rancière is the central question of how to think the aesthetic and its conditions of existence without reducing it to those conditions or transcending them.

On interests and disinterest

Between §10 and §16 of the 'Analytic of the Beautiful' the bourgeois Kant emerges most fully. This is the Kant who is then, either lionized by conservative and liberal commentators, subverted by the radical wing of the bourgeois intelligentsia or critiqued from the orthodox Marxist position. After §16 Kant returns to the question of the relationship that the aesthetic has to reason, as he transits to the Analytic of the Sublime. Because the aesthetic–reason nexus opens up the prospect of connecting the former to ideas that reconfigure reified concepts through sensuous apprehension, the question of how to think the relationship between the aesthetic and reason always tends to push Kant away from the tendency to situate the aesthetic as transcendent to the social.

§10 opens with a question: what is a purpose? In answering this question about purposiveness in general, Kant will go on to develop the concept of purposiveness without purpose (i.e. without interests). This concept appears to be a close cousin of formal purposiveness, but in fact, it lays the foundation for the bourgeois Kant. As we have seen, formal purposiveness, developed in the two introductions and linked to the capacity to make reflective judgments, was a concept that allows for the generation of a different relationship to conceptuality, not non-conceptuality per se, but a different modality of conceptuality that has a different (non-reified) relationship to the sensual. The 'formal' part is meant to designate, among other things, how the mental operation (a heuristic device) refers to the subject alone and not the object, although we also saw that Kant entertained the possibility of formal purposiveness connecting to knowledge of both natural purposes and practical purposes (the making of the social world). But purposiveness without purpose is Kant's bourgeois reinterpretation of all this in the register of aesthetic *reception*, now conceived as 'pure', and this has been predominantly read as dichotomously opposed to these other material and objective purposes (i.e. conditions and interests).

Kant defines purposiveness in general as 'the causality that a *concept* has with regard to its *object*' (Kant 1987: 65). In the first *Critique*, the transcendental subject of the understanding scrutinizes phenomena, putting together their form in order to make objects cognitively readable (i.e. purposive to the subject). This operation is of course 'interested' in the sense that it involves the subject mastering the world of nature as projected and constructed by the subject for instrumental purposes. In the second *Critique*, Kant explores the transcendental ground for the subject in their morally purposive relationship to the world. This too is an interested activity, although the interests here are more an expression of the community embodied in the moral good, rather than self-interest. In the third *Critique*, Kant coins the term 'purposiveness without purpose'. Once again, the subject must scrutinize phenomena for their meaning, focusing on the form of the aesthetic object which we presuppose has a purpose. But now in the register of aesthetic taste we must empty the aesthetic object and our response to it of any trace of interest, hence it is that paradoxical thing that it displays purposiveness without purpose. A new *as if* principle, which we saw at work in relation to formal purposiveness, comes into play.

> … there can be purposiveness without a purpose, insofar as we do not posit the causes of this form in a will, and yet can grasp the explanation of its possibility only by deriving it from a will.
>
> Kant (1987: 65)

Whereas before, with the concept of formal purposiveness, the *as if* principle seemed to be a mind expanding device, now purposiveness without purpose seems more strongly accented towards a kind of disavowal: 'I know it is the product of a purpose, a will, but in order for me to achieve aesthetic pleasure from this sensuously apprehended object, I must pretend that it is not'. The element of a mental trick designed to have a particular effect on our mental powers (formal purposiveness) now becomes, it seems, a disavowal of interests (purposes without purpose). The object, if made by human hand, is the product of a purpose but to judge it aesthetically, it must be regarded *as if* it were not the product of a purpose. The initial subjective hypothesis of formal purposiveness designed to get an enquiry going now becomes a purely subjective process and any connection to cognition is repeatedly denied by Kant in the latter sections of the 'Analytic of the Beautiful'. Purposiveness without purpose presupposes a pure subjectivity uncoupled from any reference to the world of interests. It is a presentation that requires a kind of strenuous, willed bracketing off of what the judger knows at some level to be the case: (art) phenomena imply purposes.

Recall that Kant defined reflective judgment as a process of generating new ideas through the act of comparing objects or comparing objects with our own cognitive powers. *Form* is here accented towards subjective arrangements that generate ideas that still tether the internal attunement of our mental powers towards something beyond those powers (the supersensible). This in turn opens up the possibility that the aesthetic may put us in touch with causal relations other than those empirical and linear relations which dominate the philosophical horizons of the first *Critique*. Conversely, purposiveness without purpose seems more designed to close down rather than expand our horizons. In §11, the aesthetic is dissociated from anything to do with causalities of a new and different kind and is connected exclusively with the internal play of the subject's presentational powers:

> …a judgment of taste also cannot be determined by a presentation of an objective purpose, i.e., a presentation of the object itself as possible according to principles of connection in terms of purposes…For it is an aesthetic and not a cognitive judgment, and hence does not involve a *concept* of the character and internal and external possibility of the object through this or that cause.
>
> Kant (1987: 66)

Here objectivity and subjectivity are rigorously divided off from each other, whereas the reflective judgment suggested the possibility of them feeding into one another. Furthermore, only one principle of connection or causality (familiar from the first *Critique*) is assumed in the objective world and anything not geared to *that* type of causality cannot be registering *any* mode of causality (at least one with an empirical trace). And, of course, we have again the affirmation that the aesthetic does not involve a concept, which we have already discussed in the previous chapter. Purposiveness without purpose is the concept that lies at the heart of the bourgeois Kant but, I would argue, this bourgeois Kant while plausible is quite unstable, only held in place by countless reiterations in critical discourses. Let us look again at what Kant might mean by this phrase.

Kant defines 'interest' as 'the liking we connect with the presentation of an object's existence' (Kant 1987: 45). An interested liking admits factors that are extraneous to the pure aesthetic judgment. Those factors concern the subject's non-aesthetic judgments – namely judgments that pertain to the *existence* of the object and the subject's attitudinal relationship to its existence. Kant is quite explicit about this willed bracketing of social life when it comes to aesthetic presentation:

Suppose someone asks me whether I consider the palace I see before me beautiful. I might reply that I am not fond of things of that sort, made merely to be gaped at. Or I might reply like that Iroquois *sachem* who said that he liked nothing better in Paris than the eating houses. I might even go on, as *Rousseau* would to rebuke the vanity of the great who spend the people's sweat on such superfluous things. I might, finally, quite easily convince myself that, if I were on some uninhabited island with no hope of ever again coming among people, and could conjure up such a splendid edifice by a mere wish, I would not even take that much trouble for it if I already had a sufficiently comfortable hut. The questioner may grant all this and approve of it; but it is not to the point. All he wants to know is whether my mere presentation of the object is accompanied by a liking, no matter how indifferent I may be about the existence of the object of this presentation ... what matters is what I do with this presentation within myself, and not the [respect] in which I depend on the object's existence. Everyone has to admit that if a judgment about beauty is mingled with the least interest then it is very partial and not a pure judgment of taste.

Kant (1987: 45–46)

Yet this is a complex passage and by no means quite as easily dismissed as bourgeois apologetics as we might at first suspect. Kant is distinguishing judgments of taste from two other types of judgment – the agreeable, which is based in a primarily sensuous response to stimuli (the Iroquois Indians who preferred the eating houses to the palaces they had seen in a trip to Paris) and moral-political judgments (Rousseau-type condemnations of aristocratic vanity, self-indulgence and exploitation that lies behind the palace). The aesthetic occupies a space between the sensuous and the moral-political dimensions of our being. Now, the specificity of the aesthetic might be understood as being something that is neither sensuous nor moral-political. Or, it might be that the aesthetic or a judgment of taste is a meeting point, *a point of mediation* where the sensuous and the moral/political interests at play around the inflection of concepts whose static universality is no longer given might be activated. *Everything rests on whether we understand the Kantian aesthetic as some compartmentalized sphere separate from the agreeable and reason or whether we understand it as a point of mediation between them.* The latter is obviously my argument, but this only restates the position already developed in the previous chapter. What significantly buttresses the bourgeois interpretation of Kant and seems to rescue it from the conception of it as a point of mediation is that Kant also adds that the aesthetic, unlike the agreeable or reason, is *disinterested*. Whereas the purely sensuous and purely moral-political both are shaped by *interests*, the aesthetic, Kant seems to be suggesting, is not. This would seem to emphatically rescue Kant for the bourgeois intelligentsia, allowing sensuousness to disappear into a formalism completely divorced from reason (politics). How to make sense of this supposed disinterest without concessions to bourgeois aesthetics? How to rescue the aesthetic as a kind of praxis, a point of mediation between dimensions of our social being ordinarily rendered apart, when *interest* associated with both the agreeable and the Good cannot enter the aesthetic?

The agreeable, because it is grounded only in the sensuous carries a liking that is 'conditioned pathologically by stimuli' (Kant 1987: 51). The merely sensuous is thus unfree, because of this pathological response to stimulation. 'Only when their need has been satisfied', states Kant, in terms any historical materialist could agree with 'can we tell who in a multitude of people has taste' (Kant 1987: 52). The Good, however, is free in one sense insofar as we must choose to recognize our moral duties. But it is unfree insofar as we really *ought* to act on those duties. '[W]here the moral law speaks we are objectively no longer free to select what we must do', Kant argues (Kant 1987: 52). Duties are non-negotiable categorical imperatives to treat others as ends in themselves and not means to our ends. In this sense, the Good is rational *and interested*, while the agreeable is merely sensuous and interested. Notice here how Kant's understanding of *interest* is closely associated with *compulsion*. We might then say that the agreeable is associated with immediate sensuous *need* and its satisfaction (economic scarcity) while the moral-political judgment is associated with the compulsion of what we *ought* to do. Thus Kant says,

> Neither an object of inclination, nor one that a law of reason enjoins on us as an object of desire, leaves us the freedom to make an object of pleasure for ourselves out of something or other.
>
> Kant (1987: 52)

Now, once we have recast the concept of *interest* as meaning something like compulsion, the following classic (and bourgeois) definition of the aesthetic becomes open to another kind of reading.

> Taste is the ability to judge an object, or a way of presenting it, by means of a liking or disliking *devoid of interest*.
>
> Kant (1987: 53)

Interest, now read as compulsion, recasts the aesthetic as relatively autonomous to need and politics. In terms of need, the aesthetic operates at that level that is created by any (historically specific and developed) *surplus*; after we eat and satisfy our other vital reproductive needs (the merely agreeable), we may engage in the aesthetic in which sensuousness is enlarged through a communicative form and acquires a complexity appropriate to a society that has accumulated material and cultural surpluses. But it is also the place where the compulsions of the moral (read *political*) universe to defend and obey conceptions of the Good (the distribution and order of the sensuous) are also eased. Thus the aesthetic operates in a new (for Kant) space, a space that was also historically (re)emerging in Europe but which had been absent since the times of the ancient Greeks. This space is one where sense without need and reason without a priori moral command can come together in a new configuration. The aesthetic opens up a space for reflecting *on* interests (compulsions) precisely because it is not a direct reflection *of* interests (compulsions).

Now, the aesthetic as a space where the compulsion of need (economics) and politics (the struggle over the legitimacy of the economic order) is slackened off means that the aesthetic is a practice where commonality and difference can be explored in ways that the more immediate imperatives of class membership and politics make difficult. The agreeable is a judgment wallowing in the 'private conditions' of the merely sensuous being. It has little or no social dimension about it given the structure of bourgeois civil society, while the beautiful for Kant is a code word for thinking about a more authentic social being than can be articulated by either nature/civil society or the moral-political command. Only the liking of the beautiful is 'disinterested and *free*, since we are not compelled to give our approval by any interest, whether of sense or of reason' (Kant 1987: 52). Disinterestedness opens up a social being that is intersubjective and based on communication. 'Aesthetic disinterestedness has broadened interest beyond particularity', argued Adorno in similar fashion (2004: 14) with one eye obliquely on the third *Critique*. The aesthetic implies 'a relation between interest and its renunciation' and this means that the aesthetic may function as a critique of 'the rule of brutal self-preservation at the heart of the status quo and in its service' (Adorno 1997: 14).

Interpreting Kant's aesthetic philosophy as a struggle against reification, rather than as a transcendence of the social, shifts it away from bourgeois apologetics and towards an exploration of the transcendental conditions of intersubjectivity where something analogous to (but different from) the moral good could emerge through a process of discussion, debate and dialogue. Another more productive reading of purposiveness without purpose is now possible. The formulation is designed to think of a type of will that is not grounded in individual self-interest and in the reified transcendental subject (capital, the market, the nation), which is the abstract mirror image of individual self-interest. Purposiveness *without purpose* could be read as Kant's emergent concept of non-dominative sociality and that requires rethinking the relationship of the aesthetic – as a special kind of communication – to social and collective interests as opposed to individual interests. We accord the aesthetic judgment a certain universal validity as if it were a logical objective judgment, when in fact it is merely a subjective one, but one which escapes private and individualistic subjectivity. It is *as if* the aesthetic judgment is a universal judgment (it is made as if it were objective) but it is *as if* it is not a universal judgment (it is not something grounded in empirical proofs). The *as if* principle clearly operationalizes the strategy of the parallax, the alternation between an antithesis (universality and non-universality, objective purposiveness and subjectivity) with the idea being that something unlike the *logical* universal might emerge in the oscillation. That something is clearly the social.

Taste, Kant argues, cultivates our *sociability* (1987: 163). In this it struggles to release us from the prison of egotistical judgment. Our *sensus communis*, our universal and shared powers to reflectively judge, allows us:

> *as it were* to compare our own judgment with human reason in general and thus escape the illusion that arises from the ease of mistaking subjective and private conditions for objective ones, an illusion that would have a prejudicial influence on judgment.
>
> Kant (1987: 160)

This notion that *private* conditions (and interests) have a prejudicial influence on our judgments makes Kant a rather anti-bourgeois 'bourgeois' philosopher. In reflective judgment we may override 'the private subjective conditions of … judgment, into which so many others are locked' (Kant 1987: 161) and reflect on our own judgment 'from a *universal standpoint*' which we can do only 'by transferring … [ourselves] to the standpoint of others)' (Kant 1987: 161). This movement from individual interest to some more universal interest is key, but in the first instance, the individual interest is merged with the *general* interests of a group or class. Thus the individual may be seen as a member of a genus or community (as in taxonomic classifications), a individual-general connection or circuit that is distinct from universality as such. Real universality would thus require an acknowledgement of the standpoint of others *across* substantive (and unequal) differences. Thus, and this is crucial, if the aesthetic is associated with an emerging sense of the social, it is also associated with an emerging sense of the failure of the social, the social as fractured by (class) division. I am drawing here on Kojin Karatani's reading of Kant in his book *Transcritique*. He is interested in the idea that interdiscourse across communities (generalities) represents the transcritical move (the parallax) from which we can perhaps glimpse the universal, which, as we have seen, is characterized by the fact that it is not given.

> Kant drew a keen distinction between universality and generality... While generality can be abstracted from experience, universality cannot be attained *if not for a certain leap*... the condition for a certain cognition to be universal is not necessarily that it be based on a priori rule, but that it be exposed to the judgment of others who follow a different set of rules.
>
> Karatani (2005: 100)

Universality emerges or, perhaps better, is glimpsed instead in a complex communication act *across* communities 'who follow a different set of rules' and it is the *singular* judgment which the aesthetic experience may prompt in the individual (ordinarily sunk in their membership of a particular community or group) that provides a route to a provisional universality, certainly not one that can be assumed to be given, as in the first *Critique*. For Kant, the aesthetic is the privileged nexus point between the non-logical universal and the singular (Kant 1987: 144). This 'universal' is best thought of in its aesthetic construction as a transient glimpse of structural conditions and interrelationships. In the aesthetic, the *certain leap* is achieved by metaphor (when it is working aesthetically), which is key to unlocking the secrets of aesthetic form. Thus class-consciousness always requires the emergence of a consciousness of *other* classes, since classes, by definition, exist in relationships to one another. And emergence into consciousness of others at any level, including classed others, opens up the possibility (but not the guarantee) of reflective powers in the aesthetic mode where immediate class interests can be temporally bracketed as direct imperatives and 'the standpoint of others' suddenly impinges into consciousness of the self in ways that are interesting, exploratory, critical and even anticipatory of changes implied by the un-sustainability of those class relations.

Against philosophy: Bourdieu's sociology of culture

The war between philosophy – which accuses the social sciences of a reductionist fixing of what it studies – and the social sciences, which accuses philosophy of a lack of social and historical specificity, has been particularly fierce around the work of Pierre Bourdieu. Because he had the temerity to remind intellectuals of the privileged class basis of their knowledge and tastes and even their radicalism, Bourdieu has provoked something of a backlash, not least amongst the left-wing intelligentsia. Against this backlash Bourdieu's work ought to be defended. That said, the conflict between philosophy and the social sciences does usefully illuminate the lacunae in both camps, given the traditional strengths and weaknesses of the respective discourses. Bourdieu's sociology of culture provides both the theoretical tools and masses of empirical data, albeit specific to the French national context, for understanding some of the conditions of cultural production and reception and the class-stratified nature of those conditions. At the same time, a philosophy of the aesthetic understands that the aesthetic is not identical with its immediate conditions of existence, in either time or social space. The traditional emphasis of philosophy is on ideas, consciousness and importantly communication, which is the medium for the development of ideas and consciousness (from Plato's Socratic dialogues onwards). But philosophy also examines not only what *is*, but also what *ought* to be since it always at least tacitly evokes moral reason as its compass and this gives its focus on consciousness an ineliminable utopian dimension. Benjamin's *Angel of History* can only see what capitalist modernity calls progress as a 'catastrophe which keeps piling wreckage upon wreckage' because it views events from some unarrived at future position that has left capitalist modernity behind (Benjamin 1999a: 249). Adorno evokes a similar position, what he calls 'the standpoint of redemption' that reveals the world 'as indigent and distorted as it will appear one day in the messianic light' (Adorno 2005: 247). Bloch's mammoth work on utopianism is premised on the possibility of developing an *anticipatory consciousness* that can open up the closure on both the past and the present which capitalism effects (Bloch 1995). Utopian thought is at its strongest when it finds some basis in the now which provides a point of leverage into some transfigured future. Kant's universal, as read by Karatani, finds that point in the parallax between positions of radical difference. Against the social sciences, which map the massive edifice of what is, such philosophical discourses may seem wildly idealist or perhaps merely the self-serving discourses of an intellectual elite. Philosophy can be these things of course, but it is not necessarily so. When Marx argued that philosophers have only interpreted the world, while the point is to change it, he was not abolishing philosophical interpretation, but seeking to integrate it, as a particular strata of theory in general, into action that could not be genuinely transformative without it.

As with philosophy, so with aesthetics, and thus it is no surprise to find that Bourdieu's hostility towards philosophy, whose concepts are 'half-baked, although well done enough to arouse delicious shudders of a bogus revolution' (1987: 201) is matched only by his fierce critique of aesthetics. Indeed Bourdieu's work is even more rigorously anti-aesthetic than such Marxist currents as Althusserianism, which, despite its amorphous concept of ideology, still held out the possibility, in the work of Terry Eagleton, Pierre Macherey and Alain Badiou, that aesthetic form can stress-test ideological formations and expose their contradictions.

Bourdieu's critique of aesthetics begins conceptually by reminding it of its social conditions of possibility. His important concept of the habitus is the means by which he seeks to navigate his way between the twin traditions of the social sciences, objectivism and subjectivism, whose opposition has failed to integrate their respective truths into a single system. The habitus internalizes and orientates the subject to their objective environment providing 'schemes of perception, thought, and action' that guide their practices and their representations (Bourdieu 1989: 14). Despite his anti-Kantianism, Bourdieu's concept of the habitus owes something to the first *Critique*, with its emphasis on the mental structures that allow cognitive mapping of the world. Of course, Bourdieu is not constructing a universal transcendental subject, but a more differentiated, social and historically determined transcendental (that is determinate) subject. Bourdieu seeks to bring structures and the representations which social actors bring to their daily negotiation of their structures into some sort of dynamic relationship. 'The "social reality" objectivists speak about is also an object of perception' (Bourdieu 1989: 18). The different habitus that differentially classed subjects develop mobilizes the attitudinal dispositions and competences that are available to them according to the social space that they occupy. As the competences and dispositions that are acquired 'tend to be adjusted to position' in social space, social agents 'even the most disadvantaged ones, tend to perceive the world as natural and to accept it much more readily than one might imagine' (Bourdieu 1989: 18). The habitus which agents have is shaped by the position which they occupy in social space and it in turn produces practices within that space which, within Bourdieu's conceptual architecture, can be conceived as at best, offering the line of least resistance to those conditions. Bourdieu tends to concentrate on and assume a 'quasi-perfect coincidence of objective structures and embodied structures' (Bourdieu 1985: 731) and has no real basis to theorize under what circumstances that tight fit might be fractured. It is true that he allows for a degree of 'indeterminacy and fuzziness' between objective structures and perceptual representations, not least because in real history the meaning of things 'are subject to variations in time so that their meaning, insofar as it depends on the future, is itself in suspense, in waiting, dangling' (Bourdieu 1985: 728), but the overall thrust is towards a tendential functionalism, not least because, as we shall see, Bourdieu has a rather 'sociological' view of history. The elasticity between conditions and the practices they give rise to never really causes any fundamental problems or contradictions; it merely allows a degree of latitude that gives the system (or field) a historically evolving, but stable identity. It is not that internalization of system imperatives combined with a degree of 'autonomy' is off-beam. Indeed, the idea is vital to understand the specificities of market capitalism, its combination of 'freedom' and domination. The problem comes when the internalization thesis is shorn of the conceptual instruments to posit contradiction and crisis – which are also internalized, sometimes with explosive results.

The problems with this broader conceptual architecture become peculiarly well illustrated in relation to the artistic field, which is one of Bourdieu's principal targets. A field is an objectively structured social space where a specific activity takes place (art, politics, education). It is governed by differentiations amongst classed groups according to the distribution of assets (economic, cultural, social) they have to hand and the value of those assets in a given field. Cultural capital – which is made up of formal educational training, family background and the subject's own-time investment in cultural work (as producers or consumers) – is the dominant currency, for example, in the artistic field. Volume and composition of capital (the exact mix and quantities of economic, cultural, social assets) determine the opportunities agents have in the different fields with their differential logics.

The artistic field internalizes the market logic that equates artificial (i.e. socially engineered) scarcity with a higher exchange value while also developing a language and a field that scorns proximity to the commercial, the economic, the 'vulgar' world of routine everyday capitalism and, of course, above all, to the masses. The 'pure aesthetic' of the Kantian type is founded on a disavowal of its privileged social basis. Typically the competences and dispositions for successful entry and navigation of the artistic field that have been acquired under exclusive social conditions appear to the subject as the product of personal taste, intelligence and individual brilliance. Disavowal of privilege is the norm. The autonomy of the artistic field, which Bourdieu sees as a product of capitalist modernization, is merely the institutional basis of this individual perception, writ large. 'The invention of the pure gaze is realized in the very movement of the field toward autonomy' (Bourdieu 1987: 207). Against this autonomization, which is real but also blind to its real conditions, Bourdieu insists on the importance of excavating the *history* of the artistic field, by which he means the genealogy of the special language and concepts which have been developed in order to disavow its economic and social basis. Yet, as with the tight fit between objective structures and the practical mastery of those structures through the acquired habitus, Bourdieu's historicization of the field reinforces the sense of its more or less seamless *reproduction*. There is very little in Bourdieu's work of the social and historical world *beyond* the relatively autonomous field and therefore very little sense that the aesthetic is embedded in the tumult of its times. Bourdieu is quite explicit about the need to exclude this wider historical context:

> What happens in the field is more and more linked to the field's specific history and to it alone. It is therefore more and more difficult to deduce it from the state of the general social world at the given time (as a certain 'sociology', unaware of the specific logic of the field, claims to do).
>
> Bourdieu (1987: 208)

It is not clear what sociology Bourdieu has in mind here, but a historical materialist account of art must situate the field, with all its due relative autonomy or specific logic, in that wider historical context that provides the aesthetic with its essential link to the social and to the crisis of the social. So although Bourdieu is critical of the aesthetic for its repudiation of its own social and historical basis, and although he is critical of philosophy for not enquiring deeply enough into these conditions, his own sociology of culture is premised on a problematically narrow conception of social and historical foundations.

The political economy or sociology of the immediate conditions for the aesthetic is always embedded in a wider series of differences, which disrupt the smooth reproduction of those conditions. In Bourdieu's work, there is little conceptual understanding of a communicative relation that involves awareness of difference and the *inscription of the other inside the field as a disruptive force*. Aesthetic form is the compressed and compacted inscription of wider social relations in the peculiar language of a given medium and its multiple genres. And since social relations are never – no matter how exclusive the aesthetic in question – just a matter of the internal life of a given social group, but are always about a group or a class's relationship with others, those others, even if only ever disavowed, are always inscribed as part of the communicative structure of aesthetic form. These social differences (of class, race, gender or nation, for example) produce the characteristic 'dialogic' quality of the aesthetic, as well as its internal contradictions and tensions. Indeed, we may say that all narrative starts with *difference* as its dramatic imperative.

Art cinema, for example, is a mode of film practice that is closely aligned with the middle class, although beyond noting this obvious point, film criticism predictably but scandalously has little else to say about the question of class in relation to art cinema. Instead euphemisms abound and the implications of its class identity elided. Bourdieu is right about one thing: the class basis of the aesthetic for the middle class and middle-class institutions such as academia remains an embarrassment best passed over in silence. Rather than respond to this repressive critical apparatus by reducing art cinema to the mere expression of middle-class interests as Bourdieu's model, for example, would encourage us to do, we can use Kant's concept of reflective judgment to think about how art cinema is a perennial meditation on the class situatedness of the middle class and even not infrequently on the class situatedness of art cinema itself as a cinematic institution. The dispositions and competences required for art cinema viewing tend to assume a relatively high degree of accredited educational capital and cultural capital because its formal differentiations from dominant cinema depend very largely on violating the principles of popular cinema (Bordwell 2002). But within Bourdieu's model there is no way to distinguish strategic game playing that uses aesthetic form as markers of 'distinction' and status acquisition (Bourdieu 1996) and aesthetic form as a porous and heterogeneous openness to history and reflexive awareness of social differences that need challenging. From Buñuel's *Un Chien Andalou* (1929) to Michael Haneke's *Hidden* (2005), art cinema has demonstrated that despite its material constitution as a cinema of the middle class, by the middle class, it inscribes into its very communicative architecture or form the disruptive presence of the other (the unconscious, the classed and racial other etc.) amidst the tumult of its times. In Haneke's *Hidden*, what is hidden is above all the invisible omniscient gaze of the camera – the disinterested gaze in the classic bourgeois Kantian sense – that tells the story but which is periodically unmasked as not so disinterested by the integration into the film of the 'illegitimate' *video* surveillance of the bourgeois family. Although *this* illegitimate camera is hidden from the family within the story world (and it is this that marks it as a source of threat from some *interested* other), the camera that is typically hidden from our consciousness as viewers by the denial of its presence and thus the camera which structures our point of entry into the story worlds of mass culture, our navigation of those story worlds, our sense of who and what these stories are about, in short our focalization, is the institutional camera gaze that normalizes the middle-class world view. The critique which *Hidden* directs at the erasure of *that* omniscient camera telling the story pivots precisely on the inscription of the other into the form of the film in the form of the hidden video camera. Nor is this just aimed at the media in general or popular cinema. The film is also reflecting on the implications of the middle-class focalization that is institutionalized by art cinema. Video is the form and the medium by which the uncomfortable gaze of some other literally enters the lives of the bourgeois family. Video turns the tables and empowers the marginalized against those who have access to the means of representation. Georges, the central character, is a well-known host on a television discussion programme focusing on high culture where he is happy to be the object of the official camera-gaze of consecrated institutions.

The film's refusal to explain who is behind the videotapes mailed to Georges and his family marks the film's indication that the white middle–class male around whom art cinema typically fashions its focalization strategies is intrinsically unable to *know* what is going on *beyond* its purview. Where once art cinema touched borders with radical revolutionary cinema, it can now do no more than acknowledge that the other exists outside its purview and beyond its reach. It is at most an enigmatic other, the classed and raced other who is perhaps the source of the videotapes left on the doorstep or flashing across the television screens in the background of the bourgeois family's insular private concerns, as the news reports blankly on imperialist force from Palestine to Iraq. Yet this enigmatic other from whom cryptic messages have been received also highlights another aspect of the film's formal composition: namely, the restricted nature of what we can know with certainty about the bourgeois family itself. Just as Georges hopes to conceal his guilty secrets regarding his expulsion of the Algerian child Majid from his family all those years ago, so his own family appear to have secrets from him (Is his wife having an affair? Is his son involved in sending the videotapes?). The lived experience of the bourgeois family seems to have so fragmented that it cannot be pieced together again into a coherent narrative.

It is precisely this acknowledgement by the film of its institutional, social and class limits that counts as an example of Kant's reflective judgment, as a critical interrogation into the limits of this cinematic gaze. This awareness emerges in the painful registering of the other in the form of the film, a registering that acknowledges the broken lines of communication across the divided social terrain. The parallax the film constructs between the gaze of the official art cinema camera and the gaze of the plebeian video camera can do no more than glimpse, by negating the current conditions of communication, a more authentic universal condition. Implicitly, to do that the film must allude to some 'standpoint of redemption' to make its critique. Perhaps this is one way of reading the film's final image – that enigmatic meeting between Georges son and Majid's son, which might betoken an overcoming of the divisions that structured the relationship between their respective fathers.

On one reading of Kant, it is possible to argue that aesthetic form means something like the possibility of imagining a free community emerging between the twin compulsions of economic need and political power. The agreeable is associated with a private judgment of sense rather than taste. The latter 'carries with it an *aesthetic quantity* of universality, i.e., of validity for everyone, which a judgment about the agreeable does not' (Kant 1987: 59). What makes the agreeable a judgment of sense is that it is limited to the sensuousness felt by the individual subject and therefore lacks the universality that distinguishes the aesthetic as taste. It is the complex communicative architecture of aesthetic form that makes it possible for sensuousness to be articulated across the divided terrain of the social. This distinction between the agreeable and the aesthetic proper is useful but Kant goes onto develop it in a way that helps found the bourgeois Kant that Bourdieu for one will mount his assault on.

In §14 Kant shifts the argument or distinction between the agreeable and the beautiful. Whereas before this was a distinction about communicative form that does more than merely wallow in the private–personal realm of immediate sensuous gratification, he now introduces the notion that aesthetic judgments may be empirical or pure. This is a regression on the shape of his philosophical architecture because it now enables him to revert to a dichotomy between sensuousness (associated with the empirical) and the judgment of pure form as well as lay the basis for a class-based distinction between popular and middle-class taste.

> Empirical aesthetic judgments are judgments of sense (material aesthetic judgments); only pure aesthetic judgments (since they are formal) are properly judgments of taste.
>
> Kant (1987: 69)

Tellingly, he rationalizes this new distinction by referring back to the first *Critique* where there were also empirical concepts and the pure categories of logic. By now renaming the agreeable as the site of an empirical aesthetic judgment of taste, whereas before it was 'aesthetic' only insofar as it involved sensuousness, he lays the ground for a hierarchical middle-class taste formation which denigrates the apparently merely empirical, sensuous taste of the popular classes. The way is open to build a hierarchy *within* the aesthetic by labelling certain aesthetic tastes as aesthetic, but not 'pure'. The category moves from a classification of the strictly non-aesthetic to one of a class-based *discrimination* within the aesthetic, and this is the basis for the anti-Kant argument that Bourdieu will develop.

However, this reading of Kant leads Bourdieu into a trap. He reduces aesthetic form to the class interests of the different strata within the middle class and further he collapses the difference between the aesthetic and other modes of cultural consumption. Everything becomes assimilated to the game of distinction. For Bourdieu, there is no difference between food, holidays, interior decorating and aesthetic acts of communication. Yet while the aesthetic cannot be divorced from class-conditioned contexts of consumption and production, neither should it be made synonymous with those contexts nor the difference between aesthetic works and the non-aesthetic collapsed. The more productive way of reading Kant's distinction between the agreeable and the beautiful is not to read it as a coded distinction between popular and middle-class tastes, but to read it as making a distinction between non-aesthetic and aesthetic pleasures. While socially conditioned, acts of consumption that constitute a life style (the clothes one buys, for example) are *private* experiences with little sense that they connect the subject to some sort of public conversation beyond functioning as status symbols. Kant's initial discussion of the distinction between the agreeable and the beautiful judgment of taste may be interpreted as drawing a line between private and 'public' goods. Public goods are public, not simply because they are 'non-rivalrous' as the economists would say. For this would not distinguish between an advert that everyone can consume but whose communicative architecture is primed at eliciting and satisfying only private desires and fantasies, and other forms of communication that on the contrary lever the subject back into a realm of public debate. Public goods are public because of how they connect us to the social and debates going on within it. Public goods expand our social being and are to be cherished because they are in flat contradiction to the contraction of our social being that the dominant tendencies of capitalism cultivate. The aesthetic is a public good, along with decent journalism, but it is of a special class because of its licensing of the imagination through aesthetic form. Crucially, while a pair of shoes, for example, may have some aesthetic dimension to its use value, a film may have an incomparably more complex aesthetic dimension to its form that facilitates communicative intersubjective debate (agreement and disagreement) across the divided social field. This sense that the aesthetic is part of a broader public conversation, even if that conversation is socially stratified, which it undoubtedly is under class societies, is largely missing from Bourdieu's account. Bourdieu sees culture not in terms of conversations but in terms of a game, especially as it is played between the 'objectively complicit opponents' within the dominant class, as in, for example, the conflicts between middlebrow, high brow and avant-garde markets (Bourdieu 1996: 250). For Bourdieu everything is reduced to the struggle for 'distinction' and for status between rival classes and class fractions. Despite its sociological sophistication, his model is in some ways comparable to the way the old Soviet Proletcult movement reduced culture to the expression of the interests of classes. As the more sophisticated Bolsheviks, such as Voronsky, knew, classes and their cultures are always more complexly interwoven and their fates tied together across divisions by the necessity of social cooperation as much as by the arbitrariness of exploitation (Voronsky 1998).

Against the social sciences: Rancière and the aesthetic

Bourdieu's sociology of culture offers us a sobering reminder of the classed conditions of possibility for the aesthetic, and this seems to me particularly important when thinking about both the mainstream reception of particular aesthetic works and the academic theoretical apprehension of aesthetics generally. But the aesthetic itself is not reducible to this or that example of reception or theorization of its particular conditions of existence (production or reinscription in other works or contexts of consumption). Conditions are multiple and plural and the communicative form of the aesthetic is (relative to the agreeable and the good) precisely open to such multiplicities and potentialities. Bourdieu's impoverished conceptualization of aesthetic form reduces aesthetic practices to their conditions (in this case, the field) and their functions (reproduction of class society). By contrast, Rancière's work offers us a much more suggestive, attractive and complex account of what he calls the aesthetic experience, which recognizes that practices are not identical to conditions. However, as we shall see, Rancière rescues aesthetic practices from their reduction to conditions at the expense of very largely bracketing off social and historical conditions in a traditional Kantian manner.

Rancière's discourse is in a kind of philosophic-mythic mode where Plato is his negative touchstone. For Plato prescribes the template of contemporary social scientific thought that affirms a 'relationship of reciprocal confirmation between a condition and a thought' (Rancière 2009: 17). Contemporary social scientific discourses fix people in their place, in specific spatio-temporal locations and thus reproduce the system of power that they are ostensibly trying to critique. Rancière's own method rationalizes itself as a liberation from such academic disciplines and his philosophic-mythic discourse is inspired by the aesthetic and is conceived as effecting a strategic shift in the 'discursive register' of an object, 'its universe of reference, or its temporal designations' (Rancière 2000: 120). Socio-historical enquiry thus becomes, for Rancière, the reproduction of a disciplinary prison for both the writer and object of that enquiry. In Bourdieu's deterministic sociology, for example, 'an abode must determine a way of being that in turn determines a way of thinking' (Rancière 2009: 16). The social sciences thus pacify and 'establish stable relations between bodily states and the modes of perception and signification that correspond to them' (Rancière 2009: 17).

Taking his leave from his former Althusserian structuralism that assumes a functionalist apparatus that successfully assigns the majority their place, Rancière reads Plato's anti-democratic concern about the power of (poetic) words to overrun social hierarchies, as a clue to a new methodological orientation, just as the aesthetic was for Kant, in whose footsteps he is, as a philosopher looking for reorientation, following. A key moment in Rancière's intellectual development is his book *The Nights of Labour: The Workers' Dream in Nineteenth-Century France* (1989). Here it is words written in their aesthetic modality by workers that exceeds and disrupts their identity as workers. And this is a challenge not only for the capitalist social order but also for Marxist-inflected academic discourses for whom, Rancière contends, it is equally important to keep the workers in their place as it were so that they can fulfil their 'historical mission'. *The Nights of Labour* recasts workers from mid-nineteenth-century France, influenced by the utopian socialism of Saint Simon, as dreamers, bohemians and artists, attempting to escape their identity as mere workers through their poetry and their diaries.

> I looked at these texts as inventions of forms of language similar to all others. The purchase of their political valence was thus in their revindication of the efficacy of the literary, of the egalitarian powers of language, indifferent with respect to the status of the speaker. This *poetic* operation on the objects of knowledge puts into play their *political* dimension, which elides a sociocultural reading.
>
> Rancière (2000: 116)

The division which Rancière sets up between the *political* dimension of the aesthetic and a sociocultural understanding of it is unfortunate but deeply structured into his view. The entire book is, as historian Bryan D. Palmer complained, resolutely hostile to contextualizing the workers as a *class* shaped by collective relations and historical circumstances. Instead '[w]orkers are persons adrift in the seas of individuality' (Palmer 1991: 341). At best, elsewhere, Rancière will write of the 'collective' and the 'community', but in terms that largely elide important class conflicts or only as possible future collectives without any ground in the present. For Rancière, the utopian power of the aesthetic must be conceived in terms that reject 'the consistency of coherent social groups' (Rancière 2000: 124) since a group is, by definition, for him, an entity that is already fixed in place and unable to disturb what he calls the 'distribution of the sensible'.

The distribution of the sensible refers on the one hand to the divisions of labour that assign sensual beings their place within the social order, their visibility and invisibility and the evaluations that are put on their visibility and invisibility. This dimension of the distribution of the sensible effectively renders into philosophical language the kind of sociological commonplace that philosophers censure sociologists for making, much to Bourdieu's annoyance (Bourdieu 1987: 201). But the other dimension of the distribution of the sensible refers to that peculiar (re)distribution of the sensible that is the aesthetic proper, and which on Rancière's reading of Kant, disrupts the socially determined relationship between concept and sense.

> The aesthetic experience is the experience of a specific sensorium cancelling oppositions of understanding and sensibility, form and matter, activity and passivity.
>
> (Rancière 2004: 12)

We have seen already that this is a theme within the bourgeois left-wing intelligentsia's reappropriation of Kant (Deleuze, Lyotard, Shaviro and now Rancière). It converges with my reading of Kant to a degree, but we part company on the question of how to characterize what is going on within the aesthetic as a mode of disruption and how the aesthetic relates back to the social. In the previous chapter, I discussed this around the question of cognition and conceptuality while in this chapter we are concerned with the question of interests and the reflective communication of differences. If the concept of the distribution of the sensible hovers between two modalities of experience, in order to connect them but maintain their difference, then so too does Rancière's concept of the 'aesthetic experience'.

The specificity of the aesthetic lies in two contradictory movements – one which asserts its autonomy and the other which reconnects it with 'the art of living'. The aesthetic experience is linked to both the beautiful in art *and* an engagement with the art of living. The relationship between the two is what constitutes the aesthetic experience, which is 'effective inasmuch as it is the experience of that *and*' (Rancière 2002: 134). That experience can only be embodied in a living subject that comes into contact with the aesthetic product. It is the experience itself, not the 'artwork' that achieves a degree of autonomy. This autonomy, though, is relative because the aesthetic experience opens up the possibility of transferring what is discovered in the contact with the aesthetic product, back into life and discharging something of its transformational powers into life (although not in any simple cause-and-effect manner). Here we are reminded of what Kant refers, in the third *Critique*, to the aesthetic power to develop 'material for the understanding which the latter disregarded in its concept' (Kant 1987: 185). We only have to give Kant a modest accentuation, that is that the 'understanding' disregarded material for reasons pertaining to socially determined interests, to make his philosophy useful for critique proper.

The emphasis on the aesthetic experience is a useful corrective to the avant-garde assertion that the autonomy of the aesthetic lies in its formal structure alone. From Adorno to Osborne, aesthetic form guards the artwork from being assimilated back into the commodified realm of the mass media spectacle. But it does so at the price of a retrenchment that loses contact with an audience that does not have access to the scarce cultural capital required to access such artworks. This is why it is important to stress that the aesthetic is a *communicative* experience so that we ask, who is doing the communicating, to whom and how? But the aesthetic experience is also dependent on the specific *form* or architecture that the work itself has and this locates it within the specific history of the medium, its technology, genres, institutions as well as its larger social and historical context. There is a danger that in focusing on the aesthetic experience embodied in a living subject that we collapse back into the bourgeois Kant and the 'experience' becomes individualized and uncoupled from these historically determinate conditions.

Rancière's version of the aesthetic experience is indeed, in important respects, despite its political radicalism, indistinguishable from the standard bourgeois reading of Kant. The aesthetic 'strictly identifies art in the singular and frees it from any specific rule, from any hierarchy of the arts, subject matter, and genres' (Rancière 2007: 23). To which one must ask: *any hierarchy? Any rule?* What has happened here to the medium, the genre, the technology, the institutions, in short the conditions of existence? Rather than pose a mediated relation with what exists, which I have suggested is posited by Kant's concept of reflective judgment and now disinterest, we have here a reproduction of Kantian compartmentalization. There are rules and hierarchies, and there is that which escapes rules and hierarchies. A simple division. This is the nub of the problem, the aesthetic experience is viewed as a compartmentalization not a mediation with life and its conditions. What happens within the aesthetic experience can and does cross back over into life (and vice-versa) but in this formulation the experience itself is radically non-identical with its wider conditions. For Rancière, the beautiful marks a space that is free from cognition and desire (either the interested desire of the agreeable or the interested desire of the moral Good). This is the basis of the 'free play' of the faculties for Rancière (2004: 9). Yet this conception, which can be legitimately derived from Kant, is also in contradiction with the overall architecture of Kant's philosophy in the third *Critique*, since the 'free play' of the faculties is precisely a play between the imagination and its socially determined conditions of understanding. With cognitive judgments the imagination is reproductive, assisting the understanding in its task of synthesizing the manifold of experience into intuitions that can be stamped with universal concepts. With the aesthetic, the imagination appears to be more productive, that is have some significant autonomy from the empirical world of the senses as evidenced by its play with forms. However, the imagination is still *in play* with the understanding. It is never an unconditional freedom. Taste is a point of mediation between the empirical and reason.

It is, however, a fairly unreconstructed bourgeois Kant that Rancière resurrects to underpin the aesthetic experience. Instead of thinking of the aesthetic experience as a reconfiguration of cognition (the understanding) and interest (sensuous desire and moral desire of reason), Rancière sees the aesthetic as neither cognition nor desire. 'The aesthetic state is a pure instance of suspension' (Rancière 2007: 24). What Rancière calls the 'neutralization' of the established distribution of the senses means that he associates the aesthetic with *dissensus* rather than the consensus of the socially sanctioned distribution of the senses. This is an interesting proposition and certainly a useful corrective against a version of Gramscian cultural criticism that has emphasized the role of culture in winning the consent of the dominated to their domination. If, instead, we at least contemplate that the aesthetic, like the political, begins with *dissensus*, begins with the breakdown, the gap and disturbance in the social order, it can usefully reorient us towards the aesthetic as constituted at least in part by its sensitivity towards division and disagreement, which is already implied by Kant in his introductions to the third *Critique*, where he argues that in the aesthetic the universal is *not given*. However, Rancière very explicitly rules out the idea that his concept of dissensus involves conflicting interests. To posit dissensus in terms of conflicting interests is for him to be still trapped within the terms of the hierarchical distribution of the senses that establishes the basis of the conflict in the first place.

> A dissensus is not a conflict; it is a perturbation of the normal relation between sense and sense. The normal relation, in Platonic terms, is the domination of the better over the worse. Within the game it is the distribution of two complimentary and opposite powers in such a way that the only possible perturbation is the struggle of the worse against the better.... In this case there is no dissensus, no perturbation of the game. There is a dissensus only when the opposition itself is neutralized.
>
> Rancière (2009: 3)

This is a very strange kind of dissensus indeed and one that stands outside the class struggle as it has been structured by the distribution of the senses. One can begin now to see where the tendential rejection of sociocultural contextualization and rejection of group interest as having a determining relationship to the political dimension of the aesthetic is leading. It leads in short back to a rather traditional reading of the Kantian aesthetic as some kind of transcendence of social interests, albeit now cast in the terms of a radical utopianism of the individual. This is why Rancière conceives the aesthetic effect as one of 'dis-identification', where the individual achieves withdrawal from their membership of the genus: 'The aesthetic community is a community of dis-identified persons' (Rancière 2011: 73). This is why the utopian vision of the 'aesthetic community' in Rancière's work does not seem to require a confrontation with privilege and power. One could argue in a discourse that Rancière no doubt would find old-fashioned, that the political efficacy of the aesthetic resides at one level in precisely achieving an *identification* (suppressed within the dominant universe of concepts) with a group existing in antagonistic relations with other groups. If there is any 'dis-identification' it is with the inequities of that arrangement, not with group identities, memberships and affiliations per se.

The implications of Rancière's position for thinking about the question of class interests in relation to the aesthetic are evident in his essay 'The Aesthetic Dimension: Aesthetics, Politics, Knowledge'. Here Rancière returns, as he frequently does, to his *Nights of Labour* book and cites an example of a joiner's reflections on his fellow worker that was published in a radical newspaper called *The Workers' Tocsin*.

He presents it as a kind of diary. For us, however, it appears more akin to a personalized paraphrase of *Critique of Judgment* and more peculiarly of the second paragraph that spells out the disinterestedness of aesthetic judgment. Kant documented disinterestedness with the example of the palace that must be looked at and appreciated without considering its social use and signification. This is how the joiner translates it in his own narration: 'Believing himself at home, he loves the arrangement of a room so long as he has not finished laying the floor. If the window opens out onto a garden or commands a view of a picturesque horizon, he stops his arms a moment and glides in imagination towards the spacious view to enjoy it better than the possessors of the neighbouring residences'. This text seems to depict exactly what Bourdieu describes as the aesthetic illusion.

Rancière (2009: 7)

Since *The Nights of Labour* is so resistant to socio-economic contextualization, all we have are the words of workers and our interpretations of them. And on the face of it, Rancière's interpretation of the joiner's words as a gloss on the traditional reading of Kantian disinterestedness seems questionable. At every point, aesthetic judgment seems in fact to be closely intertwined with a self-conscious awareness of class interests and the classed context in which these judgments are made. The joiner can believe himself to be at 'home' only so long as he has *not* finished the floor; he can look out onto a picturesque view and enjoy it *better* than the bourgeoisie. The reflective judgment starts with the body and sensuous pleasure that suspends the body's normal determinate relationship to the world (in this case, the worker introduces a temporary suspension of work, the condition for any cultural consumption) and reconfigures it, but with the *awareness* of class relations, the *awareness* of the classed other, which is the basis for the worker's own class consciousness, ever present. The utopian quality of the language of 'gliding in the imagination' is important, but it is a utopianism that does not transcend class interests and opposition. There is no 'dissensus' here in the peculiar and paradoxical sense meant by Rancière. Instead, there is a powerful awareness of difference and antagonism as the imagination is in play with the understanding. Rancière formulates the utopian character of the aesthetic as a 'as if' operation. 'The aesthetic judgment acts as if the palace were not an object of possession and domination. The joiner acts as if he possessed the perspective' (Rancière 2009: 8). But the Kantian and middle class 'as if' invoked here is a denial of social interest per se whereas the worker denies the *specific arrangement* of social interests which is a different question altogether. Moreover, he does not deny the social interests which motivate his denial of that specific arrangement. Nor does the worker ever lose awareness that this utopian 'as if' suspension of normal relations is surrounded and pressed in by those relations, those compulsions.

Thus Rancière may be said to reproduce his own intellectual 'fixing' of the workers, despite his critique of the reductionism he finds in the social sciences. Rancière's own discursive fixing takes the form of a denial of the relationship between the aesthetic and class interests. Rancière looked to the aesthetic to overcome the division of labour between the intellectual and the worker. The history of the past weighs like a nightmare on the brain of the living. For Rancière is quite right to argue that when this division is not overcome in real political practice, then even revolutions are condemned to reproduce the old inequalities between rulers and ruled, between those with the power to make conceptual form and those who are the passively moulded content of the understanding. Active form over passive matter (the model of Kant's first *Critique*) 'epitomizes the law of domination' (Rancière 2004: 14). Neutralization seems to be Rancière's way of dealing with the disappointments of political change, the dangers of the reproduction of political domination in new forms alternating with the 'savagery of rebellion' (Rancière 2004: 14). But neutralization amounts to no more than reproducing the conditions that perpetuate both domination and rebellion by erecting an idealist utopianism that prematurely suspends class difference *in* the aesthetic. The aesthetic is not productively utopian by abolishing class difference; it is productively utopian by recognizing it and evoking the possibility, no more than that, of an end to class difference and domination.

***

There is, then, a bourgeois Kant in the third *Critique*. We cannot deny it. But it must consolidate itself in unstable opposition to an anti-bourgeois Kant that is also at work in the third *Critique*. It does so by inflecting the concept of formal purposiveness towards purposiveness without purpose. Formal purposiveness functions in the two introductions as a heuristic device by which we can strike up an imaginative relationship to nature (and by implication, society) which can in turn stimulate our minds in new directions. Purposiveness without purpose, conversely, seems to be more about a willed ignorance, a willed bracketing of the social and historical dimension of the aesthetic. The *as if* structure of the Kantian aesthetic is thus shifted from an imaginative critical stance, to one of disavowal and fetishism. Sections §10 to §16 consolidate this bourgeois Kant around an aesthetic championing of subjectivism, interest-free judgment and an anti-empirical formalism. We have seen that the bourgeois Kant remains the dominant one in the minds of the left. Bourdieu finds in Kant's later distinction of the difference between empirical aesthetic judgments associated with the agreeable and pure aesthetic judgments associated with the beautiful, the model of middle-class hegemony in the field of taste. This is a plausible reading of how Kant has been a foundation stone for bourgeois aesthetics, although I have argued that this Kant is at odds with the anti-bourgeois Kant that is also at play in the third *Critique*. This anti-bourgeois Kant is invisible to Bourdieu.

Although he was at pains to distance himself from Marx in the 1980s, largely through some fairly cursory asides and problematic readings of Marx's methodology, Bourdieu's position on Kant is identical to the dominant Marxist position while his theorization of class was attractive to and influential on Marxists across the disciplines. The battle between philosophy/aesthetics and the social sciences turns on the question of whether practices are identical with their immediate (social, institutional, temporal) conditions of existence. I have argued that Bourdieu comes close to arguing that conditions and practices are identical and as a result, despite the crucial focus on class, his work has an unhelpful functionalist bent. His vision of aesthetic form is desperately impoverished, reducing it to strategies of exclusion and playing the game for individual social advantage. The aesthetic as a complex communicative-imaginative structure that has a lightning-rod capacity to register our social being and its relationships with broader social contexts has no place in his model. But this is also why we must reject Kant's introduction of the distinction between the empirical and 'pure' aesthetic judgment. This distinction draws Kant not only back to an emergent middle-class hegemonic position within the field of taste, but also to the logic of capital where only 'pure' exchange value is considered truly universal, while use values are merely local and empirical satisfactions of the senses. Against the subsumption of the sensuous under abstract form the aesthetic, when it is working aesthetically, builds a complex horizontal communicative act that encodes within it a possible future sociality currently unavailable to us. It is this, which unites both philosophy and the aesthetic in attunement to the non-identity, both temporally and socially, between conditions of existence and practices. In this chapter, we have explored this non-identity in the *form* of the aesthetic communicative act. Philosophy typically and implicitly speaks from a position that is other to its immediate conditions of existence and it is this that allows Marxist philosophy to insist on the reality of potentialities germinating within the present even when all the dominant empirical arrangements are so organized as to resist the development of those potentialities. Similarly, the utopian dimension is ineliminable as a tacit critical standpoint for the aesthetic. The utopianism of the aesthetic is there in the simple declaration that this or that situation causes this or that set of problems.

Unlike Bourdieu, Rancière is alive to this utopian dimension of the aesthetic. But what is largely invisible to Rancière is the possibility of a genuinely anti-bourgeois Kant from which to launch a critique of the reduction of practices to their conditions. For Rancière, Kant provides a means to critique the limits of contemporary social sciences and this takes the form of a battle between a philosophy informed by an aesthetic sensibility and the social sciences which, in the case of Bourdieu, treats philosophy and the aesthetic as casting a discreet veil over the class-conditioned contexts of all practices, including their own. Accepting the division between philosophy and the social sciences compromises Rancière's important interventions and contributions, and aligns him to an essentially left-wing version of the bourgeois Kant. His suggestive concepts of the distribution of the sensible, the aesthetic experience and dissensus are problematized by his argument that the aesthetic is not a site of mediation that is difficult to realize elsewhere, but a pure suspension of the social conditions of existence.

Against both Bourdieu and Rancière, I have argued that there is an anti-bourgeois Kant available to us. Here the aesthetic offers an experience of the universal which is inherently provisional, glimpsed in the dawning awareness of conflicting interests represented by the presence of others. The aesthetic, especially when concerned with narrative, starts with an awareness of difference, whether in terms of class, gender, race, sexuality, culture, nationality or whatever. The only question, then, is the quality of the reflective judgment that is then encouraged by this awareness of difference.

Awareness of the other, of whatever quality is inscribed in the form of the communication itself. Done well, the aesthetic enlarges our capacity for reflective judgment, for judgment to not only reflect its material conditions, but for judgment to reflect *on* its material conditions. The capacity for reflective judgment expands as our provisional awareness of the social totality is offered in the aesthetic experience and it contracts accordingly as our awareness of the other recedes from our consciousness. Since our consciousness or habitus is forged in the routine immediacy of the senses (the agreeable) we need and demand experiences which enlarge our sense of the social. Politics is one such sphere but its purpose (outside revolutionary conjunctures) tends to be the defence of the moral good as conceived by a given set of institutional arrangements. The aesthetic is therefore necessary to offer us the possibility of exploration and discovery beyond immediate individual interests and immediate interests of the class or group which politics defends. Reflective judgment in the aesthetic can be read as an imaginative exploration that takes the modes of representation beyond the (class) experience of the individual subject, situating both individual and class experience in the context of the network or relations that form the 'whole' of experience that is the essential prerequisite for the ability to reflect *on* and not be simply a reflection *of* material conditions. Reflection *on* requires coming into a peculiar kind of consciousness raising contact with the (classed) other. This painful consciousness is the open wound of the aesthetic.

5

The Sublime in Kant's Philosophical Architecture

With the entry of the sublime into the *Critique of Judgment* we come to the fault line that has divided generations of bourgeois intellectuals between the more conservative–liberal wings on the one hand and those who, to borrow from Bourdieu, have a different composition of cultural capital and who are more drawn to the avant-garde on the other which the sublime, with its stress on the breakdown of established forms and innovation of new forms, seems to lend itself to. The uncertain place of the sublime in Kant's philosophical architecture, the lack of any real substantive explanation from Kant as to why he turns to the sublime and the unconvincing arguments he gives for separating it off from the beautiful (although not, as some have claimed, the aesthetic) have facilitated this game of taking sides. On the one hand there is the beautiful, that in its popular rendition is associated with a certain languid, sophisticated calm or '*restful* contemplation' (Kant 1987: 101) and which from a certain point of view looks like insufferable bourgeois complacency. The beautiful in this rendition often comes off badly by comparison with the sublime. The latter seems to facilitate a stress on power, action, decisiveness, courage, danger, an adventurous thrusting outside our comfort zone that makes it very suited, paradoxically enough, to both popular culture spectacles and avant-garde shocks and challenges to perception and subjectivity alike. The popular and the avant-garde sublime are connected, whatever their differences, by a shared interest in 'mental *agitation*' and 'negative pleasure' (Kant 1987: 101) as Kant puts it, which is suggestive of contradiction, teetering on the edge of safety – the safety perhaps of the symbolic order itself.

The sublime is certainly one of the most multi-accentual and contradictory of all categories in Kant's philosophical architecture, capable of being read in so many different ways. Kant himself regarded the sublime as less 'rich in implications' (Kant 1987: 100) than the beautiful but this has been belied by subsequent elaborations of the sublime. It has been read as a reactionary anti-Enlightenment return to the majesty of the divine, a masculinist and individualist fantasy of imperial adventure, a bracing spur for the entrepreneurial self, the proto-outline of the coming society of the spectacle, the limit point of representation itself, a symptom of the supersensible totality of global capitalism, a celebration of Enlightenment rationality, the harbinger of a revolutionary conjuncture, or conversely, the aestheticization of political terror. Despite this diversity, there are some common themes here. In particular there is the question of the relationship between sensuous experience, understood as a culturally mediated representation, and whether that powerful sensuous experience can inspire critical reason that can *think relations* that are not directly open to sensuous experience or whether that experience overwhelms critical reason. For the sublime is virtually the paradigm case of the way the aesthetic is torn between fetishism and critical engagement. To properly understand the sublime, however, and its role within the overall architecture of Kant's thought, we need to reintegrate it back into the aesthetic of the beautiful in a way that Kant could not quite explicitly do. As a result, generations of critics have fought over the respective merits of the beautiful and the sublime, constantly posing them as antithetical opposites. For Fredric Jameson, for example, the sublime is an 'unaccountable eruption … at the end of a standard treatise on beauty' (Jameson 1998: 101). Here the sublime is seen as opening up an abstract timeless conception of beauty to the new historical forces which the sublime alludes to. This is doubly problematic, however. Firstly, the sublime functions within the overall trajectory of Kant's argument to prepare the ground for his later decisive formulation that links the beautiful to reason with the concept of aesthetic ideas. So the entrance of the sublime is not unaccountable in terms of where Kant's thought is heading even if Kant gives no explicit rationale for the entry of the sublime into his text. Secondly, once we reconceive our conception of the beautiful, we can no longer be satisfied with a simple antinomy between it and the sublime and instead we must understand their relationship as a conceptual pairing within the architecture of Kant's thought. If beauty allows Kant to socialize the individual and de-reify the social, the sublime, as we shall see, adds to the philosophy of the aesthetic both a new radical conception of temporality and a new awareness that the aesthetic, as part of the social, must also be 'de-natured' and reflexively open to change.

This is not to say that Jameson is entirely off-beam in suggesting that the third *Critique* is caught between an older model of philosophical critique based on timeless categories and an emergent sense of the historical forces stirring within the categories it is working with. But this line of demarcation is not just to be found within elements of Kant's conception of the beautiful against the sublime, but within his conception of the sublime as well. When Kant turns his attention to the sublime he seems in many ways to return to the philosophical structure of the previous two *Critiques* and affirm a strong division between abstract reason outside time and space and the senses that are on the verge of being overpowered by the sublime. It is precisely this strong dichotomy between the sensuous and reason that is typical of bourgeois society. For when the senses and reason are cleanly compartmentalized in this way, then, on the one hand, it is easier for us to succumb to the sheer visceral power of the sublime and the emotional turmoil it arouses, without filtering the experience through critical reason, while, on the other hand, it is easier for reason itself to refute its necessary material embodiment in time and space. Although Kant, as one would expect, veers towards the affirmation of abstract reason, he typically delivers a parallax critique of such reason at the same time. For when reason is so convinced of its supremacy over sensibility that it can disregard the empirical world entirely, then it tips over into the madness of fanaticism, which Kant defines as '*wanting to SEE something beyond all bounds of sensibility*, i.e. of dreaming according to principles (raving with reason)' (Kant 1987: 135). At its best, however, the sublime functions in a proto-dialectical fashion, in which new critical possibilities emerge from the relationship between sense and reason, spectacle and spectator.

Form and fear

Overcoming the dichotomy within the sublime between sensuousness and reason, or the eclipse of one by the other, requires integrating the sublime back into the overall architecture of Kant's philosophy of the aesthetic. Rancière suggests that in the sublime 'we emerge from aesthetics proper and enter the realm of morality' (Rancière 2004: 8). This is part of his polemic against the sublime on behalf of the beautiful, a position that is unusual within the left bourgeois intelligentsia, who are normally drawn to the sublime. But in fact, Kant is quite clear that the sublime judgment, and the questions it raises around reason, morality and politics, is indeed a distinct modality or dimension of the aesthetic (Kant 1987: 115). Once we acknowledge this we will be able to build bridges between the beautiful and the sublime, and therefore the beautiful and reason. But before the bridges, what about the differences? The sublime is a different modality within aesthetics of course. One of the key differences between the beautiful and the sublime rests on the question of form.

> The beautiful in nature concerns the form of the object, which consists in [the object's] being bounded. But the sublime can also be found in a formless object, insofar as we present *unboundedness*, either [as] in the object or because the object prompts us to present it, while yet we add to this unboundedness the thought of its totality.
>
> Kant (1987: 98)

The *formlessness* of the sublime, which Kant takes as being significantly different from the form of the beautiful, is divided into two types: the *dynamical* sublime and the *mathematical* sublime, which can be interpreted respectively as power and size. The unboundedness of the sublime, which is so central to its power or overwhelming size, means that clearly delineated form or form that we can *perceptually master* is breaking down. In stark contrast to the beautiful, this makes the sublime 'contrapurposive for our power of judgment', thus encouraging the mind to 'abandon sensibility and occupy itself with ideas containing a higher purposiveness' (Kant 1987: 99). The sublime is an object that defies logic and in either size or power or both is *'beyond all comparison'* (Kant 1987: 103). To call something large absolutely (the mathematical sublime), for example, suggests that 'we do not permit a standard adequate to it to be sought outside it, but only within it' (Kant 1987: 105). In the mathematical sublime the image or percept, which in the *Critique of Pure Reason* is predominantly understood as a mere fragment of stimuli that must be synthesized with other stimuli to be built up into a whole (i.e. it *must* be compared and related to other sense-percepts in the visual field), has now swelled up to a scale where it seems to be on the verge of escaping the merely linear, additive, cause-effect logic of the understanding and instead trembles on the cusp of being a self-sufficient *totality*, precisely, 'beyond all comparison', beyond our ability to contain it within a perceptible form. This totality (the signature mark of the aesthetic's relative autonomy) is different from the one intuited in Kant's discussion of the beautiful, because its form seems to be unstable, on the verge of formlessness (especially in the dynamical sublime) or a form that defies our power to grasp and comprehend it (especially in the mathematical sublime). In both cases, form threatens to exceed what perceptual sense-organs can contain in a single vision, 'directly in one intuition' (Kant 1987: 107); a percept is pushed to the very edge of what perception can cope with and this evokes or intimates (is a metaphor for) what reason can grasp more securely, namely a totality, such as our social relationships, which are similarly hard to perceptually grasp (the supersensible). Reason, states Kant, 'makes us unavoidably think of the infinite ... as *given in its entirety* (in its totality)' (Kant 1987: 111). If the beautiful also stands for a model of totality and therefore the supersensible, where parts and whole work in some kind of unity, in the sublime, the totality that is evoked is on the verge of change and possibly on the verge of crisis. Thus the unstable form of the sublime is inextricably linked with a new and potentially radical conception of temporality and history. The sublime subjectively 'does violence' to the model of linear temporal progression in the ordering of the manifold that Kant mapped out in the *Critique of Pure Reason*. Although Kant there identified simultaneity as a principle of temporal ordering, it was subordinate to the emphasis on a successive apprehension of percepts in a temporal sequence. With the sublime there is a radical shift to an instantaneous and fleeting grasping of what is simultaneous. Thus 'comprehending in one instant what is apprehended successively, is a regression that in turn cancels the condition of time in the imagination's progression' (Kant 1987: 116). The imagination in question here, of course, is the *reproductive* imagination, which is tied to empirical reality, to what is. The radical cancelling of what is generates, by contrast, the productive imagination in which the temporality of the sublime has been read in rather opposing ways. For Benjamin, the sublime appears to have been the tacit model for the revolutionary conjuncture, dialectics at a standstill, the *now* time in which a vast temporal scale, the past, the present and future, collide, as the continuum of history (Kant's successive apprehension from the first *Critique*) is interrupted (Benjamin 1999a: 252–254). Benjamin's reading of a medieval theological discourse, the *nunc stans*, suggests a fine line between *this* radical rendition of the sublime as revolutionary conjuncture and the sublime as the reassertion of a metaphysics of presence in which the subject merges with and absorbs a little quota of the infinite or God (Klinger 2009:107–108). This image of merging with the infinite is ambiguously poised within the sublime, as we shall see, between empowering and annihilating the individual.

Whereas the beautiful involves the imagination in play with the understanding, the sublime involves the imagination in some kind of relationship with reason. This is because the breaking down of sensuous form means the imagination must instead strike up a relationship with the faculty that does not involve a gathering of the manifold of sense-perception. Thus the sublime catapults the mind back to reason because the ideas it generates,

> cannot be contained in any sensible form but concerns only ideas of reason, which, though they cannot be exhibited adequately, are aroused and called to mind by this very inadequacy, which can be exhibited in sensibility.
>
> Kant (1987: 99)

The ideas of reason cannot be contained in a sensible form, according to Kant, and yet our return to a reflection on reason is precisely because a sensuous form triggers, or arouses, this reflection as it pushes up against the temporal-spatial limits of the empirical and the empirical individual. As Deleuze puts it,

> Reason puts the imagination in the presence of its limit in the sensible; but conversely, the imagination awakens reason as the faculty capable of thinking a suprasensible substrate for the infinity of this sensible world.
>
> Deleuze (2000: 63)

When the senses are overwhelmed, when sense-based faculties are confronted with size and/or power that shakes our conceptual form determination of that sensuous raw material, then for Kant, it only demonstrates that we have within us a more powerful capacity beyond sense-based faculties. '*Sublime is what even to be able to think proves that the mind has a power surpassing any standard of sense*' (Kant 1987: 106). If in the first *Critique* the problematic of the standard of sense turns on its relationship to rational cognition in the faculty of the understanding, here the sublime standard of sense becomes a relay or a metaphor that puts us in touch with our capacity for reason. In the very moment that nature impresses itself on us, the fact that we can appreciate its impact confirms our differentiation from mere natural necessity and the essential link between the aesthetic and reason. The sublime:

> is an object (of nature) *the presentation of which determines the mind to think of nature's inability to attain to an exhibition of ideas.*
>
> Kant (1987: 127)

Despite its power, despite its scale, nature is *dumb* compared to human-kind, for it does not have reason (reflexive consciousness). As Engels noted in terms that could not be closer to Kant's in their sentiment, our species is 'that vertebrate animal in which nature attains consciousness of itself' (Marx and Engels 1977: 348). It would be a mistake, I think, to see in the sublime only a complacent Enlightenment celebration of reason, although there is that as well. But there is also a kernel of materialism here. In the sublime, our ability to turn the power of nature into a metaphor for our own powers is the imaginative articulation of our real material metabolic exchange with nature. That material metabolic exchange is in turn the precondition of treating nature as an occasion for aesthetically mediated reflection on our *own* powers and our *own* relations. In short we become self-aware because we have differentiated ourselves from nature and for that self-awareness to be deep, there can be little comfort in the hubris of an abstract reason that asserts only the differentiation from nature and not also our natural creaturely continuity with nature. The dynamic between sensuousness and reason in the sublime thus embodies precisely this kind of dialectic between continuity and differentiation.

One dimension of the dialectic between our creaturely natures and reason is expressed via the sublime's association with fear, apprehension, shock and astonishment. This may seem to contradict the possibility of the sublime being a vehicle for self-reflection. Fear, as history right down to the present shows, is an excellent basis on which elites can manipulate populations and prevent them from reflecting on the fact that the real conditions that generate anxiety are connected to the preservation of the elites themselves. However, the aesthetic sublime situation is one where we can experience fear but without being in any actual danger. This is one aspect of the special *as if* modality of the aesthetic. Kant's examples are drawn from nature, but confronted with storms, the raging sea and so forth, the sublime simulates a fearful situation that is 'all the more attractive the more fearful it is, provided we are in a safe place' (Kant 1987: 120). The 'safe place' is an indication that reason in the form of culture has thrown a protective barrier around us that mediates our experience with nature at its most powerful. And, of course, in our own time the cultural mediation, the protective barrier and 'safe place' in which spectacles of the sublime are rather common, is the cinema. If we were not in a safe place but were actually really experiencing fear, then the sublime would less likely be an occasion for reflective judgment as the need for self-preservation takes priority. In the aesthetic sublime, fear and apprehension can be experienced *as if* it were real but without real danger and so fear can be (although as we shall see, there are social impediments to this) subjected to reflection as to its social roots and consequences.

The sublime, like the horror film, teeters on the edge of the monstrous. For when our ordinary perceptual forms break down, so too do our conceptions of order, normality, safety and security. 'An object is *monstrous*', Kant suggests, 'if by its magnitude it nullifies the purpose that constitutes its concept' (Kant 1987: 109). We saw in the previous chapter that purposiveness of a special type is characteristic of the beautiful. For one thing the purposiveness of the beautiful is more orientated towards the utopian. The nullification of purposiveness in the sublime pushes it more towards the dystopian. Anything that threatens comprehension because of its size or power threatens to nullify our conceptualization of that thing or our powers of conceptualization in general. The monstrous sublime may thus be viewed as a means of calling into question the universe of dominant conceptualizations, just as the beautiful does, although in different ways.

The beautiful and the sublime

So much for the differences between the sublime and the beautiful. What now about the bridges? Kant himself actually identifies what ought to be for him, some very substantive links between the beautiful and the sublime (Kant 1987: 97). He notes that both use reflective judgment, which is to say that both use form metaphorically to reflect upon some other aspect of nature (including ourselves). Both involve the power of exhibition, which the productive imagination has at its disposal – for in order to perform reflective judgment we cannot be slaves to nature just as we find it, just as we apprehend it in the senses. Both are singular judgments, which is to say both require the unique capacities of the individual judger to form an opinion on the basis of an experiential engagement with the beautiful or the sublime that is not foreclosed by a universal concept of cognition or morality. Yet both are also universally valid, which is to say these judgments have a significance that is more than a merely individual opinion, but which bear within them some subjective apprehension of an objective situation. Despite this Kant believes that the sublime is a mere appendix to the beautiful (Kant 1987: 100). This attempt to marginalize the sublime is clearly a containment strategy, as Fredric Jameson would say, an attempt to keep the disturbing implications of a crisis in form and the political implications of bringing reason *explicitly* into alignment with the aesthetic, corralled.

Kant's containment strategy does not work, even for Kant, who later brings the beautiful (albeit without the radical temporality of the sublime) into a relationship with reason via his concept of aesthetic ideas. Tacitly within the overall architecture of Kant's philosophy, the beautiful and the sublime converge, not least in that both are intimations of a concept of totality which neither the understanding or reason can generate on their own, hence the need for the mediating work of the aesthetic. In the previous chapters, I have shifted the beautiful philosophically away from its more popular and dominant conceptions. We have seen that it is not all calm tranquility, composure and harmony. The beautiful has been redefined as *that feeling which it is pleasurable to communicate because it is the affective trace of objective social relationships that have been rendered palpable by a creative act which de-reifies those objective social relationships and opens the subject up to an encounter with otherness.*

Once the reified conceptual universe is suspended then the beautiful is, from the start, posing a question for reason, for it is reason that must now step in, albeit in a sensuous imaginative form in which the categorical imperative or command of moral reason is opened up to intersubjective debate. The beautiful is not just about the play between the understanding and the imagination since that play already presupposes a relationship with reason which provides the principles by which that play meaningfully occurs. This reading is justified because the purposive unity of the beautiful is actually borrowed by the imagination *from* reason. The understanding cannot itself generate up the sort of purposive concept of the arrangement between parts which characterizes the beautiful. Aesthetic purposiveness is emphatically not the instrumental exercise of causal power by an individual agent, but is instead a concept that is closer in meaning to the necessary reciprocity between things that make up an organized being (including social organizations). The understanding, by contrast, is more 'linear', more atomistic and thus grasps only the phenomenal forms of appearances, which is to say only those characteristics which our conceptual powers are equipped to grasp and to grasp in particular combinations that fall under the remit of empirical-individual and logical-abstract universal relations.

Kant grasped that the limited focus on the forms of appearance within the faculty of the understanding implied a model of part–whole relations antithetical to the idea of the totality.

> [We,] given the character of our understanding, can regard a real whole of nature only as the joint effect of the motive forces of the parts.
>
> Kant (1987: 292)

For the understanding the whole is never more than the sum of its parts and this signifies the absence of a praxis-orientated consciousness materialized at the level of the whole. The significance of this is that reason is the source of our ability to grasp the whole as necessarily interdependent, exercising a determining power on the parts and not just the result of the parts being added together. However, as we have seen, reason is consigned to impotent marginality when confronted by the massive edifice of nature, including social nature, built by the understanding. Hence the need for the aesthetic to give reason a palpable presence in the world, to 'exhibit the idea of reason' (Kant 1987: 114) otherwise banished from a reified universe.

Within Kant's philosophical architecture, reason is tacitly indicted for its failure to make its presence felt as moral principles in the world that the understanding builds. Both the beautiful and the sublime bring reason back into a relationship with the world, but in so doing, they alter reason precisely because it now strikes up a relationship with the sensuous which it could not do before. In the case of the beautiful, reason loses its demeanor of making categorical demands and opens up instead an intersubjective realm of debate around 'taste'. With the sublime an even more explicit *worldly* politics of reason is kick-started. When sensuous form or our capacity to apprehend sensuous form breaks down under the power of the sublime, the mind is vividly reminded of 'the scope of rational cognition or human artifice', argues Paul Crowther (1989:74). But this formulation, along with Kant's, is a little too comforting for reason, a little too complicit with the complacency of Enlightenment rationality. Although Kant presents the sublime as a moment of rational self-confirmation, what is also breaking down is the idea of reason that the imagination borrowed and turned into a sensuous palpable form. The breakdown and mutation of form in the sublime requires that critical reflection of reason is also critical reflection *on* reason, on what has been suddenly called into question by new events, new forces, new large scale and powerful experiences. There can be no return to a serene reason abstractly independent of the experiential as Kant would seem to want when he discusses the sublime. If both the beautiful and the sublime evoke a totality that neither understanding nor reason can do on its own, then, as we have seen, the sublime also adds to that totality a radically new conception of temporality. There is, however, a second characteristic that distinguishes the sublime experience from the beautiful. If the beautiful is a sign that the universal has been suspended, the sublime is a sign that this suspension of the universal now extends to the aesthetic itself, which has been reason's special medium. Hence the sublime tends to have an ineradicable self-reflexive dimension to it, as part of its reflection on the sensuous and creative form that reason takes in the aesthetic. When aesthetic form breaks down or is disturbed in some way, we are in effect drawn to asking questions about the terms on which we had previously engaged with those forms when they were not, to our eye, 'breaking down'.

Kant's sublime is therefore a precursor to the Brechtian aesthetic practice of *Verfremdungs-effekt*, as Ernst Bloch noted sometime ago. He suggested that the Kantian sublime is an early example of the dialectic between distance and closeness, strangeness and familiarity, estrangement and 'its dialectical opposite – the recognition, or "Aha!" experience' (Bloch 1970: 124). The science fiction genre regularly constructs temporal (future) or spatial/other-worldly distanciation devices that provide us with a new view on what is close to us in the familiar here and now. With the beautiful, the 'aha' experience is turned outward onto the world around us; with the sublime, it may at its best continue to include that but it now also turns on aesthetic form (or in popular genres, content) itself. As perceptible aesthetic form breaks down so too habituated ways of aesthetic seeing are called into question. The sublime anticipates the pedagogical possibilities of astonishment at the circumstances under which we live that Brecht's stagecraft specialized in (Benjamin 1999a: 147). In this conception, if all the world is a stage, then the stage has to be made strange, its forms broken down and rearranged, if we are to reawaken our critical reason vis-à-vis that world.

Fetishism and the sublime

The sublime as a means of provoking critical reason into action when confronted with that which challenges our normative-conceptual classifications of nature, including the nature we make, has been widely used within popular culture, especially in the genres of the fantastic, horror and science fiction, for example. But the sublime also teeters on the edge of fetishism and must often enough plunge into fetishism, as the sublime also plunges us into fear and apprehension, as the risk to be taken if some more critical reason is to emerge. In popular culture, the supersensible which the sublime evokes and provokes thought about can just as easily take the form of God, the original fetish that capital subsequently took as a template for its own commodity fetishism. That the sublime dances on the borderline between promoting and suffocating critical reason is ambiguously and fleetingly registered by Kant with his concept of subreption. In the first *Critique* Kant refers to 'the subreptions of sensations' (Kant 1996: 90/B53), which involve the surreptitious process whereby we believe sensations such as colours and sounds inhere in an object independently from the role that the transcendental subject has in mediating our relationship to external reality as forms of appearance. The emphasis in the first *Critique* is on the relationship between the empirical subject and empirical sense data and its conditions of possibility that lie in the transcendental aesthetic (pure space and time) and the categories of the understanding. The concept of subreption, then, refers to the misrecognition that occurs when the transcendental conditions for the possibility of experience are bracketed off and instead we take the content of sense data as inhering in things in themselves, independent of our aesthetic and cognitive organization of perception. For Kant, of course, things in themselves cannot be registered in the realm of sense data. However, this latent theory of fetishism (the bracketing off of the conditions of sensuous objects) becomes more interesting once it moves away from the relationship between sense data and the transcendental subject of the understanding.

In the third *Critique*, the question of subreption is raised in relation to extraordinary sense data and the faculty of reason. This more explicitly raises the question that what is being bracketed off is not the abstract, formal transcendental cognitive subject of the first *Critique*, but the social, historical, intersubjective and political subject that is emerging in the third *Critique*. In §27 Kant writes of the vocation of the imagination to be adequate to an idea of reason but at the same time the condition of the imagination is its inadequacy to do so. What might it be about the imagination–reason relationship that blocks or frustrates the dynamic by which this very inadequacy of the imagination becomes a dialectical, contra-purposive spur to awakening reason's idea of the supersensible?

> But by a certain subreption (in which respect for the object is substituted for respect for the idea of humanity within our[selves, as] subject[s]) this respect is accorded an object of nature that, as it were, makes intuitable for us the superiority of the rational vocation of our cognitive powers, over the greatest power of sensibility.
>
> Kant (1987: 114)

'Subreption' has its roots in two Latin words: *sub* (secret) and *rapere* (to seize). Via subreption a secret, surreptitious seizure occurs: 'respect for the object is substituted for respect for the idea of humanity within our[selves, as] subject[s]', a line that tantalizingly hints at the secret seizure of power by the commodity-object that Marx would write about as fetishism in *Capital*. Note that the word 'substituted' seems to imply that the *relationship* between the subject of reason and the object has in some way been disrupted and the *meaning* of the sublime (as a way of reflecting on our own powers) has been suspended because 'respect for the idea of humanity' has been rerouted from the subject into the object.

Yet the second part of the paragraph seems to contradict this idea of a fundamental misrecognition. For Kant continues that it is precisely this investment in the sublime object of perception as the source of impressive power and might that 'makes intuitable for us the superiority of the rational vocation of our cognitive powers'. Yet for the sublime to have *that* particular outcome, for us to be able to reflect on our own powers of reason as the true subject of the sublime, we cannot rest with the initial substitution of respect for humanity with the respect accorded to the sublime object. So perhaps subreption or fetishism is best understood as kicking in when a circuit between imagination in crisis and reason fails, and instead the metaphorical spur to critical thought stalls in some way. When the circuit of meaning gets stuck in the object (the spectacle, the special effect, the film star, for example) then we have subreption; then we also have a systematically engendered opaqueness between human beings, that bracketing off of our social relationships in which fetishism thrives. If we think of reason as Kant's invocation of our collective relationships (the totality), then this stalling may be seen as the failure of the sublime to explore our profound *social* existence and instead substitute for that all the theological niceties of commodity exchange (Marx 1983: 76). It is clear that the intensity of the experience of the sublime is extremely congruent not only with a shock to our conceptual categories, but also with the individual subject's exchange relation with the luminescent commodity. In this relationship, social context is bracketed off and appropriated as the characteristics that inhere *in things as if* they were the intrinsic property of those things. In this relationship only the relationship between the lonely isolated monadic bourgeois subject and the equally isolated object counts, not the relationships between people that mediate the relationships we have with the sublime object. This is the secret seizure of reason indeed.

Typically within bourgeois relations this isolated act of exchange is framed in two rather antithetical, contra-purposive but also mutually beneficial ways (for capitalism). On the one hand this exchange relationship is framed by an abstract and uncritical rationalism (which Kant may indeed be contributing to) that is grounded in the economic base of capitalist production and exchange. Although this rationalism can produce the technological sublime, and can therefore be responsible for 'wonders of the world' there is always the sense that its proximity to economic interests and accumulation compromises it or even robs it of authentic meaning altogether. Thus rationality split off from reason requires abstract moral discourses to issue forth from the various superstructures and provide some more authentic *meaning* to buttress a life lived under the sign of amoral accumulation. The most powerful and sublime moral discourses available to capitalism are of course religious ones (and increasingly so as reason retreats under neo-liberal capitalism).

All the positions within this ideological matrix, that is the lonely isolated monad trapped between an uncritical rationalism tied to the economic base and a transcendent theistic impulse triggered by the power of *nature*, are at play in a film like *Sunshine* (Danny Boyle 2007). The ultimate reconfiguration of the form of nature by the powers of reason aligned to and expanded by our productive powers would be to restart a dying star. To be able to create or at least rejuvenate a star would put humankind on an almost equal footing with the vast forces involved in the creation of the universe. This is the presupposition of *Sunshine* in which the sun, for some unexplained reason, is dying. The narrative of the film concerns a small crew of a space ship (significantly named *Icarus*) travelling towards the sun with the intention of launching a huge nuclear bomb into it which it is hoped will jump-start the sun once more. The isolation not only of the crew from humankind but from each other is conveyed in numerous ways: from the cold colours of the ship interior and the green and blues associated with the ship's electronic devices (contrasting with the warm end of the colour spectrum, the yellows, reds and whites of the sun); the relative silence of the film (alternating with bursts of loud action); and the dispersal of the crew in their different spaces within the ship associated with a strong intellectual division of labour that also pushes them towards their own individual obsessions (so that, for example, Searle, the psychological officer, is associated with the observation portal where he seems to be subjecting himself to a psychological experiment with the sublime power of the sun, while Corazon, the biologist, is associated with the ship's garden, whose destruction hits her hardest in emotional terms, or Capa, the physicist, whose occupational space is the massive nuclear bomb which is to be delivered into the heart of the sun to kick-start it into life). Typically in these situations, characters are cut off from communicating to base and/or to loved ones and this reinforces the sense of isolation and loneliness. The small crew/large ship ratio also seems to be a requirement for the generic inclusion of the ship's computer, whose omnipresent monitoring of systems, unemotional dialogue with the crew and occasional assertions of autonomy in the name of the 'mission' also adds to the sense of an impersonal system operating at the expense of individual lives, all the way back to *2001: A Space Odyssey* (1968). Yet all these thematics of 'alienation' remain sunk in an a-social, a-historical framework in which an implied rationalistic hubris is contrasted with the power of nature/God.

Contrasted against this representation of the interior of the ship, with its collection of monads who are rather opaque to each other, is the ever more immense presence and power of the sun, a golden unity or totality in which life and death seem to be conjoined. In an early image in the film the space ship is shot in silhouette as it heads towards the sun, its circular back-end placed in the centre of the larger burning yellow/white circle of the star, thus creating a visual metaphor of a giant eye. This link between the star and looking, between sight and the sublime, is immediately underlined by our introduction to Searle in the observation portal, watching the sun, which already looks very different from our usual view of it: more like a molten ball of lava. Searle asks the ship's computer to turn down the filters protecting him as far as possible without damaging him. The scene ends with Searle being engulfed in the yellow and white-hot rays of the sun in a way that virtually obliterates his body by sheer light. This is one of the key images or motifs of the film, replayed on several other occasions. The crew's captain, Kaneda, will die when he is blasted by the sun's rays when he is performing a repair job in space on the hull of the ship. As Kaneda is exposed to the sun, Searle, from inside the ship, demands that Kaneda tells him what he *sees*. At one level what Kaneda sees is obvious and well known to Searle, but clearly, just as the sublime functions as a metaphor in Kant's philosophy, here the sun is being transformed to mean something else and something more than its mere physical materiality. Thus, death in the form of the annihilation of the individual and a profoundly meaningful moment for the individual that is in fact ineffable and cannot be communicated (Kaneda does not answer Searle) converge. The theological orientation of this image of the sublime is obvious as is its simultaneously bourgeois affirmation of an intensely *private* uncommunicable experience. The real basis of this moment of private meaning is to be found in the social relationships that are only symptomatically present in the representation of the ship and its crew. These social relationships, based on the category of the private dominant in the mode of production, allow the individual to discover in the sun something that appears to be *there* independent of those social relationships and allows the individual, in an act of subreption, to *possess* that something (that sublime meaning) albeit at their moment of disintegration as they are blasted by intense heat.

That the film is trapped within the bourgeois relations whose meaninglessness it tries to transcend is evident not only in the representation of the crew as a collection of atoms, but also, perhaps more importantly, in the entrance of Pinbacker. He is the captain of the first ship, the *Icarus 1*, that went out to perform the same mission but which mysteriously disappeared. Pinbacker clearly travelled all the way down the road that Searle looked to be embarking on and, having killed his own crew, lures *Icarus 2* to dock and then sets about completing the job. Pinbacker explicitly states that it is not for humans to play God and he is presented like some kind of avenging angel, all burnt and blistered, bathed in light from the observation portal of *Icarus 2* where Capa discovers him and 'shimmering' in multiple images. Pinbacker seems quite the reverse of the puny and fragile individuals whose bodies have been blasted by the sun or frozen by space, his strength and ability to survive (on *Icarus 1* for years) casts him into a superhuman register. It is as if he has absorbed some quota of the power of the sun from having spent so much time gazing at it, an exchange relationship that the spectacle of consumer capitalism constantly promises. The film has strong intertextual references to the horror film and perhaps the monstrous Pinbacker is like a Frankenstein's monster, turning on the humans as punishment for scientific hubris. Beneath the overtly theological meaning of Pinbacker as avenging angel lies a long running strand to sublime imagery that connects it with madness and fanaticism, of either a secular rational kind (such as neo-liberalism and its techno-culture) or a religious kind (such as fundamentalisms of the Christian and Islamic kind). The link that Kant made between the sublime and fanaticism (dreaming according to principles) connects to a much longer and broader history concerning the power of the aesthetic to provoke delirium in a way that may be regarded as inspirational or profoundly dangerous. Such ambivalence structures *Sunshine*. For Pinbacker is both clearly marked as insane and yet at another level he is the film's own muse, representing the film's own investment in the theologically tinged meaning of the sublime, just as the Romantics saw the poet as one 'deemed to possess a special affinity with nature' (Burwick 1996: 27).

Finally, though, the film does give equal affirmation to our human productive powers when the nuclear bomb explodes just as the sun seems about to engulf it, thus saving humanity. Capa, the physicist, is positioned physically in-between these two forces and ideologically as a point of reconciliation between a theistically tinged nature and an uncritical rationality that gives nuclear power of all things an unexpected public relations boost at a time when vested interests are trying to sustain public funding for it as an alternative to fossil fuels.

The confusions and contradictions around power and size which suffuse bourgeois culture means that very often the critical potentiality latent within the sublime requires a kind of relativization of power and size via some strategy of miniaturization. This strategy offers us the possibility of a (very broadly) 'Brechtian' defamiliarization of our relationships with the forces which we make and which are at our disposal, for good or ill. In fact, however, Kant himself anticipates this process of miniaturization or relativization opened up by the new technologies of seeing he was familiar with:

> *That is sublime in comparison with which everything else is small.* We can easily see here that nothing in nature can be given, however large we may judge it, that could not, when considered in a different relation, be degraded all the way to the infinitely small, nor conversely anything so small that it could not, when compared with still smaller standards, be expanded for our imagination all the

way to the magnitude of a world; telescopes have provided us with a wealth of material in support of the first point, microscopes in support of the second.

Kant (1987: 105–106)

Discussing the need to confront large-scale political terror through 'negative' presentations that view the traumatic event obliquely and indirectly, Gene Ray, in his discussion of the sublime as political terror, takes as his example the atom bomb that was exploded over Hiroshima by the United States in 1945. In practice, the indirect presentation of an almost incomprehensible action turns out to be a strategy of looking at the large scale from a miniaturized perspective. In this way the sublime can recover its 'demand, something like an objective *social imperative*, to radically politicize the notion of mourning' (Ray 2009: 136). A photograph by Seiji Fukusawa of a watch recovered from the rubble of Hiroshima and now exhibited in the Peace Memorial Museum is an example of this negative presentation. This blasted relic, the hands of time frozen at the moment of detonation, has the potential to put us in touch with the trauma of the event and thus prick critical reason and feeling into action in a way that eludes more 'positive' representations:

> Unlike positive images of mushroom clouds that apprehend the awesome detonation through a long, God's-eye perspective, this image of a blasted watch does not present itself as the record of a visibly comprehensible event. It shows itself, rather, as a clue to something else that lies beyond it and remains invisible. To reach that something else, a labour of reflection is needed. As a negative presentation, the watch comes with no pre-given, pre-digested narrative. Interpretation is left to the beholder, who must construct the narrative and meaning.
>
> Ray (2009: 143)

The God's eye perspective on the atom bomb is more analogous to the subsumption of the percept under the concept in the machinery of consciousness that Kant maps out in the first *Critique*. Here all the moral-political implications of the 'mushroom cloud' are drained away leaving only a reified registration of a fact: an atom bomb explosion. But confronted with the watch, shot against a black background, all brown and rusted, with some flecks of black and white, the face of the watch largely smeared away with only the 8, 9 and 10 visible, we now have different relationship to this large-scale act of terror, one in which the watch as fragment does not pretend to master the incomprehensible dimension of suffering unleashed by the bomb. Metonymically, the bare survival of the watch testifies to the obliteration of the singular human being it was once attached to. As with *Sunshine*, we see again the theme of the annihilation of the individual subject, here by awesome technological power and political terror. Metaphorically, its fossil like quality, which suggests that apprehending it is an act of recovering some prehistoric artefact, is in jarring contradiction with the fact that it is a modern technological product. Like all fossils, time has stood still for it and yet this is *our* time, this is modernity, this is progress that has been frozen or, as Kant put it, cancelled by the temporality of the sublime, its linear unfolding violently interrupted not by revolution, as Benjamin had hoped for, but by colossal state terrorism unleashing an element of our productive forces against humanity. This contradiction between productive forces and human needs is precisely the contra-purposive challenge to perception, understanding and reason that the sublime can evoke.

Popular culture is awash with the ambivalent and contradictory dynamics that the clash between productive forces and social relations stirs up. Our relationship to both nature and the nature that we make have become so habitualized and normalized that to put us in touch with these contradictory dynamics, we often need a strategy of miniaturization to turn what we know so well into that mixture of fear and wonder that is the sublime. The child, in which scale can be overlaid with a fantastic reimagining of power and size, is a recurrent strategy. Esther Leslie discusses the comic strip character Little Nemo drawn in the early twentieth century for *The New York Herald*. Little Nemo enters his fantasy adventures through sleep and escapes from them by waking up. For Leslie, the location of Nemo's adventures in icy terrains indicates that snow and ice are transient and fluid forms that allow them to be annexed 'to powerful fantasies of transformation' (Leslie 2009: 38) that are common to the popular sublime. For Kant too nature is subjectively purposive for our imagination, its diversity, forms and processes acting as a stimulant to ideas of reason. The transition from fluids to solids and vice-versa in nature Kant called *fluid at rest* (Kant 1987: 222). He cites water freezing as the commonest example. Nature becomes an image or a metaphor for thinking about contrary processes going on at the same time: 'formation then takes place, not by a gradual transition from the fluid to the solid state, but as it were by a leap' (Kant 1987: 222). Once again, we see how for Kant nature was a subjectively purposive image for reason which here begins to imagine dialectical relations of rapid transformation. Nemo, meanwhile, also has adventures amidst the nature that we make, in the city, where his size transforms the urban environment into a threatening and oppressive landscape of 'constant disasters' and 'novel, rapidly changing' forms (Leslie 2009: 41), such as when he and his friend are pursued by buildings that seem to have grown stilt-like legs.

The cartoonist's 'cities and wilds are alike sites that evoke terror and ecstasy: the sublime is an experience to be relished in the context of first and second nature alike' (Leslie 2009: 43).

An example from popular film, *The Incredible Shrinking Man* (1957), deploys a strategy of miniaturization to offer something like an optical pedagogy. The film begins with a bourgeois idyll, the happy couple on a motorboat on holiday. But when Scott Carey has an unfortunate encounter with a mysterious radioactive cloud in the middle of the sea, his relations with bourgeois life start to change as he himself begins to shrink. What was once homely and comfortable becomes dangerous and insecure. The domestic interior is transformed by nourish lighting and wide-angle lenses as Scott's relationship to material commodities undergoes rapid changes and as debts become unpayable. Along with second nature becoming dominating and imprisoning, first nature too launches its attacks, first the house cat and then as Scott shrinks further, the spider in the basement. Alterations in the normal scale relationships of people and things trigger the allegorical impulse. The strategy of miniaturization in film runs all the way through to *Night at the Museum* (Shawn Levy 2006). Here Larry Daley (Ben Stiller) takes the job of a night guard at the Museum of Natural History. However during the night, Larry discovers that the museum exhibits come to life, and he in effect becomes the custodian of a living and active past that allows the film to rework American national identity in a more liberal direction. Among the exhibits are two miniatures, a cowboy called Jedediah (Owen Wilson) and a Roman centurion, General Octavius (played by the British actor Steve Coogan, thus perhaps evoking the British Empire as well). Now, these two iconic images, one of America's belief in 'Manifest Destiny' that clearly did not stop with the nineteenth-century conquest of Native American Indian lands, and the other of the historically extinct Roman Empire (with which American power was being constantly compared to in the mainstream press) cannot be seen as coincidental in the context of the George Bush years (by that time, starting very much to slide into decline). Much of the comedy around these two miniatures, who both naturally enough dislike each other and Larry, revolves around the disjuncture between their hyper-aggressive stance towards all would-be competitors and their diminutive stature. For General Octavius and Jedediah, their agency in the world has significantly diminished when measured on the normal anthropomorphic scale, but they have failed to adapt accordingly, and thus they are prone to what we might call 'imperial overreach'. The miniaturization of the political sublime is a timely reminder that all empires have limits.

***

One of the main themes of this chapter is to challenge the traditional split between the beautiful and the sublime, a fissure which has served well the different cultural politics of the bourgeois intelligentsia, left and right, but which does not help us understand the place of the sublime in Kant's thought, its relationship to the beautiful or be true to that dialogue between the popular and the avant-garde that the best political modernists, Benjamin, Brecht, Eisenstein and so on, grasped. Accordingly, I have suggested how we might reintegrate the sublime back into our (suitably modified) understanding of the beautiful. Both the beautiful and the sublime involve reflective judgment, the productive imagination and singular experiences that are more than merely private ones. Both the beautiful and the sublime share the same aim of challenging the cognitive grids of the understanding when they have hardened into reified structures of universal assent. For the beautiful, the universal is not given, but the play of sensuous forms generates new thinking about our social relationships that the *concepts* of the understanding are blind to. The beautiful is not ideology and the sublime its critique – that schema must be laid to rest. If the beautiful challenges conceptual form the sublime does both that and it challenges aesthetic form itself, the means by which the beautiful questions the so-called universal. The emphasis on contradiction, the mixing in of displeasure, the breakdown of form and a radical cancelling of ordinary temporal unfolding give the sublime its characteristic aggressiveness. If in the beautiful the imagination borrows from reason principles that govern its play of forms, in the sublime, the mind is abruptly returned to the source of those principles in reason itself as awareness of the historical *limits of the forms* by which reason has made itself palpable in the beautiful become available to us. Thus both the beautiful and reason are implicated in the crisis which the sublime speaks to. Aesthetic form becomes the 'content' of the aesthetic experience most evidently in the avant-garde, giving the sublime its characteristic self-reflexive movement, while in the popular the *form of the sublime* tends to be more 'contained' within the narrative form as the content of spectacle, although even here, there are usually innovations in form to be detected due to the very 'pressure' on perception which the content of the sublime brings. There is, then, a sense in which Kant's sublime is embryonically 'Brechtian', insofar as the relationship between the spectacle and the spectator becomes in some way the issue. But to relink the beautiful and the sublime once again, in both cases, our relationship to nature is no longer what it was outside the aesthetic experience. As Kant puts it in a hugely suggestive passage when he is discussing genius,

> For the imagination ([in its role] as a productive cognitive power) is very
> mighty when it creates, as it were, another nature out of the material that actual

nature gives it. We use it to entertain ourselves when experience strikes us as overly routine. We may even restructure experience; and though in doing so we continue to follow analogical laws, yet we also follow principles which reside higher up, namely, in reason (and which are just as natural to us as those which the understanding follows in apprehending empirical nature). In this process we feel our freedom from the law of association (which attaches to the empirical use of the imagination); for although it is under that law that nature lends us material, yet we can process that material into something quite different, namely, into something that surpasses nature.

Kant (1987: 182)

Here the productive imagination reshapes nature in the manner of the Russian formalists performing *Ostranenie* when experience, including aesthetic experience, becomes 'overly routine'. In the aesthetic we 'restructure experience', at once following empirical and analogical laws of association, but also activating higher principles within reason (such as totality and the supersensible) which come alive in the aesthetic and work by different laws of association (metaphor in fact).

Ideologically the sublime is fundamentally ambivalent, bifurcating in one direction towards fetishism. This may take the form of the theistic mixed in with the modern bourgeois cosmic enlargement of the individual and/or uncritical rationalism in the celebration of the technological sublime. Or the sublime may go in another direction, concerning critical thought about our social relationships. The ambivalence of the sublime is inescapable and Kant himself articulates this ambivalently with his concept of subreption. Here, the object secretly seizes what are social conditions for its existence and expropriates those conditions as its own inherent characteristics before then offering the isolated and helpless bourgeois monad a little quota of imaginary power back in a spectacular visual exchange relationship with said object. This is the culture of consumer capitalism and it would be absurd not to think that it impacts on cultural production as well. Yet in its potential for critical reflective judgment, the play of forms in the sublime, as with the beautiful, is essentially a metaphorical operation that awakens reason. It is a play that works according to principles (of reason), not 'factual' knowledge. The starry sky is mobilized not so that we can think about astronomy but so that it is seen 'as a vast vault encompassing everything' (Kant 1987: 130). The ocean is mobilized not so that we can think about marine science but so that we can see it as 'a clear mirror of water' or 'as being like an abyss threatening to engulf everything' (Kant 1987: 130). Like reason, the aesthetic is liberated from merely factual knowledge and logical relationships. As Paul Ricour argues in *The Rule of Metaphor*,

The imagination mingles with reason by virtue of the rules of correlation
governing the translation of statements concerning the secondary domain
[vaults, mirrors, the abyss -MW] into statements applicable to the original
domain [the starry sky, the ocean -MW].

                                                             Ricour (1978: 241)

This play with forms, this different law of association, which bypasses the
reified real speaks to a supersensible reality, namely our relationships with one
another and nature. The metaphorical operation does not just imaginatively
suspend what is given but opens the imagination up 'towards a dimension of
reality that does not coincide with what ordinary language envisages under the
name of natural reality' (Ricour 1978: 211). The aesthetic is our way back to
the disavowed social dimensions of our being and the sublime introduces the
whole thematics of time as change, crisis and transformation. In the popular
sublime especially, utopian desires concerning the possibilities of productive
forces and simultaneously fear concerning how those productive forces might
be mobilized against us by capital are mixed together in complex arrangements
from which there is the possibility for the aesthetic to provide critical reflection
on the sources of our hopes and fears, when the latter is a mere simulation
of the real thing. We saw that miniaturization is one strategy by which the
critical potential of the sublime may be recovered from a cultural scene awash
with fetishism around power and size. Adorno associated the beautiful with
'micrological perception' (Adorno 2004: 91) because its form, in contrast to
the sublime, is compact, vividly finite and something that attunes perception
to tiny details: hence in nature beauty is found in a rose, a crystal formation
or organized being. This would suggest that the strategy of miniaturization is
actually the beautiful and the sublime working together in aesthetic practice just
as ultimately they work together within the architecture of Kant's philosophy.
Conceptually, although Kant sees the sublime as a mere appendix to the beautiful,
his acknowledgement that it is part of the aesthetic prepares the ground for his
later and final twist in the 'Dialectic of Aesthetic Judgment', where he makes
explicit what is tacit within the architecture of his thought. There the concept
of the aesthetic idea acknowledges that the beautiful is an operation that draws
on and is analogous to reason's own principles and powers. In reconstructing
the usually suppressed connections between the beautiful and the sublime, we
have completed our reconstruction of Kant's aesthetics. What we must turn to
now is the basis of the aesthetic itself in human labour. Unexpectedly, here too,
Kant is our guide.

6

Labour, the Aesthetic and Nature

The absence of human labour, of that productive activity unique to our species, marks Kant's philosophical project from the outset and is the central reason why his first two *Critiques* suffer from debilitating dualisms. In the *Critique of Pure Reason*, we saw a fundamental dualism between the faculties of the understanding and of reason. The faculty of the understanding constitutes the world of the given according to the causal laws and complexes of nature, but these laws and complexes tend, in an early sign of reification, to extend imperiously into the social world of human practices robbing them precisely of their basis in human freedom that makes them possible. This leaves the faculty of reason retreating in Kant's philosophy to the private citadel of the individual moral conscience.

This fracture between understanding and reason was reproduced in the dualism between concept and sensuous apprehension of the empirical world *within* the faculty of the understanding. Yet despite this overwhelming tendency in his thinking, Kant noted in the *Critique of Pure Reason* that human knowledge has, as he put it, 'two stems': one was sensibility and the other was conceptual recognition. The metaphor of the two stems helped Kant to make a revealing aside, namely that these two stems 'perhaps spring from a common, but to us unknown, root' (Kant 1996: 67/B29). Given the otherwise dichotomous structure of his philosophy, this is a remarkable statement. For the common but unknown root could provide the basis of a reconstruction of his philosophy that might overcome the dualistic fissures within it. The root that was unknown to Kant – because the historical conditions were not propitious for him to know it – is of course human labour.

So it is remarkable and hugely significant that the question of labour – in the shape of artistic labour within the fine arts – makes a surprising, brief but significant entrance into Kant's philosophy in *Critique of Judgment*. The moment, which is nothing short of a revolution in philosophy, occurs within the section that is supposed to be dedicated to the Deduction of Pure Aesthetic Judgments.

With the Deduction apparently complete, Kant suddenly turns to the question of labour in §43 and grounds the aesthetic in the materialist relationship between labour and nature. This brings Kant even closer to Marx as his philosophical precursor. As we shall see, there is little doubt that Marx read Kant's passages on the labour of fine art and incorporated Kant's ideas into his own ontology of labour in both his early work, *The Economic and Philosophical Manuscripts*, and his later, mature work, *Capital*. This means we must reassess the widespread view that Marx's philosophical account of labour is drawn exclusively from Hegel's work.

Kant's own turn to labour was driven by the need to distinguish between natural beauty and the beautiful which human beings produce. For it was clear to Kant that the former presupposes the latter kind of beauty. We can only find nature beautiful because we ourselves apprehend it as such. That *reception* of nature in turn presupposes a culture and society that has humanized nature. In §43 Kant's materialist turn, which his aesthetic turn has opened up, is confirmed by acknowledging that the humanization of nature (the basis for that special mode of communication which Kant calls beautiful) rests on *production*. One of the most important issues that is at stake in linking the aesthetic to production is that it simultaneously materializes the aesthetic and aestheticizes (in a good way) questions around production, putting questions of creativity, freedom and imagination back into the question of labour as its general condition. Since the industrial revolution until quite recently, those normative issues were excluded from mainstream considerations of work. More recently, with the rise of cognitive capitalism, the culture industries, the rise of intellectual and symbolic labour and so forth, values once associated with the aesthetic and pitted against production since the Romantics have now been incorporated into mainstream celebrations of 'creative capitalism' (Raunig, Ray and Wuggenig 2011). Direct engagement with this discourse is not possible here, but instead I hope that what follows may be a contribution to sketching out a philosophical foundation for a different vision for thinking the relationship between the aesthetic and labour. As Jason Toynbee argues, 'to the extent that cultural work encompasses an idea about what work in general *could* be like then we ought to take it seriously' (Toynbee 2013: 94).

§43: Kant's materialist turn

Kant initially defines *art* in a general sense as *work*, thus linking it explicitly to human labour and differentiating it from *nature*. Precisely because it is a product of human labour, is the product of rational, conscious thought with a designed intention behind it, it must be differentiated from nature which is either the product of no intentionality whatsoever, or in the case of animals, is governed by instinct alone. Art is 'work', nature is merely 'an effect', that is the product of causal forces that are not open to conscious change, but only what Engels would call the blind forces of natural evolution. Kant goes on, in terms that should be familiar:

> By right we should not call anything art except a production through freedom, i.e., through a power of choice that bases its acts on reason. For though we like to call the product that bees make (the regularly constructed honeycombs) a work of art, we do so only by virtue of an analogy with art; for as soon as we recall that their labour is not based on any rational deliberation on their part, we say at once that the product is a product of their nature (namely, of instinct), and it is only to their creator that we ascribe it as art.
>
> Kant (1987: 170)

The famous comparison that Marx makes in *Capital* (Chapter 7) between bees and architects is rarely traced to its origins in Kant's *Critique of Judgment*. As Marx will do, Kant here distinguishes human labour from the work of natural creatures on the basis that the former involves 'rational deliberation', while the latter is the product of their instinct and therefore involves no freedom, no choices or deliberation and therefore no reason, in the specifically human sense of the word. The comparison between what bees produce and art proper is simply that an analogy that paradoxically helps us think about how we are differentiated from the rest of nature by starting with a structural resemblance between products. This, of course, is one of the *as if* characteristics of judgment for Kant, the ability to compare nature with art or our cognitive powers in order to hypothesize either about nature or about our own powers (Kant 1987: 390).

Like Kant, Marx uses nature as a metaphor to reflect critically on what is specifically different about human labour. Marx argues that it is conscious intentionality that differentiates human labour from animal labour. Nature may have perfection on its side (it is doubtful whether there are many spiders that are lousy at spinning webs) but it is the choices that have to be made (and which open up the prospect of failure and the likelihood of flaws) that makes human labour superior to the products of nature. Interestingly, Marx writes not about reason in the famous passage from *Capital* but about that much more aesthetic category, the imagination:

> ... what distinguishes the worst architect from the best of the bees is this, that the architect raises his structure in imagination before he erects it in reality.

> At the end of every labour-process, we get a result that already existed in the imagination of the labourer at its commencement. He not only effects a change of form in the material on which he works, but he also realises a purpose of his own that gives the law to his modus operandi, and to which he must subordinate his will.
>
> Marx (1983: 174)

It is the ability to form an image of something that does not exist in the form imagined that is important. Imagination is central to the reflective judgment's ability to exceed the material conditions that make it possible, to realize what is possible within the actual. Imagination is a faculty that catapults us out of the cycle of instinctual activity that characterizes the 'labour' of animals, where practices are indeed reduced to material (physical) conditions. Marx's use of the imagination is very close to Kant's productive imagination from the first *Critique*, which is differentiated from the reproductive imagination precisely by the autonomy it achieves from the empirically given in time and space. Notice, too, that the imagination is here tied closely to the production (first in the mind, then in material terms) of *forms*. This too is very close to Kant's position. For all Kant's talk of the play of the understanding and the imagination as a purely 'mental state' in parts of the third *Critique* (Kant 1987: 62), Kant's turn to the activity of making gives his otherwise reception-orientated philosophy of the aesthetic a decisive materialist turn. The imagination, as both Marx and Kant use it, is a socially cultivated capacity essential for production. The final sentence where Marx thinks dialectically about how changes in form realize a purpose while at the same time that purposive form in turn provides the 'law' to the labour process itself to which the worker 'must subordinate his [sic] will' is nothing other than a rewriting of Kant's *'free lawfulness* of the imagination' (Kant 1987: 91).

The reproductive imagination may be thought of as the active selection by the senses of the most salient features of the environment in order to negotiate the already existing, the already known. The productive imagination, then, may be seen as the capacity of the problem solver and the artist to discover a new more appropriate form within the situation. Rudolf Arnheim, concerned to overcome the separation between the conceptual and perceptual by which a dominant rationality becomes detached from experience, put it like this:

> A problem solver ... is driven by the need to obtain from the given situation something it seems unprepared to give. ... In the problem solver, the image of the goal situation exerts pressure on the image of what is presently given

and tries to force a transformation in the direction of what is required by the task. The demands of the goal image justify the reorganization of the present structure. The primary obligation, then, is to what is presently given. In one of Hank Ketcham's newspaper cartoons the ingenious but formidable boy, Dennis the Menace, pulls out the drawers of a chest stepwise in order to construct a staircase, which will allow him to climb to the cookie jar on top of the steps. The usual image of the drawer resists being seen as a set of steps, but the goal image of 'getting up there' draws the ingenious discovery of the steps from the potentialities of the given resource.

(Arnheim (1972: 194–195)

The goal image exerts pressure on what is actually given within the reproductive imagination, which in turn releases the potentialities that can be discovered in the situation through the process of transformation in which one form (the drawers) is altered (against their 'resistance' as a specific material form) by the productive imaginative act of making them resemble another form (stairs). Once again, metaphor is central to this productive capacity. Kant names this productive transformation of forms *technic*.

> Art, as human skill, is also distinguished from *science* ([i.e., we distinguish] *can* from *know*), as practical from theoretical ability, as technic from theory (e.g. the art of surveying from geometry).
>
> Kant (1987: 170)

Here Kant is arguing that human skill is an embodied practical knowledge that develops as we transform the laws of nature as codified by natural science into use values (the art of surveying from geometry) and it is this that lies behind the distinction between *can* and *know*, *technic* from theory. Theory refers here to natural science theory concerned with the determinate constitution of phenomena which we did not have a hand in making (the inner constitution of nature, and/or nature that pre-exists our emergence on the planet (such as coal) or the universe, such as the atomic composition of matter). The problem comes when this perfectly correct model for natural science is overextended to society, for here we do have a hand in the making of what we are also studying and expunging our ineliminable subjective participation in the production of this social nature leads to reification. This, of course, was Kant's problem and he refers to it in both the first and second introductions of the third *Critique*. What he hopes is that art plays a mediating role in the strong division between theoretical philosophy (which includes the *technically practical*) and practical (moral) philosophy. Hence the importance of the distinction between theory and *technic*. The latter term refers to the power of practical arrangement that requires deliberation and creative choices. The concept of *technic* would later be crucial to Benjamin in his reflections on the complex dialectical relations between nature, technology and social relationships, and how technologies and their techniques cultivate distinct modes of subjectivity appropriate to their remaking of the world the subject inhabits (Leslie 2000: 73–79). If for Kant *technic* embodies the subjective capacity to remodel nature, the crucial mediating role of technology is not entirely absent from his thinking either. He notes in relation to the sublime, for example, how the telescope and microscope have respectively altered our way of seeing size and of positioning ourselves in relation to the world (and universe) around us (Kant 1987: 106).

The concept of *technic*, then, can be broken down to encompass a number of interconnected attributes within a process. Firstly, it encompasses technology, that is the tools that have been developed to work on nature. Secondly, techniques, that is the body of skills that have clustered around the particular uses of the technology. Kant suggests that when techniques have developed to a particular level of complexity, as with craft skills, a mixture of talent and experience is required to deploy techniques successfully. 'We refrain', he suggests,

> from calling anything art that we *can* do the moment we *know* what is to be done, i.e., the moment we are sufficiently acquainted with what the desired effect is. Only if something [is such that] even the most thorough acquaintance with it does not immediately provide us with the skill to make it, then to that extent it belongs to art.
>
> Kant (1987: 170–171)

This is important because the techniques of *technic* are to be differentiated from Kant's concept of the technically practical. The latter is a narrowly instrumental idea of techniques where the ends to be achieved are already known in advance. In the first introduction Kant discusses in a footnote how the techniques that are involved in the development of subjectivity, such as happiness, rule out such instrumental application of techniques because 'here we have the additional task of determining what this purpose itself (happiness) consists in [not just how (we are) to achieve it' (Kant 1987: 390). Thus the form of happiness is for Kant an open question and this makes it analogous to the aesthetic. The more questions of craft, culture and subjectivity become integral to material production in the course of human history, the more the means and ends of techniques become a site of discussion and debate.

Techniques associated with particular technologies are in turn governed by particular sets of rules that are specific to the technology and/or techniques in question. Rules are more plural than techniques as they amount to the differentiated codification of what can be done with the techniques associated with tools. For example, editing is a technique associated with the technology of film, but continuity editing or montage are very different rules (or conventions) implementing that technique. If we follow Kant and differentiate *technic* from the instrumental application of rules, then again we can see why the aesthetic is linked to craft labour without necessarily being identical to it. Aesthetic rules, even more than the rules of a craft, open up a space in which the effects to be achieved require more than the acquisition of knowledge but also judgment that is finely attuned to the precise context of the work. This necessary attunement to the specificity of work introduces (when the aesthetic is working aesthetically) friction with the quantitative logics of capitalist exchange that aspires towards equivalence, not difference.

Having started with a definition of art in general, one which encompasses work *and* aesthetic production, Kant has established a materialist framework for thinking about the relationship between aesthetics and ordinary work. But he goes on to make a distinction between fine art and craft work which also lays the basis for thinking about how the aesthetic may act as a repository of critical energies concerning the fate of ordinary labour when our creative relationship to nature starts to be unnecessarily compromised by social relationships. The distinction Kant makes is between *free* art and *mercenary* art or craft.

> We regard free art [as an art] that could only turn out purposive (i.e., succeed) if it is play, in other words, an occupation that is agreeable on its own account; mercenary art we regard as labor, i.e., as an occupation that in its own account is disagreeable (burdensome) and that attracts us only through its effects (e.g., pay), so that people can be coerced into it.
>
> Kant (1987: 171)

The distinction between art and mercenary art clearly stands for the distinction between art as aesthetic activity and art as work under a given set of historical conditions (capitalist class society). Art is characterized as play, as agreeable and as something that is done for its own account. Craft, by contrast, is occupation, not play; burdensome, not agreeable; done for and subject to external ends (especially mercenary exchange); and it involves coercion. Let us remind ourselves that this is Kant, not Marx, and yet this apparently unambiguously bourgeois philosopher seems here a very long way from unproblematically endorsing the capitalist mode of production. But neither is this a bourgeois romantic flight of fancy, for Kant emphatically does not counterpoise the rules to be found in craft work with an apparently absolutely rule free zone of fine or free art. Kantian scholars often argue that 'there are no rules, methods, foundations, or criteria for the creation and appreciation of beauty. All we have are examples of what is beautiful' (Shaviro 2009: 13). But although beauty is for Kant the product of exemplary acts, these acts of creative labour are *not* rule free.

> It is advisable, however, to remind ourselves that in all free arts there is yet a need for something in the order of a constraint, or, as it is called, a *mechanism*. (In poetry, for example, it is correctness and richness of language, as well as prosody and meter.) Without this the *spirit*, which in art must be *free* and which alone animates the work, would have no body at all and would evaporate completely.
>
> Kant (1987: 171)

Kant does not associate 'mere play' as the defining feature of art. Here he is being consistent with his definition of the aesthetic of the beautiful as a *play* between the imagination and the understanding. Without structure and constraint, the spirit that animates the work 'would have no body at all and would evaporate completely' (Kant 1987: 171). So art is a practice in which creative agency is in a dialectical relationship with constraint, with technical structures and the conflicting rules of aesthetic production where much of the cultural politics of the aesthetic is to be found. Kant is writing specifically about the techniques of artistic production, such as rhyme and rhythm in poetry. But coming so soon after the broader discussion of the institutional constraints that are at work in craft, we are inevitably left to wonder how those constraints and structures of fine art differ from those of craft work. Extrapolating from Kant's argument, we may say that the difference between constraint/mechanism in fine art and craft (ordinary labour) is that in art the determinate conditions are (or ought to be) in some way *internal* to the productive activity itself while in craft the determinate conditions (which Kant explicitly describes as commodity exchange relations) are external, imposed and therefore they *foreclose on play*. The implicit argument in Kant is that constraint should be de-reified. But what does this mean and how can we distinguish between determinate freedom (free lawfulness) and reification (unfree lawfulness)? As a first formulation in trying to address this, we may say that structures should in principle be open to moral-political consideration (democratization) within a given level of historic development, rather than arbitrarily foreclosing on the subject because of capitalist class relations which express themselves precisely as a priori unmastered imperatives (especially the profit motive and class-differentiated access to material and cultural resources). This ought-utopian impulse is inscribed in the aesthetic play of the imagination with the understanding, in *the production of a form that does not foreclose on the recovery by the subject of the socially available cultural resources.* At this philosophical level the aesthetic act is always deeply political.

For us today, when commodity exchange has become more universal and more pervasive, one can only suggest that to fall short of Kant's position on commodity exchange implied by his distinction between fine art and mercenary art suggests accommodation to our historical predicament rather than an advance on Kant. The connection between freedom, choice and reason and commodity exchange under capitalism is patently tenuous, despite all the ideological rhetoric surrounding the so-called 'creative industries', and at best may be described as (a) accidental, emerging in the occasional gaps that open up due to 'anarchic' competition, gaps that are strictly (b) time-limited within certain situations due to monopolizing tendencies and powers and (c) restricted according to unequal purchasing power and stratified access to other resources. Finally, we may add that (d) capital against its will, begrudgingly and always on terms open to revocation, must cede some limited power to the creative labour it buys because of its nature and the nature of the process it is involved in that produces aesthetic products. As Deleuze writes in relation to film,

> however great the controls which bear upon him [sic], the creator has at his disposal at least a certain time to 'commit' the irreversible. He has the chance to extract an Image from all the clichés and to set it up against them.
>
> Deleuze (2005: 214)

To extract an Image from all the clichés: that is a nice Kantian formulation but we must always situate aesthetic labour in a dialectical relationship with ordinary labour. The relationship between tools, techniques, rules and their application is relatively more instrumental in the case of material production if a desired outcome that is functional for a specific set of needs is to be achieved. And yet, despite the fact that work is a response to need, we must remember that Kant still begins §43 by insisting that it involves 'a power of choice' that differentiates work from nature. In doing so, he has broken with his earlier position (repeated in the first introduction) that the technically practical, which also involves a 'power of choice' merely shadows the laws of nature (Kant 1987: 389). Instead, now labour, art as work, demonstrates that creative element, that capacity for some original causalities to interrupt the natural cause-effect relations of nature, and this is the basis of our social being, the basis that is of society (any society) itself.

Thus the aesthetic as creative arrangement is part of material production, what Marx and Engels called the '[t]he first historical act ... the production of the means to satisfy ... needs, the production of material life itself' (Marx and Engels 1989: 48). As that production becomes more complex and developed so the material basis for creative arrangement to separate itself as a specific activity outside 'the first historical act' also grows and develops into the aesthetic proper. With that all sorts of problems about how to conceive and capture their essential connection also develop along with the division between manual and intellectual labour, but the two types of art remain closely linked in their development and meaning, as this passage from Marx's 1844 *Economic and Philosophical Manuscripts* makes clear:

> An animal forms things in accordance with the standard and the need of the species to which it belongs, whilst man knows how to produce in accordance with the standard of every species, and knows how to apply everywhere the inherent standard to the object. Man therefore also forms things in accordance with the laws of beauty.
>
> Marx (1980: 168)

Unlike animals, our species being is not trapped to produce according to an inflexible standard but rather we are able to be inspired by the 'standard of every species' (architects inspired by bees), creatively adapting what we discover in nature through our conscious practical activity. The 'inherent standard to the object' that we can discover and refine refers to the specific prototypes that underline the functionality of all and various use values. These standards of functionality (inherent, say, to a bridge, an axe or a space ship) also lay the basis for the development of beauty, where a non-instrumental functionality comes into play, in relation to both material production (design, for example) and the aesthetic proper. What Marx draws our attention to here is that the seeds for aesthetic production and appreciation are inextricably linked to *the appreciation of form in the sphere of material production* by which we meet the needs of daily reproduction. Here the rules of material production mediated by techniques and technologies come into contact with the laws of nature and through that engagement the forms of nature become the testing ground for freedom through the creative discovery and transformation of nature.

Form and purposiveness

The standard inherent in the purposiveness of something is a source of beauty. On this both Kant and Marx agree. In §48 Kant asks how the standard inherent in the purposiveness of something produced only by nature differs from something produced not by nature, but by art. The difference lies in how we read natural beauty and artistic beauty. Natural beauty does not require us to wonder at the purposiveness (Arnheim's goal image) responsible for the production of a beautiful form. For no species being that we know lies behind the colour and shape of crystals or the setting sun. With art, whether understood as material work or artistic work, this is not the case: 'since art always presupposes a purpose in the cause (and its causality) … the harmony of a thing's manifold with an intrinsic determination of the thing, i.e., with its purpose, is the thing's perfection' (Kant 1987: 311). If we take Kant here to be referring to art in the general sense of work, as we are entitled to given everything else that has been argued, then this statement is a precursor to Marx's argument in the *Economic and Philosophical Manuscripts* that beauty is a capacity that is fostered in the production of use values where we learn to produce 'the inherent standard to the object' in order to satisfy needs. As we have seen, artistic beauty is then defined by Kant as purposiveness without purpose, a specific type of practice where our relative autonomy from nature is then doubled as a relative autonomy from the production of material life. The aesthetic is a type of activity where specifically, a mode of communication, sociability and reflection on our relationship to nature and ourselves as mediated through the production of use values can be cultivated in a way that economic need and political order otherwise make difficult within a class-divided society.

Kant also notes that 'certain objects of nature, above all animate ones, such as a human being or a horse' (Kant 1987: 311) do also provoke in us purposiveness as a criterion for judging them. As organized beings with their own powers of movement, such natural things do seem to have an 'objective purposiveness' to their *form* and we take this into account 'in order to judge their beauty' (Kant 1987: 179). Again, Kant is making the same point regarding the standards inherent to nature, as Marx also makes in relation to the standards inherent to the objects we produce out of nature. In such cases of natural beauty, where we posit objective purposiveness as a criterion for judging the form of a horse, for example, when appreciating its power, speed and grace, we are no longer making a 'pure' aesthetic judgment. Instead, we make a 'teleological judgment that serves the aesthetic one as a foundation and condition that it must take into account' (Kant 1987: 179–180). Again, insofar as Kant is identifying objective purposiveness as a 'foundation and condition' for the aesthetic proper, he seems remarkably close to Marx, or Marx seems remarkably close to Kant. Kant is mapping out a complex relationship between nature, the nature we make (material production) and the aesthetic. What defines the specificity of the latter against nature and material production is the complex communicative formal structure of the aesthetic. For example, fine art, says Kant, is superior to the objective purposiveness of nature and art (ordinary production) in that:

> it describes things beautifully that in nature we would dislike or find ugly. The Furies, diseases, devastations of war, and so on are all harmful; and yet they can be described, or even presented in a painting, very beautifully.
>
> Kant (1987: 180)

Beauty, despite all the connotations which bourgeois aesthetics has loaded around the word, is here understood as a mode of communication that cultivates our understanding of ourselves as social beings rather than refined individuals with innate personal taste. This means that we must explore the meaning, the purposiveness of the formal structure. The beautiful is 'actually only the form of a concept's exhibition, the form by which this concept is universally communicated' (Kant 1987: 180), writes Kant, explicitly linking the pure aesthetic judgment to some mode of conceptuality that is yet different from the conceptuality that dominates the understanding. That difference resides in the play of the imagination with the understanding (and with reason). But the 'imagination' is not to be reduced to some purely internal psychological faculty, empirical or transcendental. The imagination is materially embodied in the *form* of the artwork, that is in the outcome of a productive activity.

We can use this discussion around the production of forms by which we judge the purposiveness of material life and aesthetic reflection to introduce two categories of reception: recognition and reinterpretation. We have seen that the standard inherent in the purposiveness of objects that we make develop our capacities for thinking the beautiful. Such objects also constitute the raw material and object world of the aesthetic which we recognize as particular syntheses of forms, but which the aesthetic then extends by its peculiar laws of play between the productive imagination and the understanding. Kant's aesthetic philosophy is not therefore narrowly serviceable for the aesthetics of naturalism and cognitive psychology. On the contrary, it seems perfectly compatible with a wide range of aesthetic practices, including modernist critiques of naturalism. Take, for example, René Magritte's famous painting *Ceci n'est pas une pipe*. Foucault says of the painting:

> who would seriously contend that the collection of intersecting lines above the text is a pipe? Must we say: My God, how simple minded! The statement is perfectly true, since it is quite apparent that the drawing representing the pipe is not the pipe itself. And yet there is a convention of language: What is this drawing? Why, it is a calf, a square, a flower. An old custom not without basis, because the entire function of so scholarly, so academic a drawing is to elicit recognition, to allow the object it represents to appear without hesitation or equivocation.
>
> Foucault (1982: 19–20)

It is not a pipe. It is not as the Kant of the first *Critique* might say, the thing itself, but a picture or presentation of a pipe, a series of intersecting lines that are synthesized into a form, the standard inherent in the purposiveness of which we recognize as a pipe. But thought has a habit of leapfrogging over the *picturing* process of the aesthetic act (Kant's formal purposiveness) and settling for the more comfortable habits of mere recognition that dominates the first *Critique*. We *know* it is not a pipe itself and yet, says Magritte's painting, we have a powerful urge to suspend our knowledge of the implications of that knowledge – which would or should lead us to address the *formal conditions of the aesthetic picturing process* – and invest instead in the comforts of identification (it *is* a pipe) which seems in turn to confirm our own identity (as classifiers who can bring the manifold of elements into a causally intelligible relation and name the object – a pipe!). Here in short we have in summary form the entire debate about fetishism, which was played out particularly fiercely in film studies due to the photographic realism of the medium's moving image. The argument of the psychoanalytic critics did not in fact depend, as many cognitive critics have subsequently contended in the backlash against 'Theory', that audiences mistook the image for reality. Instead the argument was that the spectator was trapped into an unproductive duality in which 'I know' (it is not reality, it is not, as Kant would say, the thing in itself) cannot be mediated or integrated with the 'I nevertheless believe' in the compelling illusionistic quality of the image. Since dualism breaks the mediating *play* between positions in favour of static opposition, no integration of knowledge with belief (the seeming *presence* of the thing depicted in the cinematic image) is possible. This compartmentalization of knowledge from belief, which protects belief from critical interrogation, is fetishism. What is thus known (I know the women does not have a penis, I know the image is a formal construct, an effect of an apparatus that is technological, cultural, etc.) is then disavowed and displaced *with interest* into the belief side of the opposition (the women does have a symbolic penis! This story is so compelling! So real! So immediate!) affording the image a peculiarly intense power over the subject which in turn helped cultural theorists of the time (circa 1970s) come to the conclusion that feeling and emotion are dangerous to critical reason.

The psychoanalytic critics (Heath, Metz, etc.) were essentially asking spectators, film theory and film practice, to do what Magritte's painting does and explore the tension (Kant's 'play') between the picturing *process* and the thing pictured. At least that, I think, is a productive interpretation of the psychoanalytic critique of fetishism. It is a gloss on their project that acknowledges the critical thought which motivated it, whatever problems the critical apparatus has. One of those problems remains its idealism and subjectivism that did more than differentiate formal purposiveness from the intelligible thing depicted in the name of nourishing critical thought, it actually uncoupled representational systems (language, film language) *entirely* from their social and material conditions. The same arguments and problems were played out in art criticism and post-structuralist theory in the attack on the symbol, with its fetishistic appearance of presence that abolishes language, its apparent plenitude and completeness of meaning. Against the symbol there was the recovery (inherited from Benjamin) and affirmation of allegory, with its contrasting stress on fragmentation, its playful merging of visual and linguistic relations and undermining of their traditional hierarchical ordering (Day 1999, Tambling 2010).

Foucault's own version of this is to make a distinction between the principle of resemblance that dominates painting where the painting 'posits an equivalence between the fact of resemblance and the affirmation of a representative bond' (Foucault 1982: 34) and *similitude*. The latter (close to Lyotard's *simulacrum*) unmoors images and words from their referential security while also playfully teasing us with the visual similarity between image and referent. 'Magritte dissociated similitude from resemblance, and brought the former into play against the latter' (Foucault 1982: 44). But as with the psychoanalytic and the post-structuralist critics, Foucault loses the necessary tension with resemblance in the play of similitude against it. One can only appreciate Magritte's disruptions to causal intelligibility, to the gathering together of the manifold, by holding in our heads the norms of intelligibility that obtain outside the universe of the aesthetic act itself. When I say 'hold in our heads' this is not a collapse into cognitive psychology, since what we 'hold in our heads' (consciousness as

Marx called it) is also related to and determined by our social being. For all the hilarious playful brilliance that Foucault displays in his reading of the multiple paradoxes, ambiguities and uncertainties engendered by Magritte's painting (his formal purposes) and its unravelling of 'all the traditional bonds of language and the image' (Foucault 1982: 22), Magritte's entire operation depends on the very practices of imagistic resemblance, recognition and linguistic referentiality that it seeks to raise questions about. After Foucault is done with it, the

> 'pipe' that was at one with both the statement naming it and the drawing representing it – this shadow pipe knitting the lineaments of form with the fibre of words – has utterly vanished.
>
> Foucault (1982: 29)

Except the 'shadow pipe', Marx's prototype, the form inherent to the objective purpose of the pipe, has not utterly vanished because if it had then so too would Magritte's painting as an artistically intelligible product that is opening up a aesthetic communication act about how we relate through art to the world we make through art in general (as work). Magritte's painting is obviously not about pipes per se but about our relationship to the object world we make through art as work. Art as aesthetic thus expands the range of ways we have of relating to nature (and our own material productions), which allows us to explore that nature in ways we could not easily do outside the aesthetic experience (where we are bound by objective purposes – yes, *this is a pipe*, or yes these are Kant's 'Furies' of nature that oppress us) and which cultivate the utopian desire to *change* our objective relationship to such nature. Art as aesthetic is merely a heightened mode of consciousness regarding our relationship to nature as it is produced through art as work. This ultimately is aesthetic reinterpretation.

The counter-attack on conventionalism within film theory was not led as one might have thought (or hoped) by historical materialists, not least because Marxism insofar as it existed in the field seemed to be very close to conventionalism. Instead conventionalism was critiqued most cogently by cognitivism (Bordwell, Carroll, etc.). The materialist kernel that underpins the cognitive interest in recognition, memory, inference and other cognitive powers is that these capacities must be the complex outcome of a real practical relationship with the world around us and the world we make. As Bordwell writes, 'given certain uniformities in the environment across cultures, humans have in their social activities faced comparable tasks in surviving and creating their ways of life' (Bordwell 1996: 91). Thus the key ideas underpinning conventionalism – that all symbolic constructs are entirely arbitrary, that nature is identical with or a mere outcrop of culture and that there is no world of forces independent of our apprehension of those forces – are difficult to sustain. Furthermore, the perceptual-cognitive capacities required for reading at least certain aspects of the film image (the intelligibility of perceived objects) seems to indicate the possibility of something approaching a cross-cultural universalism that calls into question the implicit subordination of the image, from film studies to visual studies, to the methodologies devised to analyse the more evidently arbitrary structures of written language (Jay 2002: 271). The photographic image of a horse is at least recognizable to virtually everyone on the planet in a way that the words 'horse', 'caballo' 'Άλογο' and 'الحصان' probably are not. The cross-cultural intelligibility of the iconic sign indicates that there is a determinate 'baseline' in our dealings with nature from which cultural variability, and beyond that, variability in our social relations, are played out. The dialectic between determination and freedom vis-à-vis nature is thus redoubled in the nature that we make. While the meanings attributed to the images we make may well be context sensitive, in relation to both the work it appears in and the wider culture that produced or receives it, the medium's iconic intelligibility and reproducibility lays the foundations for cross-cultural communication and shared understanding at even this more sensitive register of *meaning* as well.

But if cognitivism is happier to think about the film image as having meaning at least in part due to a continuity between everyday sense-perception and the image, it often ends up marginalizing the power and extent of conventions or symbolic sign systems to shape the culturally specific and at least potentially ideologically inflected meanings of the image. From there it becomes difficult to mount a sustained interest in the social, political and historical conditions of the aesthetic, which one feels, for many cognitivists, is precisely the point. Although happy to draw on cognate fields within the natural sciences, the fields of politics, society and history are typically viewed as beyond the remit of film scholars. In his critique of the conventionalism of Umberto Eco, Gregory Currie argues,

> Umberto Eco gives the example of an image from Fritz Lang's *M*, in which the girl's balloon is caught in overhead wires. This image, he says, 'stands for' the capture of the girl by the murderer, but it does so only by convention; that is, it does so only because in our culture 'wires recall ropes, ropes capture, and so on'. The example isn't helpful to Eco's case, since there really are no conventions associating wire with ropes and ropes with capture. Wires and ropes are alike in their function and appearance, which is nothing to do with convention, and it is by no kind of convention that ropes are useful for capturing things.
>
> Currie (1995: 131–132)

In fact the example is not particularly helpful to either Eco's conventionalism or Currie's cognitive naturalism, at least in the way both account for the meaning of the image. Neither grasp the play in Kant's terms, between objective purposes that form the basis of intelligibility and formal purposes that reflect on and reinterpret those purposes. In the antinomies of bourgeois culture, cognitivism and naturalism line up on one side at the expense of the cultural-political specificity, variability and construction that goes on in aesthetic reinterpretation, while on the other, conventionalism has an awareness of these in spades, but very little sense that a practical relationship to a lawful world of recognizable forms lays the basis for common understandings or at least a baseline from which intelligible disagreement (and conflicts) can proceed.

In the shot from *M* (1931) we recognize the object 'balloon' and the object 'wires', and also recognize that the path or movement of the air filled balloon in space is being impeded or obstructed by the wires. But beyond this recognition *and on the basis of it*, convention (formal purposiveness) is indeed at work in the *reinterpretation* of this object world. Firstly, it is precisely a cinematic convention that objects metonymically associated with children, when they are subsequently seen separated from the child, portend that something ominous has happened on the basis that the child's will has been blocked in some way by some other force. Secondly, it is a convention that we associate things in the air with freedom. The juxtaposition of the balloon's flight being impeded by the power lines stands in metaphorically for the child's entrapment by M. No linkage to ropes (which are hardly the same in either form or function to power lines) by convention or logic is going on in this shot. Indeed the power lines are significant because they form part of the object world of the modern city, out of whose anonymous crowds M emerges, a symptomatic figure for a Germany in economic and political crisis. When the balloon (or rather two balloons stuck together to form the head and body of the human figure) is blown out of shot by the wind, cause-effect relations in the natural and social world form the basis of intelligibility for the metaphoric resemblance between the balloon leaving the frame and the girl leaving this mortal life.

A balloon is a material product designed to be filled with air, and as a result, immersed in other natural forces such as wind and gravity it will float upwards unless tethered to the hand or something else. This set of natural/material cause-effect forces is the basis for the conventional interpretation we have ascribed to the balloon, formerly in the possession of the child, now prevented from its natural upward trajectory by the wires. In other words, without a set of natural/material qualities and forces and forms, the conventional meaning of the image would be impossible. And without the conventional associations that the image generates, it would be impoverished and perhaps too odd and nonsensical (why are we looking at this instead of the murderer killing the child?) But then we would be strange creatures indeed, extremely literalist and without that essential quality required for the aesthetic: the imagination. Recognition and reinterpretation always go hand in hand and there cannot be one without the other. There can be no interpretation without recognition of objective purposes – the interpretation would evaporate since it would have no material basis. And there can be only a very functional and impoverished recognition (that could not generate the aesthetic) without reinterpretation. Thus Kant's play between objective purposes and the aesthetic, between the understanding and the imagination (as materialized in the form of the aesthetic act), lays the basis for a historical materialist philosophy of the aesthetic. All we need to do is understand this play as a model of production and as the materialization of products whose forms are social communicative acts that reflect in a special way on the wider culture that we have made.

Singularity

Kant associates the aesthetic at the point of reception with singularity.

> No one can use reasons, or principles to talk us into a judgment on whether some garment, house, or flower is beautiful. We want to submit the object to our own eyes, just as if our liking of it depended on that sensation.
>
> Kant (1987: 59)

In the beautiful, however, the embodied sensuous experience of the thing registers more than the sensation itself (which is merely the agreeable) but has universality or a socially communicative dimension at work as well. But does this element of singularity vis-à-vis social communicability survive within mass media culture, or is it crushed by a reified social mechanism that Marx called value relations? It is well known, of course, that industrial production techniques and standardized cultural templates such as genres have been extensively developed in order to minimize the risk of capital investment in mass cultural production. Nevertheless, as has been noted by many writers, each cultural product is its own prototype, which is to say that the standard inherent in its purposive form has some elements of uniqueness to it. Even at the height of Fordism which was in some respects embraced by Hollywood during the 1930s and 1940s, and which was, of course, the paradigm of horror for Adorno and Horkheimer in their work on the culture industry, there was a limit to how far standardization and mechanization (precisely the predetermined application of techniques) could go, as Allen Scott suggests:

> There was to be sure, a prevailing attitude among the top echelons of Hollywood executives that fordist principles of manufacturing could eventually be applied to the production of motion pictures.... Studio managers enthusiastically endorsed this quest for efficiency, and they succeeded in streamlining many kinds of work processes. However, they were unable to push the process to its logical end and install mechanized assembly-line methods, for the very good reason that no commercially viable film can be exactly like any other.
>
> (2005: 4)

To that extent there is an irreducible singularity to all cultural products. To speak of singularity in terms of the aesthetic is immediately to court disaster, however. From the perspective of reception/consumption, the notion of singularity is part of the language of the middle-class elite market in aesthetic goods that seeks to differentiate themselves from the mass market and reproduce class divisions (Bourdieu 1996). From the point of view of production, capitalist commodification of the aesthetic, institutionalized in terms of copyright, for example, has founded a powerful ideology around 'originality' and 'uniqueness' as a means of legitimizing private property rights (under threat by digitalization) and collecting rent on intellectual property (Toynbee 2013). Adorno, replying to his critics that he and Horkheimer had dismissed too quickly the difference between cultural artefacts and the production of automobiles, revisited his 'culture industry' thesis and admitted that 'individual forms of production are nevertheless maintained' within cultural production. But he then went on to argue that such artisanal modes of working only serve as the basis for an illusory ideology of individuality that conceals what is 'completely reified' (Adorno 1991b: 87). This is a salutary warning and perhaps we always need Adorno at our shoulder to keep us honest about the dominant tendencies or logic of the system (Ray 2011).

Yet both aesthetic labour and the outcome of aesthetic labour, the product itself, has a singularity to it which we need to retain. Precisely because the rules that govern techniques in aesthetic production require context-specific judgments, the aesthetic may throw up defensive barriers to capital's instrumentalization of work.

The difference between this notion of singularity and the bourgeois notion of singularity, enshrined, for example, in copyright, is that in the latter, singularity is tied to the *individual* author as a discrete entity cut off from the collective and social traditions as well as historical context that are its conditions of possibility. By contrast, I want to suggest a notion of singularity that is not antithetical to the social and collective relations that constitute it. Deleuze writes of singularities that have nothing to do with the individual and individuations that have nothing to do with the personal (1998: 111–112). Singularity is 'a point of inflection or ... discontinuous transformation' as Steven Shaviro puts it when invoking Deleuze (Shaviro 2009: 18) and it is from such moments that something new enters the world. However, this notion of singularity from the left wing of the bourgeois intelligentsia reproduces the same problem of eclipsing the conditions of practices that was discussed in the previous chapter around the work of Rancière. For me singularity refers to that *fine-grained* registering (in the aesthetic work as 'structures of feeling') of any movement, shift or moment in our *collective* relations and *historical* experience.

This irreducible singularity could be posited on many different levels, such as the personnel involved in making a film. Key creative roles, such as the director, the star, the cinematographer, the writer and so forth, will significantly affect the final outcome and counterfactually at least, we can imagine how a given film would have differed had the complex logistics of organizing the crew and cast ended up with such and such a person being replaced by someone else. Indeed there is a popular subgenre of film history on famous films in which leading on-screen roles might have been played by other people who were at some point under consideration. But let me give an example that is governed less by chance and logistics than by history itself. This is the singularity of the *temporal window* within which a film can be made and *be* the film that it is. Consider the film *Casablanca*. It was made in 1942 and it is the classic film that we know because it was made in that year. It could not have been made earlier in the way that it was because the Americans only joined the war right at the end of 1941 after the attack on Pearl Harbour. Nor could it have been made later in the way that it was, because the entire situation within the film is dominated by the broader historical context in which the fate of the Allied powers, especially in Europe, hung in the balance at that time. By 1943, the situation was tilting towards the Allies with the Axis powers suffering a series of retreats and defeats in Asia, North Africa and above all at Stalingrad, which changed the balance of forces. The film that we *know* as *Casablanca* is unlikely to have been produced in this less imperiled context. For a start there is the key mood of encirclement of the heroes combined with the cocky arrogance of the Nazis. By 1943, the balance of forces had changed and such a mood of entrapment and encirclement and such arrogance on the part of the Nazis, would have made less sense to the producers and their contemporary audience. In addition the story line of the film is all about getting Rick, the American, to commit to fighting the fascists. Again that would not have made sense to an American wartime audience *after* 1942. By 1943, that commitment was already well under way. So in fact the temporal window for the production of the film that we are familiar with was 1942 and *no other year*.

Paradoxically, if the production and the emergence of the aesthetic product is finely tuned to a brief temporal window and an invariant set of conditions which make it the product *just as it is*, this contrasts with the temporal window of the product's reception. This is potentially as long and as wide as there are human beings alive to receive the work. The conditions of reception, although determinate are, in contrast to the conditions of production, highly variable. A dialectical tension exists between the relatively invariant conditions that have shaped the product just as it and the highly variable conditions of reception, which re-inscribe the aesthetic product in numerous contexts, multiplying the possibilities for different aesthetic experiences. This re-inscription emerges as a dialectic between preservation of the original artefact and its internalization of its original socio-historical context *and* transformation (large or small) in its new context of reception. The institutions of bourgeois cultural conservation and heritage tend to have a problem with appreciating the 'transformation' side of this process. The historically specific nature of the production and conversely reception of aesthetic products and the differences between them, as well as the specific material conditions outside the text that sustain the receptiveness of the receivers to the film or other aesthetic practice, are not particularly high on the agenda of bourgeois criticism. Typically continuity of meaning and universal themes are the order of the day. For example, in his assessment of *Casablanca* Umberto Eco puts its continued success with audiences down to its eclectic melange of universal archetypes (Eco 1985). But since most popular Hollywood films mobilize characters and situations that could be said to be a hybrid of archetypes with intertextual relations to previous stories, this hardly explains why *this* film continues to exert such a hold on the popular imagination. I would suggest that any explanation must start precisely with its preciously brief temporal window of possibility. The film catches that fleeting historical moment in its 'structures of feeling' when the balance of forces were against the Allies and the power of the Nazi war machine seemed to be on the verge of victory. This gives the 'message' of the film (a message which it was designed to produce as a propaganda film) that now was the time to take sides in the name of freedom despite the difficulties of the current situation, a particularly powerful and poignant expression that is at some level preserved (but also transformed) for audiences many years later in many geographically and socially different contexts of reception. European audiences, for example, especially those that were under Nazi occupation, no doubt read the film somewhat differently from American audiences.

***

In sketching out the genealogical connection between Kant and Marx's ontology of labour, we not only gain a fuller understanding of the seeds of Marx's thought that go back further than Hegel, we also rethink our standard version of Kant. For example, the play between understanding and imagination has been reconceptualized not as a model for an internal cognitive psychological approach but as a model for grounding the aesthetic in production, in labour and in our metabolic exchange with nature. What the understanding provides is the intelligible gathering of the manifold according to cause-effect relations. The relationship between intelligibility and imagination is not to be understood as that of nature and culture. Intelligibility certainly does involve nature, both the nature around us and our own nature, our species being with certain sensuous-cognitive powers that differentiate us (although not absolutely) from dogs or monkeys. But it is also part of our species being that we are social creatures who can engage in a distinct form of non-instinctual labour. This distinct metabolic exchange with nature, which includes our own nature, has a foundation in our socially objective understanding and capacity for creative imagination, even if material production requires that creative imagination to be subordinated to nature and historically determined need. It is this that is captured by Kant's concept of the reproductive imagination in the first *Critique*. The productive imagination, by contrast, has a relatively more autonomous relationship to nature and social need and the politics formed to regulate both. It marks a cognitive shift, what Lukacs called, in his late unfinished work on the ontology of labour, 'an act of arising freedom' (Lukács 1980: 117) from the causalities of already existing nature that 'elapses "automatically"' (Lukács 1980: 33). The productive imagination is the actualization of potentialities that have been discovered within materials and a given set of circumstances. In the aesthetic the arising freedom of the productive imagination is preserved and expanded rather than turned back into the service of material production. The aesthetic preserves both the creativity inherent in all labour and a unique, singular response to a set of conditions (e.g. the temporal window) that make the product the thing just as it is. But while it remains a determinate thing and preserves in some form its original historical relation, this preservation is not fixed and static but relatively mutable according to what subsequent, highly variable contexts of reception might make of the aesthetic product.

Freedom, of course, is closely associated with the capacity to make judgments. Under capitalism, the intricate web of decisions and the weighing of alternatives that go into making something, anything, comes up against a set of social relations that are not open to the same kind of scrutiny and alteration that the labour process is in principle built on. The aesthetic is also drawn into the same imperatives that govern material production under capitalism, despite its special character. The threat of mercenary commerce is already hinted at even in Kant. But however narrow the scope for choices that a given set of circumstances impinge on agents, 'the act of the alternative contains a moment of decision, a choice, and … the "place" and organ for this decision is human consciousness' (Lukács 1980: 39). Where at the point of production, judgments, choices, selections harden into something that resists reflexive justification (through economic pressures and institutional doxa) there the capacities we have for making judgments become sclerotic and we suffer from an inversion typical of capitalism, where the ontological process or capacities that distinguish our species being and that even make capitalism possible are turned upside down in order to make capitalism not only possible, *but safe*. Here a second nature emerges, or what István Mészáros calls our historically specific alienated second order mediations (2006) in which causal relations again elapse automatically and resist reflexive interrogation. Nevertheless, in principle, even under the pressure of institutional doxa these 'conditioned reflexes', as Lukács puts it, can have their bases in the making of choices and deciding between alternatives, open to recall (Lukács 1980: 34). It is the special characteristic of the aesthetic that it opens up values that have acquired the automaticity of the conditioned reflex, to some sort of questioning, some sort of reinterpretation. In the space between cause and effect, reflective judgment is allowed to flourish. Although contemporary capitalism has now appropriated the concept of 'reflexivity' in its cultivation of a subject fit for the 'permanent revolution' that the domination of market relations requires, this is of course a false reflexivity since it can never call into question the terms of that revolution in the first place. In between cause (capital) and desired effect (more capital), there can be only the most limited form of consciousness.

By contrast, the aesthetic is ineluctably drawn to exploring the contradictions from which it emerges in part because it is itself a kind of labour, a kind of work that Kant correctly connected to art in general, and which therefore gives it an ineliminable materialist orientation. The aesthetic, beauty as an appreciation of form in relation to social purpose, grows from within material production itself, what Marx called our appreciation of the 'inherent standard to the object', the prototype idea that underlies numerous empirical examples of what we produce. This specific interest in form determination is what links aesthetic labour to labour in general, especially craft labour of which the aesthetic may be said to be a branch. But with aesthetic production we have the opportunity to reflect on our self-production and ask whether this is the best of all possible worlds. This questioning dimension of the aesthetic is linked to the fact that the condition of possibility for the aesthetic is a historically determined surplus above conditioned needs. As Terry Eagleton argues,

> The gratuitousness of art, its transcendence of sordid utility, contrasts with enforced labour as human desire differs from biological instinct. Art is a form of creative surplus, a radical exceeding of necessity.
>
> Eagleton (1997: 204)

Necessity is of course historically determined and variable. But whatever the social level at which needs deemed necessary are set, the aesthetic always stands as a call back to what is necessary to reach beyond itself and attain, as a general condition, the surplus which makes the aesthetic possible in the first place. This connection to the social surplus gives the aesthetic a powerful utopian thrust despite the class relations in which it is embedded. The condition of possibility for the aesthetic in class-divided societies is precisely that it and its creative agents are the beneficiaries of an unequally divided surplus. That is a problem that consciously or unconsciously haunts the aesthetic. The utopian desire to overcome it may be said to be what underlies the act of communication between those the 'artist' encounters in the course of making their work and the communication between the work and those who receive it. The innumerable faces of the poor staring back at the camera testify to this, from photographs of America in the 1930s Depression all the way through to the black and white semi-fictional character portraits of people the young Che Guevara has met who stare back at the spectator at the end of *The Motorcycle Diaries* (Walter Salles 2004). These blur the 1950s setting for the film with our own contemporary moment, just as the form seems ambiguously blurred between the style of the still image portrait shot and the fact that these are not stills at all, but the moving image.

Production, Brecht says somewhere, is something that bureaucrats everywhere fear, because something might be produced that was not anticipated, that overflows and exceeds what is strictly serviceable to the system. This is the problem with the creative imagination: its unmanageable overflows. Capitalism at every level has to work with agents and their capacities which it absolutely needs in order to turn a profit but which it truly wishes it did not have to depend on. It needs use value but is indifferent to it; it needs labour but cannot abide it; it needs consciousness, creativity, initiative, but knows full well that these things are dangerous and must be managed, restricted and stratified at all costs; it needs reason, or at least its split off and degraded cousin, rationality, but overall it breeds irrationality; it needs exchange, to realize surplus value but does not produce for consumption; it needs social relationships but is fundamentally a mode of production utterly hostile to sociality. The list could be extended, but the point is that the list has as its indispensable foundation the emphasis on production, on labour (and its fate under capital). And yet contemporary theory is extremely wary of a philosophy grounded in an ontology of labour. In part this is because ontology has been so thoroughly attacked by waves of conventionalism (structuralism, semiotics, post-structuralism, post modernism). But the ontology of labour also has something specific to it which has become something akin to a great crime in contemporary theory to evoke: what Arnheim called the goal image and what Lukács called 'teleological positing'. This is more than the becoming conscious of causalities and reacting to them since that would not sufficiently differentiate our species being from the animal. Rather teleological positing refers to a purpose that involves the *conscious transformation* of causalities in 'the overall process and in its details' (Lukács 1980: 5).

Ever since Althusser's critique of teleology, production has been cast as the bourgeois subject affirming itself writ large (an argument also made by Adorno and Horkheimer in *Dialectic of Enlightenment*). Accordingly, Althusser argued that the mature Marx, who had broken with his earlier Theoretical Humanism, conceived history as a process without a subject (Althusser 1982: 185). I quoted the early Marx of the *Economic and Philosophical Manuscripts* on aesthetic beauty having as its ground form determination for functional use values (purposiveness with a purpose). Here is the next paragraph from that quote, and it stands as a typically offending example of the early Marx's so-called Theoretical Humanism. Marx writes,

> Thus it is in the working over of the objective world that man first really affirms himself as species-being. This production is his active species-life. Through it nature appears as his work and his reality. The object of work is therefore the

objectification of the species-life of man; for he duplicates himself not only
intellectually, in his mind, but also actively in reality and thus can look at his
image in a world he has created.

                                                              Marx (1980: 168)

Here we can see all the supposed crimes of the early Marx: the affirmation of
the species being, the object as the product of the subject, the duplication of the
subject in the object and the object as a mirror in which the subject can see an
image of the world they have created. This image, this mirror, becomes of course
the very essence of ideology via Lacan's critique of the Imaginary and Althusser's
critique of the misrecognition intrinsic to this specular relation.

As Liu Kang notes in his discussion of Kantian-influenced Chinese aesthetic
Marxism, 'Insofar as Marx's notion of a humanized nature is eschewed by
Western Marxism for its outmoded productivist tendency, a constructive view
of practice as a utopian vision is unlikely to emerge' (Kang 2000: 139).

But is teleological positing too affirmative, too uncritical, too incompatible
with a negative dialectic so necessary in a world of technological and scientistic
fetishism for a constructive view of practice to emerge? Does the capacity to
posit goals abolish the difference between subject and object, affirming the
homogeneity of the object to the subject as Kant's first *Critique* tended to do?
Or can we think teleology while remaining committed to what the late Lukács
(1980: 124) called the heterogeneity to the subject of the material complexes
teleological positing works with? Is teleology's purposiveness always closed
and predetermined, or does it especially in the aesthetic act retain a certain
openness and mutability (another way of thinking purposiveness without
purpose)? Does teleology commit us to an internally unified subject and abolish
the unconscious, contradiction, the decentred subject and the subject subject to
unintended consequences?

I would say not. For there are numerous and conflicting teleological positings
at work in any situation, and what is more the most consistently powerful ones
are institutionalized, collective and shaped by the contradictions of capitalism.
Despite the origins of teleology in theology (God as the creator) and the
appropriation of Christian teleology by early capitalism (where each individual
becomes like God's representative on earth, a *sovereign*) and which clearly attach
to the concept of teleology all sorts of unwanted uses and abuses, it seems that
without the idea that we can have minimally successful teleological positings of
various kinds, then most of what we take to be human activity, including writing
books that denounce teleology, becomes inexplicable.

But beyond the empirical fact that minimally successful (in the short and immediate term) teleological positings are routinely possible, there is a deeper issue. The critique of teleology takes the dominant form of causality – the efficient causality that takes natural science as its model for society – as the only kind and conception of causality. In 'The Question Concerning Technology' Heidegger reminds us of the ancient Greek model of making and creating which involves the interplay of four modes of causality: the causal properties of matter, the causal form which matter is transformed into (the form inherent to the objective purpose of the product), the socio-cultural purposes and uses in which the product is embedded (what Kant calls final cause) and the causality which the consciousness of the maker brings to this interrelationship of co-responsibility and indebtedness between all the causes (Heidegger 1977: 6–8). This is a model of causality which is antithetical to production as the bourgeois subject writ large.

In the productive imagination, we have a teleological positing that does not simply reproduce the empirical but generates something new, original, a singularity that is saturated with its social conditions but not reducible to them. One way of grasping the productive imagination as a cognitive shift, as reinterpretation of what is recognized, is in terms of the shift from metonymy to metaphor. The former is more immersed in the causalities of nature (Kant's gathering together of the manifold) although the social subject that organizes those causalities into intelligible relations means it is by no means identical with nature. But metaphor constitutes a certain leap above the causalities of nature from which it emerges (Lukács' metaphor of arising freedom) without ever uncoupling itself from nature. Unlike metonymy, metaphor involves the more actively generated comparison of non-contiguous domains rather than the gathering of the causally related and usually spatially proximate manifold:

> every experience and application of causal connections, i.e., every positing of a real causality, while in labour it figures always as the means for a particular end, has objectively the property of being applicable to something else that may be completely heterogeneous.
>
> (Lukács (1980: 18)

Lukács' example is that the development of Chinese astronomy was dependent on the invention of the wheel, which provided a model for thinking about something completely heterogeneous: the universe and its planets (Lukács 1980: 19). This is an example of the power of the metaphorical act of the productive imagination within the realm of material products and natural science. In the aesthetic register, the productive imagination magnifies that creative power (and the possibilities it opens up) many times by dint of its orientation towards intersubjective and non-functional communication about the world we have produced rather than in the service of producing that material world (as in material production or natural science). It is time to now turn to various theories of aesthetic Marxism and explore how specific strategies of metaphor provides the often barely acknowledged problematic around which so many writers in the Marxist tradition have orientated their work on the politics of the aesthetic.

7

On Marxism and Metaphor

Technic, as we saw in the previous chapter, was the productive transformation of matter. In our relationship to nature and the nature we make, we saw that aesthetic labour was grounded in the productive imagination, an act of arising freedom within determinate conditions that discovers and generates potentialities to be found within our relationships to the material world and each other. Now we take those lessons about the relationship between artistic labour and the dialectic, utopianism, negation (of what is) and social interdependence into aesthetic language and explore the question of metaphor, which I characterized in the conclusion of the last chapter as a certain imaginative leap above the causalities of nature (including the nature that we make) from which it emerges.

We have seen that analogy is central to the break that Kant makes from the problems of rationalism and empiricism that structured the first *Critique*. In the third *Critique* Kant sought to avoid the methodological weaknesses that corresponded with rationalism and empiricism, namely deduction and induction. Deduction as we saw subsumes the particular under some a priori abstract concept without any regard to the particularity of the particular. Induction conversely is able to engage with the particular but is unable to posit the foundational causal conditions for the particular. It remains mired in the merely empirical or at most observes regularities. Both deduction and induction remain in turn dichotomously cut off from the supersensible realm of ideas (moral-political reason). In the third *Critique* Kant combines the deductive and the inductive. A judgment of taste is deductive insofar as it is not only intelligible to others but that it makes a claim to the assent of others 'as if it were an objective judgment' (Kant 1987: 145). This 'as if' bears within it the trace of the judgment's social roots. But a judgment of taste is also inductive because it starts with the singular experience of the judging individual. However, Kant then added in a third element, which has often been overlooked, which opened up sense experience to what was formerly excluded from it: namely the supersensible.

That third element was, as we have seen, analogy, which is essentially what the reflective judgment brings to the table in the third *Critique*. As Kant puts it in the first introduction of the third *Critique*,

> To *reflect* (or consider [überlegen]) is to hold given presentations up to, and compare them with, either other presentations or one's cognitive power [itself], in reference to a concept that this [comparison] makes possible.
>
> Kant (1987: 400)

Analogy posits resemblances between 'given presentations' drawn from different domains of experiential life. In still dealing with particulars and in noting their differences it does not rush to subsume them under a priori principles. At the same time, insofar as resemblances between different particulars can be identified, this infers, at least hypothetically or subjectively that there are some higher order laws (if we are dealing with natural science) or ideas (if we are dealing with anything that we are responsible for making) which unites the particulars despite their differences. That this break from the problems of dualism between rationalism and empiricism associated with his philosophical architecture was achieved by Kant's *aesthetic* turn is not, of course, a coincidence. But Kant returned the favour aesthetics paid him by outlining in embryonic fashion the ideas that would later ferment into such Marxist aesthetic concepts as the dialectical image and mimesis, where the play of resemblance and difference is at the core of the politics of representation.

In §59 'On Beauty as the Symbol of Morality', Kant argues that to exhibit a concept via sensible intuition takes two forms. Either it subsumes the intuition under the empirical concept using schemata and formal logic as in the first *Critique*, or it is *symbolic*. In the latter case what needs to be represented cannot be done so directly because it belongs to the realm of the supersensible (the realm of ideas) which neither concepts nor empirical particulars can represent. The supersensible can only be represented indirectly by comparing one form or set of relations with another form or set of relations (Kant 1987: 226). Building on his earlier formulation that the aesthetic works as a kind of 'schematizing without a concept' (Kant 1987: 151) that is without the sort of determinative concept of the first *Critique*, Kant argues that:

> Schemata contain direct, symbols indirect, exhibitions of the concept. Schematic exhibition is demonstrative. Symbolic exhibition uses an analogy (for which we use empirical intuitions as well), in which judgment performs a double function: it applies the concept to the object of a sensible intuition; and then it applies the mere rule by which it reflects on that intuition to an entirely different

object, of which the former object is only the symbol. Thus a monarchy ruled according to its own constitutional laws would be presented as an animate body, but a monarchy ruled by an individual absolute will would be presented as a mere machine (such as a hand mill); but in either case the presentation is only *symbolic*. For though there is no similarity between a despotic state and a hand mill, there certainly is one between the rules by which we reflect on the two and on how they operate [*Kausalität*]. This function [of judgment] has not been analyzed much so far, even though it very much deserves fuller investigation.

Kant (1987: 227)

There is no real similarity between a despotic monarchy and a hand mill but the rules of the schema by which we reflect on each in turn and synthesize the predicates of each into a unified intuition onto which the concept 'hand mill' and 'despotic monarchy' can then be stamped, form the basis of a further aesthetic play with forms. In this second-order operation, certain imaginative symbolic similarities, certain 'subjective' resemblances by which the hand mill comes to stand in for despotic monarchy can be articulated (schematizing without the schema). Anticipating the later work of linguistics and cognitive psychology, Kant notes that in the 'transfer of our reflection on an object of intuition to an entirely different concept' the latter is one to which 'perhaps no intuition can ever directly correspond' (Kant 1987: 228). In other words, the abstraction of the concept of despotic monarchy is an idea that requires metaphorical thought to help develop it and make it concrete, vivid and perceptible, to us. Marxist cultural theory is necessarily interested in this process of making the abstract (i.e. social and historical relations) perceptible so that it can become a proper object of consciousness (interwoven with praxis). At the heart of the many terms which Marxist cultural theory has developed to explore this possibility within aesthetics, such as allegory, mimesis, montage, the dialectical image and even narrative realism, has been a more often than not, tacit debate about different strategic mobilizations of metaphor.

From Kant to cognitive linguistics

The work of Mark Johnson and George Lakoff has been instrumental in putting the question of metaphor at the heart of cognitive linguistics and psychology. Their philosophical debate is largely with the limits of the Anglo-American analytic tradition, ignoring the European or rather French-dominated linguistics associated with post-structuralism. Instead they conceive their intervention as a critique of the positivist prioritization of propositional statements that are deductive, literal and logico-empirical and the consequent marginalization of the body, experience and the imaginative power of figuration (finding resemblances between things, or things and ideas). Johnson and Lakoff's whole project is to bring 'non-propositional' structures, previously regarded as marginal to meaning, to the core of their cognitive linguistics by grounding schemata in the body and showing how metaphor and images underpin and enmesh our propositional language in a dense web of implicit and tacit comparisons and analogies. They ground Kant's image schemata as emerging out of reoccurring bodily movement, orientation, physical manipulation and motor-coordination interaction with the world around us. 'Image schemata *are* those *recurring structures of or/in, our perceptual interactions, bodily experiences and cognitive operations*' (Johnson 1987: 79).

Verticality, for example, is an abstract schematic template grounded in our upright bodies and which can be flexibly applied to everyday phenomena. Metaphor transfers our bodily grounded cognitive structures around verticality to ideas (such as equating height with power or quantitative increases (Johnson 1987: XV). The schemata for containment/boundedness are again based on our experience of our bodies as finite and relatively fixed in its parameters and provides the basis for metaphors around crossing thresholds, or (as with the sublime) breakdown (Johnson and Lakoff 1980: 29). Concepts such as front and back are bodily based and only make sense 'for beings with fronts and backs' (Johnson and Lakoff 1980: 34). Lakoff and Johnson explore the relationship between this bodily substrate and our own meaning making processes and inferential strategies. What they call embodied sense-making patterns provide the physical basis for making inferences to more abstract, non-physical, non-perceptual, more intangible ideas, principles and theories.

Metaphor is 'a process by which we understand and structure one domain of experience in terms of another domain *of a different kind*' (Johnson 1987: 15). For Johnson and Lakoff metaphor is not restricted to the 'poetic imagination' or writing but rather is the fundamental thought process by which we make the world around us meaningful and navigate our way through it. Metaphor suffuses our conceptual systems and 'allows us to conceptualize one domain of experience in terms of another, preserving in the target domain the inferential structure of the source domain' (Johnson and Lakoff 1999: 91). Unlike the deconstructionist model of the metaphoricity of language, Johnson and Lakoff see metaphor as emerging out of a formalization of experiential patterns (Johnson 1987: 38) and this means that language is not seen as entirely arbitrary but is instead constrained by reason that emerges from that experience. Theirs is a philosophy of the flesh rather than the word, still less the sliding signifier. The emphasis on cognition and experience through analogy gives metaphor a more realist ground than the mainstream of the 'linguistic turn'. Our inferential, figurative and creative relationship with the world we find through our bodies makes what Johnson calls 'metaphorical projection', this ability to map meanings across domains, a powerful means by which we 'project structure, make new connections, and remold our experience' (Johnson 1987: 169).

What cognitive science calls basic-level categories, the highest level at which a single mental image can represent a category, provides the basis for one domain to be mapped across to ideas that are not limited to specific instances of basic-level categories (Johnson and Lakoff 1999: 27). Thus chair, table, sofa and so forth are basic-level categories of a higher category – furniture – which no single image can adequately represent. Basic-level concepts constitute the 'level at which we are maximally in touch with the reality of our environment' (Johnson and Lakoff 1999: 555) although crucially one should add, *at the level of empirical experience*. In metaphor, perceptual and empirical experience typically forms the ground for more abstract propositions (Lakoff and Johnson 1980: 159). The grounding of meaning making and metaphorical projection in particular in our bodies and sensory–motor capacities has a materialist kernel to it that strikes a blow against idealist theories of language. They call their position 'embodied realism'.

> At the heart of embodied realism is our physical engagement with an environment in an ongoing series of interactions. There is a level of physical interaction in the world at which we have evolved to function very successfully, and an important part of our conceptual system is attuned to such functioning.
>
> Johnson and Lakoff (1999: 90)

The relationship between the embodied conceptual structures and our inferential metaphorical projections are analyzed by the distinction they make between 'emergent concepts' and metaphorical concepts. The former are concepts that arise 'directly from our bodily sensory-motor-systems and their interaction with the physical world' (Johnson and Lakoff 1980: 56–57), so that up–down, in–out, front–back are concepts that are closely tied to how we are constitutively structured as organisms. They caution that even emergent concepts are suffused with cultural predispositions but suggest that 'we can still make the important distinction between experiences that are "more" physical, such as standing up and those that are "more" cultural, such as participating in a wedding ceremony' (Johnson and Lakoff 1980: 57). Emergent and metaphorical concepts, they suggest, are best thought of as a spectrum rather than a division. Even concepts core to natural science such as causation are both emergent and metaphorical. Causation (a sub-category of one of Kant's pure categories) is emergent in the sense that it arises out of our daily pragmatic negotiation of the world which starts at the stage of infancy when we begin to acquire basic motor control over our bodies. Causation as a concept emerges as a 'experiential gestalt' (Johnson and Lakoff 1980: 70) in which the various component parts or elements that make up any act involving causation, for example, goal orientation, a change in a physical state, mobilization of physical powers and bodies to effect a cause-effect relation, fuse together (Kant's process of synthesis in the understanding) into a meaningful unity. But since being is never separated from consciousness, Johnson and Lakoff are right to stress that this emergent concept is suffused with metaphorical patterns and elaborations as well. In terms that any historical materialist should appreciate, they suggest how *making* is a process which can be viewed metaphorically in a variety of ways. For example, 'The object coming *out of* the substance' stresses the transformation of the substance into something else and determination by the substance *on* the object that emerges from it (Johnson and Lakoff 1980: 73). Conversely the metaphor 'The substance goes into the object' stresses less the process of production and more the finished object as if the object existed prior to the substance that makes it. We may suggest that the first metaphor is more proto-typically dialectical than the second.

All this suggests that conceptual metaphors have profound 'entailments' or consequences for the way we think and act out our thinking. Metaphorical elaborations can go in different directions, pulling our conceptualization of our relationships to the world in directions that are potentially politically charged. At the same time, these entailments are not the arbitrary movements of an autonomous sliding signifier. Metaphor is constrained by our experience of real physical relations.

> A metaphor can serve as a vehicle for understanding a concept only by virtue of
> its experiential basis… which ones are chosen, and which ones are major, may
> vary from culture to culture.
>
>   Johnson and Lakoff (1980: 18–19)

But although they acknowledge that there are cultural, social and historical dimensions to this embodied cognitive relationship to the world, such dimensions are only very weakly and usually rather inadequately registered in their work, as one might expect from philosophers drawn largely to the cognitive sciences. Their methodological framework means that the politics of metaphor is very underdeveloped. They do not engage in the question of the varying cognitive power of certain metaphorical strategies. In their determination to ground metaphor, rightly, in everyday experience and inferential meaning making, there is very little sense in their work that the aesthetic might operationalize our powers of metaphoric projection differentially from ordinary everyday experience. They acknowledge that Kant's concept of reflective judgment is essentially a metaphorical operation that 'enlarges the concept, opening up new significance in a creative generation of new structure and order' (Johnson 1987: 163). However, they miss the cultural politics implicit in the third *Critique*'s methodological break with the reified structure of the first *Critique*. Perception via the basic-level categories has been extended not just by scientific technologies of seeing, such as telescopes, microscopes and spectroscopes, as they note (Johnson and Lakoff 1999: 91) but also by aesthetic technologies and aesthetic ways of seeing such as the film camera. Metaphor is a way in which we can 'project beyond our basic-level experience' and generate abstract reasoning (Johnson and Lakoff 1999: 556) but this takes us into the whole fraught debate about cultural politics, different aesthetic strategies and critical reason. Or at least it should.

That the limitations of cognitive linguistics as a bourgeois social science are built into its methodological assumptions and cannot be overcome merely by extending the framework to the aesthetic is demonstrated when a Marxist theorist tries to work within it. Galvano Della Volpe's materialist poetics is very much in the tradition of Kantian-Marxism discussed in Chapter 1, and he was influential on the thinking of Lucio Colletti. His book *Critique of Taste*, despite its title, attempts to produce a Marxist reading of poetry via a mixture of Saussurean linguistics and Kant's first *Critique* rather than the third. *Critique of Taste* opens with an attack on the romantic prioritization of the image over conceptuality in poetic criticism and insists that the imagery that is distinctive of poetry always has an intellectual, that is conceptual dimension. It is for this reason that Della Volpe is critical of Kant's third *Critique*, because there he argues Kant lapsed into romantic mysticism and confused the semantic immediacy of poetic speech with a kind of intuition shorn of conceptuality (Della Volpe 1978: 178–179). We have seen that it makes much more sense to understand the third *Critique* as not abandoning conceptuality per se but as developing a critique of the reified conceptuality of the first *Critique*. In line with the positivist bent of Kantian-Marxism, Della Volpe is unable to gain sufficient critical distance from the first *Critique* and thus misses, like Johnson and Lakoff, the critique of the first *Critique* that is available to us in the third.

Della Volpe is hostile to the concept of the imagination as the means by which we apprehend poetry and instead argues, invoking the Kant of the first *Critique*, that what is sensuously apprehended as images requires concepts that order, arrange and make images meaningful. The language of the imagination, of intuition, of the senses, is for Della Volpe too compromised by a romantic distrust of conceptuality. This is a form of aesthetic mysticism which must be demolished to establish an 'epistemology of art'. (Della Volpe 1978: 20). Such aesthetic mysticism fails to study the real material ground of poetic images: words. It is words that form that materialist semantic bedrock of meaning. The 'materialism' that Della Volpe has in mind here is the same materialism that Kant develops – albeit through the idealism of the transcendental subject – in the first *Critique*, namely the *logical relations* between physical material reality which words are said to capture. So far this sounds like a radically unproductive basis for a theory of poetry. It also appears to be at variance from the cognitive linguistics of Johnson and Lakoff, whose project is to make the imaginative dimension of meaning making via embodied metaphorical projection central to their work. However, differences aside there are similarities in their philosophical starting positions. Images, Della Volpe reminds us, depend on logical relations, the literal-material without which their meanings would be meaningless. Similarly, as we have seen, for Lakoff and Johnson metaphorical concepts have a relationship with emergent concepts that derive from embodied experience of the literal-material. For Della Volpe the unity and order of percepts is derived from rational structures which gives them some sort of communicable intersubjective meaning.

Yet while grounding poetry in the conceptual-perceptual process that Kant establishes as the basis for objective knowledge, Della Volpe does not deny that poetry and the aesthetic is a mode of discursive practice that *differs* from ordinary everyday semantics on the one hand and scientific and philosophical semantic practices on the other. Della Volpe argues that what distinguishes poetry from these two other discourses is that it is *polysemic*, whereas scientific or philosophical discourse is *univocal* and ordinary everyday speech is what he calls *equivocal*. For Della Volpe the aesthetic has a distinct formal structure that is specific to itself – it fashions its own context and establishes the terms of its autonomy. He thus calls poetic discourse *organic-contextual*. By comparison equivocal discourse of everyday speech does not structure itself into its own formal unity but is *omni-textual*, which is to say that it partakes of the mass of discourses in circulation around it and on which it depends and hence it tends to be discourse that has a certain 'random' determinate quality, made up of bits and pieces of discursive formations with which it is criss-crossed in an unsystematic (but still determinate) way. Its 'random aggregates of meanings, ensembles of equivocations' (Della Volpe 1978: 124) are the product of this formal structure that lacks its own distinct structure. A lot depends on whether we measure the weaknesses of ordinary everyday speech against the standard of natural scientific discourse against which the omni-textual is found wanting, or against critical philosophical discourses. Because for Della Volpe the natural scientific is the unproblematic basis for the philosophical, he does not make this important distinction. But if we perhaps think of Gramsci's critique of everyday consciousness as lacking philosophical self-reflection and systematization, then Della Volpe's critique of the omni-textual equivocations of everyday discourse has some value.

Polysemic poetic discourse, by contrast, fashions its own context out of its own elements but relative to the pragmatically orientated and relatively less autonomous (formally and socially) discourse of everyday life, it achieves 'a *surplus* of meaning' (Della Volpe 1978: 124). Both equivocal and polysemic discourse are distinct from the univocal discourses of science and philosophy which Della Volpe describes as *omni-contextual*. This means that like organic contextual polysemic discourse its linguistic units are not 'randomly textual' but are forged by a linguistic structure that has sufficient form to determine its own meaning as the objective correlation to the literal-material world. However, its meanings are *not* tied to the unique context of the singular utterance, as with the aesthetic structure, but can operate in innumerable contexts and across contexts, hence its omni-contextual character, or what Roy Bhaskar would later call the *transfactuality* of scientific discourse. The univocal discourse of meteorology operates in its essence without cultural specificity in and across many contexts, in relation to both geography (it is a science that can be applied from Arkansas to Zanzibar) and various other scientific discourses such as maths, physics and data modelling. By contrast within any one poetic/aesthetic text, a storm has the meanings it has (intertextuality with other singular aesthetic structures notwithstanding) only within the organic context set up by the text. Its polysemy is related to *that* context and does not depend for its validity on having any real omni-contextual reach. The storm in *King Lear* and the storm in *Frankenstein* (James Whale 1931) are aesthetic constructs whose meanings (e.g. the breakdown of the feudal order or the moral transgression of modern science) is dependent on the contexts in which they are placed. And these contexts are independent aesthetic universes or miniature totalities.

Both polysemic discourse and univocal discourse have their basis in the common-sense semantic humus of equivocal discourse, which is itself grounded in literal-material logical relations which Kant formulated as a priori categories and which Johnson and Lakoff call emergent concepts. Both polysemic and univocal discourse transcend the literal-material relations through their own specific mode of operation or formal structures.

> It follows that the circulation of historical (univocal) thought in poetic thought and vice versa, since it consists in the mediation of the literal-material, or reference back to the latter as their common basic semantic value, in no way prejudices their independence of and distinction from each other. That distinction is semantic.... This independence and distinction is realized in the semantic-formal transcendence of the literal-material peculiar to each, whether polysemic or univocal: from which we have *polysemic typical abstractions*, or poetic genera, and *univocal typical abstractions*, or scientific genera.
>
> Della Volpe (1978: 131)

For Della Volpe, then, 'taste' is defined in anti-bourgeois and anti-individualist terms as the ability to register 'the transition from the random and equivocal sense of the literal-material to the formal rigour of the polysemic' (Della Volpe 1978: 132). The *switching* from the literal-material axis to that of the polysemic discourse of the poetic is primarily the operation of metaphor. Take a couplet from a Burns poem:

The wan moon sets behind the white wave,
And time is setting with me, Oh:

Della Volpe notes that the effect of poetic melancholy is generated by the metaphorical transference of the setting moon to time and the further metaphorical transference of the literal and logical congruence between the waning of the moon and the colour white (implied by the reference to the moon and specified in reference to the wave) and the fading away of the individual human life (mortality). As Della Volpe remarks, to remove the 'logical congruence between the elements of the two propositions' (Della Volpe 1978: 135) the moon as subject and its predicates waning/whiteness/setting and time and the human lifespan, by for example writing of a 'gold' moon, would destroy the basis for meaningful polysemic values: waning, whiteness and setting are the predicates of the subject (the moon); they are its logical, necessary extensions. The *synthesis*, however, that is being made (between the moon and time and between whiteness and death) is metaphorical rather than logical in just the way the third *Critique* suggested. Thus a technical definition of metaphor would be that it involves the imagined correspondence between the predicates that constitute radically different subjects.

Della Volpe's theory of materialist poetics is able to differentiate between everyday, scientific/philosophical and aesthetic discourse while still seeing how they depend upon and interact with one another, as well as how scientific/philosophical and aesthetic discourse depend upon the literal-material semantic foundation. He formulates two modes of abstraction from the literal-material, the univocal and polysemic. However, there is no critique of the univocal or a recognition of its limits when extended to the sphere of the social in a way that robs the subject of their critical autonomy and faculties. This is because Della Volpe elides the distinction between natural science and a critical social science or philosophy. In extending univocal values to social relations, he rules out the possibility of the social as a site of contradiction, because the univocal is the systematization of logical relations that rule out contradiction in nature and therefore are unable to explore the contradictions of the nature that we make. Della Volpe sees univocal and polysemic discourses only as different and complimentary, each offering truths within their own contexts while feeding off each other as sources of inspiration. Polysemic discourse is discourse that creates multiple meanings within a self-sufficient context established by the semantic-formal structure of poetic discourse. There is no sense in Della Volpe's *Critique of Taste* that polysemic discourse might critique and challenge univocal discourse because he has no critique of the unwarranted extension of univocal discourse to social relations. Similarly, the common-sense semantic humus of equivocal discourse cannot just be grounded in the literal-material world, but also the social and historical world which 'common sense' frequently accepts in uncritical terms. Della Volpe has no critique of the first *Critique* but accepts that the configuration between abstraction and perception is unproblematic and can be applied to social life as easily as it can be applied to natural relations. Therefore, Della Volpe does not break with the logical positivism already implicit in Kant's first *Critique* and misses the implied break and critique with that earlier framework in the third *Critique*. If Johnson and Lakoff help us to materialize Kantian concepts such as schema and metaphor and apply them to everyday conceptual structures, Della Volpe tries to specify the differences between the aesthetic and everyday discourse. But both are unable to theorize the aesthetic as a critique of social relations, common-sense understandings and the limits of positivist knowledge.

Kracauer and Benjamin: Metaphor and decomposition

For Siegfried Kracauer, the division between theoretical philosophy in Kant (which is dominated by nature) and practical philosophy (the terrain of moral reason) was a historical contradiction as it was for Lukács. Under capitalism reason has been hijacked by technical rationality (what Kracauer called the *Ratio*) reducing reason to an empty formalism poorly mediated with the real nature of things and as indifferent to the self as the transcendental Kantian subject of the understanding. Kracauer's back-story to the way contemporary technical rationality penetrates everyday life and mass media spectacles is mapped out in his celebrated essay 'The Mass Ornament' (first published in 1927). During the early stages of bourgeois/capitalist production (the Enlightenment) reason gradually penetrates nature and breaks down the 'boundaries which nature has drawn' on changing the basis of social life (Kracauer 1995: 79). Significantly, from the perspective of the prefigurative role that the aesthetic can play, Kracauer believes that the advance of reason is already latent in pre-modern narratives such as fairy tales with their wish-fulfilment for social justice to triumph over poverty, scarcity and cruelty (Kracauer 1995: 80). Yet the promises of the Enlightenment to fulfil the utopian images of fairy tales went unrealized as capitalism more and more captured reason for its own purposes and turned it into technical rationality. Taking the Tiller Girls as his example, Kracauer associated the abstract formal rationality of *Ratio* with 'linearity' as opposed to the unity of genuine reason – thus once more echoing the distinction between the mechanical sequencing of matter in Kant's faculty of the understanding and the moral consciousness of the world to be found in the faculty of reason:

> The more the coherence of the figure is relinquished in favour of mere linearity, the more distant it becomes from the immanent consciousness of those constituting it.
>
> Kracauer (1995: 77)

Linearity, the mechanical and mathematical organization of matter dispels consciousness from the arrangement in favour of the abstract *Ratio*, thus leaving reason marginalized from material reality just as it was for Kant. When Kracauer uses one element of the mass ornament or spectacle (photography) as a metaphor to critique the social conditions which the spectacle as a whole represents, he demonstrates its potential political and educational value:

> The ornament resembles *aerial photographs* of landscapes and cities in that it does not emerge out of the interior of the given conditions but rather appears above them.
>
> Kracauer (1995: 77)

Here mass culture, as the embodiment of the *Ratio*, takes up the same position as the transcendental subject in Kracauer's critical reading of Kant. The subsumption of empirical experience to a rigid and abstract transcendental subject that is external to experience and dominates the individual subject from 'above' is graphically translated into this image of the aerial photograph.

In his 1928 review of Walter Benjamin's recently published books, *The Origin of German Tragic Drama* and *One Way Street*, Kracauer identifies Benjamin's strategies of de-reification. Against the Kantian transcendentalism of the first *Critique* with its subsumption of the particular (sense-impressions) under the universal, Benjamin pursues a 'monadological' approach that is strikingly similar to Kracauer's materialist phenomenology. Benjamin's approach (and by implication Kracauer's) is 'the antithesis of the philosophical system, which wants to secure its grasp of the world by means of universal concepts, and the antithesis of abstract generalization as a whole' (Kracauer 1995: 259). Yet if Benjamin and Kracauer are critical of Kant's transcendental subject from the first *Critique*, they both use the overall *structure* of his problematic in which the division between objective material reality and moral-political reason is addressed via the mediating role of the aesthetic. Even within the *Critique of Pure Reason* Kant acknowledges the limits of the faculty of understanding, with its linear sequencing of sense impressions (synthetic judgments) subsumed under logical relations (a priori synthetic judgments). Besides the painful fissure between understanding and reason, another site where Kant's misgivings emerge is in the distinction between phenomena and noumena, the latter functioning as a rebuke to the limitations of Kant's own logical-empiricist philosophical structure. Similarly, Kracauer and Benjamin turn their critical gaze against the transcendental subject of the understanding and evoke instead a radically reconfigured Kantian subject of political-moral reason – the subject of ideas which are a 'discontinuous multiplicity' to be found in 'the murky medium of history' (Kracauer 1995: 259). The murky medium of history must be recovered from the phenomenal world as it is presented according to the faculty of the understanding whose combination of empirical immediacy and abstract universalization reveals virtually nothing of the essentials of social life, but is instead a model of ideological thought. Clearly, we are a long way here from the cognitive linguistics discussed in the previous section. As Kracauer puts it, 'he who faces the world in its immediacy is presented with a figure that he must smash in order to reach the essentials' (Kracauer 1995: 260). Film, despite its role within the mass ornament, provided a potential aesthetic instrument for this smashing, as Benjamin suggested in 'The Work of Art in the Age of Mechanical Reproduction':

> Our taverns and our metropolitan streets, our offices and furnished rooms, our railroad stations and our factories appeared to have us locked up hopelessly. Then came the film and burst this prison-world asunder by the dynamite of the tenth of a second, so that now, in the midst of its far-flung ruins and debris, we calmly and adventurously go travelling.
>
> Benjamin (1999a: 229)

Here Benjamin stresses the potentialities of the medium as a productive cognitive augmentation of the human eye which in transforming our relations to material nature is at the same time registering new social meanings, relations and possibilities slumbering within that material nature but unrecognized because we are 'locked up hopelessly' within it. Film explodes this reified world, turning it into 'ruins and debris', which is to say montage elements that can be reconfigured dialectically for cognitive travelling.

In the motif of the ruin, which Benjamin linked to the Baroque period and which romanticism subsequently secularized, the remains of previous human existence speak to the transience of the body and civilizations. In the romantic 'impulse ... to valorize the very decay of the classical artifact' (Dillon 2005), the architectural remains of previous civilizations (the Greeks, the Romans, the Egyptians) are enigmatic fragments of a life that has passed and which can now only be assembled tentatively and in fragments in the imagination. In European painting of the period, the detritus of the past speak perhaps of some disaster that overtook previous civilizations and this inevitably evokes premonitions of future decline. As stone buildings and statues are reclaimed by nature, the dialectic between nature and society becomes visible once again, by its very reversal. What Benjamin and Kracauer do is read the earlier fascination with the ruin as a germ of historical consciousness that in both form and theme is reconfigured in the contemporary photographic media.

The concept of the ruin reminds us that for Benjamin the inert qualities which reified material nature acquires under capitalism can be counteracted when that material nature breaks down in some way. A key term through which we can understand Benjamin's conception of the dialectical image is *decomposition*. This is a double death: the death which the commodity brings to the living and the potential to in turn bring the living back to a more authentic life via the death of the commodity. Decomposition as death in this double sense and as a methodology are linked, for example, in Benjamin's theory of the collector. The collector lovingly brings back obsolescent commodities whose original uses and exchange values have died, reconstructing their history as a 'magic encyclopedia' that traces the 'fate of his object' (Benjamin 1999a: 62). The collector has an intense personal relationship with the commodity ambiguously different from the way the commodity interpellates the subject when the commodity is in its full glory as the 'prodigies' of their day (Benjamin 1999b: 203). Death makes the commodity more receptive to the living, its powers over the living weaken with its historical displacement into the collector's arrangement of artefacts. Benjamin quotes Marx in the Convolute on The Collector in *The Arcades Project*: 'I can, in practice, relate myself humanly to an object only if the object relates itself humanly to man' (Benjamin 1999b: 209). The emergent concept here is something like reciprocity and its negation. The physical relationship to things is also a relationship to other people who make those things. Under capitalism, those things, basic-level percepts like a table 'evolves out of its wooden brain grotesque ideas' (Marx 1983: 76) where things dominate people and occlude their reciprocal relationships with one another. The metaphorical elaboration of this relationship in terms of a dialectic around death and decay expands our understanding of the implications and effects of this social arrangement.

In his brilliant 1927 essay 'Photography', Kracauer uses the motif of death to recover a political lesson from the mass ornament. Juxtaposing a contemporary photograph of an unnamed film star, a public property who everyone 'knows' with a photograph from the personal family album, a picture of a dead 'grandmother' taken in 1864, Kracauer creates a dialectical image between past and present, the living and the dead. Unlike the film star who is alive, the body of the grandmother, because it has no indexical relation to a living body, seems to dematerialize leaving only something of a museum piece – a mannequin in a glass, labelled, telling the viewer 'how women dressed back then: chignons, cinched waists, crinolines, and Zouave jackets' (Kracauer 1995: 48). The contemporary image of the film star is, by contrast, bolstered in its apparently self-sufficient meaning by the fact that the film diva herself is still alive – her 'corporeal reality' conceals the hollowness that Kracauer wants us to confront via the 1864 photograph (Kracauer 1995: 54). By contrast, the photograph of the grandmother 'has been emptied of the life whose physical presence overlay its merely spatial configuration' (Kracauer 1995: 54–55). Spatial and temporal configurations reside merely at the level of forms of appearances, as with Kant's faculty of the understanding. But through the juxtaposition of the two photographs, their 'surface coherence' (Kracauer 1995: 52) can be disrupted and the noumenal truth of capitalist commodity society revealed. The essential emptiness of the 'public' figure of the film star enshrouded in the secrets of private property is glimpsed while the private photograph reveals something interesting about our historical condition under commodity production. Death drives a wedge between the image and that which it resembles and in effect opens the image up to a genuine historical consciousness. Death hollows out the unity and linearity of the image. 'The contiguity of these images', says Kracauer, evoking Kant's sequential ordering of sense-percepts under abstractions, 'systematically excludes their contextual framework available to consciousness' (Kracauer 1995: 58). One achieves a similar effect today watching popular American films from the 1980s. Now that the superficial fashions of the times are so noticeably out of date (the perms, the leggings, the gyms, the loft apartments, the actors,) the ideologies of the times (the contextual framework) are laid-bare all the more starkly for a critical pedagogy to investigate.

Marx and Adorno: Nature and society

We have seen that cognitive linguistics argues that metaphor is grounded in the corporeal experience of real physical relations which are then imaginatively projected from this domain of life to other less tangible relations or ideas. What interests historical materialism is the possibility of conceiving this imaginative projection as a movement from the materialism of physical relations to the non-empirical materialism of social and historical relations. At the very least this requires a critical practice, in the register of philosophy, social science or the aesthetic, to engage in combat with the dominant positivist-orientated framing of nature as a support structure for capitalism. We saw that the cognitive linguistics of Johnson and Lakoff and Della Volpe could not make this break with positivism. Kracauer and Benjamin, by contrast, both reconceptualize the body and the body of the commodity in terms of ageing, death and decay into a constellation of polysemic possibilities which attack capitalism's 'eternal present', its historical amnesia and fetishism of the now. Through decomposition, Kracauer and Benjamin prise nature out of their literal-material relations to forge new relations and connections. Capitalism mobilizes an ideological rendition of nature in making it an accomplice to capitalism, a repression of nature's true nature (entropy) because it is a painful reminder of its own potential mortality.

In *Capital*, Marx uses a different strategy, a metaphor drawn from natural science to critique the inadequacy of social science discourses when they do not situate the empirically perceptible within a broader totality of relations. In *Capital* Marx appeals to the natural science which had loomed so large for the first *Critique*: Newtonian physics. We have seen that conceptual metaphors have entailments, and Marx very deliberately selects a particular aspect of Newtonian physics to play with metaphorically. He uses Newton's theory of gravity as a way of trying to exhibit the idea of value as a *social* force operating at distance, rather than drawing on the more applied dimensions of Newtonian physics in which the relations of force and motion depend on mechanical parts interacting with each other. This latter aspect of Newtonian physics resides at the level of the sensible, whereas Marx draws on Newton's theory of gravity to say something about the social supersensible forces acting on us. For Marx natural science could still be a metaphorical model for a critical social science in the sense that both seek to penetrate beneath empirical forms of appearances to their deeper underlying conditions (the social a priori).

Marx constructs an analogy between weight and its determination by gravity and exchange value and its determination by value relations.

> A sugar-loaf being a body, is heavy, and therefore has weight: but we can neither see nor touch this weight.
>
> Marx (1983: 62)

As with weight, value is measurable, but it cannot be touched or seen because it exists as a relation of forces between physically perceptible matter. It is, in Kant's terms, a supersensible force that is invisible and yet it is a constituent part of the body of the commodity in the same way that weight is to the body. Just as weight is determined by a gravitational force generated by the relation between an object (here sugar-loaf) and the mass of the planet, so exchange-value is determined by the relation between a commodity object (sugar-loaf) and the totality of value relations within which it is determined. This totality has a 'mass' and therefore force 'at distance' (i.e. mediated through all parts of the social system) just as gravity is the product of mass and exerts its force in an all-encompassing (but microscopically differential) way at distance (between the object and the centre of the earth). Weight on planet Earth, like value, within capitalist society, is a totalizing power.

How, though, is value measured? Rather like weight in fact. Traditionally, weight was measured by bringing an object, here sugar-loaf, into a *relation* with various pieces of iron. Of course the iron as iron 'is no more the form of manifestation of weight, than is the sugar-loaf' (Marx 1983: 62) but it has become the measure or equivalent of weight for other goods by convention and custom. Similarly, certain objects become by convention forms of money that measure the value of goods. Both the iron and the sugar-loaf have weight and were it not so, 'the one could therefore not serve as the expression of the weight of the other' (Marx 1983: 63). This means that 'when taken in proper proportions, they have the same weight' (Marx 1983: 63). Thus the sugar-loaf stands in the same relation to iron as weight, as the commodity sugar-loaf stands in relation to another commodity that will measure its value that will be equivalent to it. That other commodity will no more, in its essence, be the form of manifestation of value than iron is weight, but will become so by custom and convention. This other commodity (today what we know as money in the form of coinage and notes) measures a commodity like sugar-loaf on the basis that both have value, otherwise notes and coinage could not serve as the expression of the value of sugar-loaf. Just as the weight relation between sugar-loaf and iron is ultimately determined by a totality of forces far greater than *either* of the two objects, so the *value relation* or exchange-value between sugar-loaf and money, two physical objects open to the senses, is also determined by the nexus of value relations that are supersensible and that stretch far beyond the temporal-spatial moment in which they become exchanged. What is most perceptible to the senses is not weight, but the physical structure of the sugar-loaf. But when we are aware of weight, we tend to perceive it as something that belongs to the sugar-loaf and iron discretely, something that inheres in them independent of a relationship of forces. Even when we put them into a relationship to measure their weight, it is not obvious to our 'pre-scientific' everyday perception that this is a relationship not only between the objects in question (Johnson and Lakoff's basic-level categories of perception) but also between the objects and a more all-encompassing gravitational force. The same is true, on all these counts, with value, which appears to be inherent in the commodity or at most a relationship between the commodity and its money equivalent struck up at the moment of exchange. That this exchange is in turn shaped by the supersensible global struggle of competitive accumulation between capital and between capital and labour is far less evident to our senses. Finally, just as the sugar-loaf only has the weight it has on planet Earth, so the commodity sugar-loaf only has value on planet Capitalism.

The intensification of reification after Marx's death meant that natural science as a resource for critical thinking became more and more problematic and instead, for Adorno, in his late work *Aesthetic Theory*, natural beauty (rather than science) is explored for its possibilities to sustain dialectical thinking. For Adorno if art's autonomy is a historical product then that autonomy and indeed art itself may be transitory and annihilated by new historical conditions – such as the 'universal' value relations of late capitalism. The social conditions everywhere imperil the existence, meaning and purpose of art. Even if it manages to sustain itself within capitalism, its autonomy is profoundly ambiguous. For it at once establishes both itself and the empirical world from which it has detached itself as two autonomous realms, 'whole and self-encompassing' (Adorno 2004: 2) and in an ironic historical fate art becomes a secular version of religion, providing a complimentary solace to a world which it never challenges or questions. Art is thus confronted with a huge dilemma – its autonomy (Della Volpe's organic-contextual structure) is immanent to its very contemporary existence, yet this autonomy, so hard won, threatens to render it a pleasant decorative function that can only mask the contradictions and anti-human imperatives of the social order. Yet art, through its form, also critiques the social order: both consolation and critique are dialectically intertwined into the very fibre of the aesthetic.

Following Kant, Adorno prioritizes the question of form. Art is defined by what it is not, that is the empirical world, the semantic-humus of Della Volpe's equivocal discourse or what Gramsci called common sense. 'Art acquires its specificity by separating itself from what it developed out of; its law of movement is its law of form'. (Adorno 2004: 3). Thus inscribed into the aesthetic is a kind of negative dialectic in which it retains an openness to difference which empirical reality and the dominating concept attempts to crush. This immanent openness to difference inheres in the very autonomy of art from empirical reality; inscribed in its every formal gesture is an awareness that it has differentiated itself from the empirical reality to which it indirectly refers. The outlines of the Kantian interplay between understanding and the imagination are evident when Adorno writes:

> Art negates the categorical determinations stamped on the empirical world and yet harbours what is empirically existing in its own substance.
>
> Adorno (2004: 6)

The organizational principle of the artwork is related to the organizational principles of society as a whole but with this crucial difference: the principle is not 'forced on its elements' but rather the elements are organised in such a way that they are able to 'communicate with one another' (Adorno 2004: 9). This normative image is redolent of a non-coercive organization in which each element is both a means for other elements and in the terms of Kant's moral philosophy, *an end in themselves*. An element which is both a means and an end is Kant's attempt to resolve the relationship between the individual and social in ways that neither one displaces the other. The notion of art as a normative model comes direct from Kant's *Critique of Judgment* where it emerges via a metaphorical mediation with a life form or organized being. '*An organized product of nature is one in which everything is a purpose and reciprocally also a means*' (Kant 1987: 255). Should we be in any doubt that Kant is discussing social forms of organization via the metaphor of the 'organized body' then that is dispelled by a footnote in which he refers to the newly created United States of America as a historically novel form of association among people in which one sees at least the utopian *idea* of a better (more democratic) political organization of 'the people'. In this normative image or ideal, the people are both ends in themselves and are means for the organization of the whole.

Here we see the seeds of the concept of mimesis that was to be so important for Benjamin and Adorno. Although mimesis was interpreted in the late nineteenth century as copying and reflecting reality, its true and historical meaning lies more in the realm of achieving a dynamic and productive representation of reality (Suvin 1967). But in stressing an activist conception of aesthetic practice, mimesis also means, especially for Adorno, something like an affinity between things or a sympathetic correspondence that does not annul difference. Thus the representation is not to be confused with the represented while within the representation a play of forms between things instructs the mind in the dynamics of resemblance and difference. As Paul Ricour put it in relation to metaphor, 'To see *the like* is to see the same in spite of, and through, the different' (Ricour 1978: 148). This reconciliation/tension between resemblance and difference within metaphor has a broader philosophical and political import. 'Affinity', remarks Adorno in *Negative Dialectics*, 'is the point of a dialectics of enlightenment' (Adorno 1973: 270). Our productive relationship to nature is based on just such an affinity and the extent to which we find beauty in nature that inspires our own efforts in aesthetic production is in turn a mark of our own difference from nature due to our subjectivity and our reason. In terms of cinema, for example, we may view it as the technological augmentation of social and cultural ways of inhabiting the world. The frame has an affinity with both the nature that we make, such as the geometric shapes of industrial modernity that we find so pleasurably composed (buildings, machinery, etc.) in the 4:3 ratio especially and conversely with the nature that we do not make which the frame can equally accommodate (landscapes, horizons, etc.) especially in the 16:9 aspect ratio. Kracauer found that mutability in the *form* of the medium (here the frame) and its sympathetic reconfiguring of the different forms of nature central to the aesthetics of cinema in his later work *Theory of Film*. He noted how in the early reception of cinema, it was widely appreciated that the new medium had an affinity to the movements of external nature (the wind moving the leaves being a favourite motif) and our own nature such as the urban street which featured the crowd 'whose incalculable movements resemble, somehow, those of waves or leaves' (Kracauer 1997: 27–28). The camera's mimetic affinity or receptiveness to either waves or crowds makes an affinity between waves and crowds possible. The camera, then, is something like its own transcendental aesthetic subject, its techno-cultural basis constructing affinities across nature (Wayne 2013: 79).

Whereas Benjamin and Kracauer were attracted to death and mortality as a way of using nature against capital, Adorno returned to that more evidently Kantian concept of natural beauty, which Hegel had banished from aesthetics. Adorno recognized, of course, that nature and natural beauty has enormous ideological possibilities for commodified aesthetics such as with advertising and the tourist industry which offers neutered consolation and pseudo-escape from alienation. 'Natural beauty is ideology where it serves to disguise mediateness as immediacy', writes Adorno (2004: 89). This escape is ideological for many reasons, not least because nature now functions to bracket off the social relations that inevitably shape our relationship to nature. It is then an extremely fine line between positing natural beauty as outside the *dominant* social order in order to mount a critique of it and positing natural beauty outside the *social order completely*, which in reality disguises the extent to which natural beauty is secretly integrated into the dominant order as commodity. Nevertheless, Adorno balances the ideological possibilities of nature within capitalism, with the argument that however 'dubious and antiquated' its image may be, the 'longing' for gratifications denied by the dominant order which it is a sign of means that it retains 'an element of corrective justice' (Adorno 2004: 84–85).

Natural beauty is a socially determinate response to the beauty that the social dominant (capital) is expunging from the social world. The intermingling between nature and culture in the category of natural beauty provides the model for art to learn not just the dialectic between those categories but also the dialectic between the objective and the subjective, self and other, just as it is for Kant. In natural beauty the subject has the possibility of breaking out of their 'monadological confinement' (Adorno 2004: 90) and engaging with 'authoritatively binding' (Adorno 2004: 92), that is social experiences. In short like Kant, the aesthetic is a site where the individual and the social can recover a liberating dialectic, rather than one eclipsing the other or eliminating the difference between them.

Let us take an example of how a popular cultural text may handle the themes of nature, difference, death, decomposition and beauty, and the relations of these terms to our broader social relationships in George Romero's *Land of the Dead* (2005). Here a brutalized class-divided city, the remnants of civilization, sends out raids seeking food supplies beyond the electrified fences. Arriving in a small town early on in the film, the raiding party finds zombies shuffling around, still dressed in the clothes of their former life and performing, badly, some of the gestures and routines which once made them human. The humans meanwhile have a weapon of *distraction* that allows them to manipulate the zombies, shoot them and grab supplies. This weapon is the spectacle of fireworks that they fire from the militarized vehicle or quasi tank that they travel in. The fireworks – or 'skyflowers' as another significantly simple-minded character calls them – refer to something beautiful which the human characters by and large can no longer appreciate but only use instrumentally. The zombies stare at the skyflowers thus indicating that despite their bestial state, they retain, ironically, a trace of human feeling for what they once were that the humans themselves have in many ways inured themselves to because of their brutal conditions of life. The eyeline match that takes the viewer to the fireworks/skyflowers, which we ourselves cannot help find attractive, is from the look of the zombies, a cut that infers our own wounded social being and positions the spectator in an ambiguous position which the rest of the film's narrative plays upon.

The fireworks/skyflowers, then, can be thought of as a dialectical image of our contemporary media whose spectacles distract and manipulate the masses – but even to formulate the allegory in the words of a cliché often associated with Adorno himself is to do an injustice to the richness of the image just elaborated, with its dialectical switching between the zombies and the humans in terms of those who still retain a *feeling for beauty* within the mechanism of distraction. The humans are in fact less human than the dead in this regard, a feeling underscored by the reversal of our expectations as to which group – the zombies or the humans – pose a threat to the other. For the humans, with their weapon of distraction, tear through the town shooting it up and taking what they want in an image that self-consciously echoes the US projection of military power around the world. The trace of a feeling for their former life by the zombies, their former humanity shown by their interest in beauty, is then amplified and developed by the raid, as the zombies begin to organize and march on the city (led by a black working-class zombie, a former garage mechanic). The narrative trajectory of the zombies towards (class?) consciousness of themselves and their interests means that at the end of the film, when the skyflowers are launched once more the zombies again look up and the trapped humans celebrate a moment of hope, only for the zombies to then turn their heads back to earth and lock their gaze on human flesh. Sensing now the ideological manipulation within the skyflowers, the trace of the feeling of beauty which hinted at their capacity to develop their consciousness, now has to be set aside, in a Fanonian moment of necessary violence, at least momentarily, if their liberation is to be achieved. Since we have seen enough of the city to know its corruption and brutality, the spectator has been given every opportunity to feel dialectically ambivalent about its destruction. As in the best horror films, our initial certainties regarding the firm division between the human and the monstrous, precisely the line drawn by those universal concepts that the aesthetic declares is *not given*, are subverted and a more complex dialectic and reconfiguration of the meaning and relations between terms (here zombies and humans, the dead and the living, the civilized and the bestial) is explored.

But it is not only natural beauty that functions as a means to reflect critically on the domination inscribed into the customs and conventions of a world made by us. This is also true of natural disasters (the prelude to the ruin). In our preparedness for them and especially in our responses to them, natural disasters or rather their aesthetic representation throw into sharp relief our social relationships and the different, especially class-based values, which people have, the dominant imperatives and priorities at work within the social set-up and social stratification in the differential impact which disasters visit upon people. In the aesthetically apprehended disaster, it is as if nature tears away the illusions and façades of business as usual, the semantic humus of common sense is smashed open as the phenomenologically solid life-world is turned upside down. In its very otherness as nature untamed, social critique finds a purchase outside the dominant universe of concepts, a universe that still spins its wheels in the moment of the disaster (political pronouncements, media discourse, relief officials, etc.) but which now stands revealed as falsely 'universal' and merely self-serving. Nature untamed and striking back is not natural beauty but closer to the sublime, and although its power might leave us in awe, the scale of the disaster leaves us with little sense of conventional clichéd 'wonder'. What makes a documentary such as *Trouble the Water* (2007), about the flooding of New Orleans following Hurricane Katrina, so unique, is the non-professional participant-witness perspective of its black working-class authors and protagonists. Shot on consumer camcorders, this encounter with untamed nature by those on the receiving end of it is an example of what the Cuban filmmaker Julio García Espinosa famously dubbed 'imperfect cinema', which is to say a cinema which inscribes the imperfections and tensions of the social environment that is the context of the film into its very formal structure (García Espinosa 1997). In one of its cultural manifestations, the video camera as non-professional tool of diary record is saturated by class resentment, as *Hidden* (Michael Haneke 2005) and the interesting anti-superhero film *Chronicle* (Josh Trank 2012) suggest. *Trouble the Water* is a documentary offshoot of this tension between the mass distribution of the means of audio-visual production and the prevailing social relations that consign the majority to marginalized positions of power and *classification*. The natural disaster as the basis for the aesthetic is a good example of the latter taking as its starting point dissensus rather than consensus (Rancière 2007). The Kantian concept of 'disinterest' is very evidently here, for our main protagonists and authors, the suspension of the everyday social interests that have hitherto acted on them in compulsive ways that have limited their perspectives and their ambitions (e.g. What to do with the means of representation that are now available to them?). Disinterest here means paradoxically expanding their horizons (enlarging their sense of what *interests them* and what is *in* their interests) and instructing themselves and the audience on how their brutal exposure to nature is heavily mediated by social determinations and social interests. An affinity is constructed between the devastation caused by the flood and the devastation caused by social inequality.

***

The purpose of this chapter has been to demonstrate how central metaphor is to the aesthetic. Our starting point was that it was metaphor that enabled Kant to break with the dualities of deductive and inductive thought. It allowed Kant to think sideways into a network of associations by which supersensible moral-political abstractions could be made perceptible through certain linguistic or imagistic arrangement in which the predicates associated with one perceptible thing ('basic-level' categories of the empirical world) are projected into the supersensible domain (the idea). To materialize metaphor at one level, it must be grounded in everyday experience and our corporeal relationships to the physical world. But to materialize it at another level, the level of social and historical relations, we must conceive its projective reordering as having entailments that can open up a reified world to possibilities that the dominant order seeks to close off. In such uses our relationship to the perceptible basic-level concepts of empirical experience is transformed by metaphoric projection into the domain of ideas which are themselves also transformed by being brought into contact with the domain of the sensuous body. It is this dialectic that potentially at least opens up the abstract conceptual infrastructure, which underpins the Kantian understanding to political-cultural critique or the kind of moral-political inflection of empirical concepts which Kant's philosophical architecture had blocked before the third *Critique*. Both Adorno and Della Volpe agree that the aesthetic emerges in its play of forms, its rupture from the empirical that Della Volpe calls *organic-contextual* form and Kant calls the play between the understanding and the imagination. But whereas Della Volpe sees the aesthetic in traditional Kantian terms as merely a different modality of practice within a division of labour, Adorno, Benjamin and Kracauer see it as harbouring critical energies effaced by empirical existence and positivist frameworks alike. The polysemic possibilities of the aesthetic include the possibility of prising images away from their embeddedness within the death grip of commodification and domination and reordering their relationships and thereby our perceptions of relationships. Within the philosophy of culture developed by Adorno et al., a complex of poetic-critical insights are developed by metaphorically rethinking nature: nature as timeless, eternal, fixed, grandiose and given and as the model for human nature and the nature that we make is reconfigured. Nature becomes transient and changeable, as ruin or disaster it punctures the smug complacency of the dominant order; it undoes the opposition between nature and technology and for Adorno, Benjamin and Kracauer is the spark to ignite historical reveries. As the mortal body ages and decays it reveals the repressed underside of the social order, the glittering mask slips to reveal the skull beneath, in the same way that George Romero's living dead are the dialectical alter-egos of the living who do not know they are socially dead. Adorno also defends that most unfashionable of categories, natural beauty, along similar lines. It becomes the subjective repository of what we endanger objectively and this becomes a model for negative critique and utopian possibilities in the artwork.

If the German triumvirate discussed in this chapter conceive of metaphor as an avant-garde form of breaking down abstract unities into fragments that can be reassembled into new configurations, the question of metaphor is just as central to Marxist theorists of the aesthetic who are more interested in storytelling. For Jameson, allegory means something quite different from the decomposition of material nature which is how Benjamin used the term.

For Jameson, allegory is about making supersensible social and historical relations perceptible through the narrative development of character (Jameson 1986: 69). Similarly for Lukács if a concern with storytelling differentiated his aesthetic preferences from the modernist sensibilities of the Germans, he in turn differentiated what he called realism by a formal narrative structure that mobilized metaphor in cognitively more adequate ways than naturalism. In his essay 'Narrate or Describe', Lukács compares the metaphor of the horse race in Zola's *Nana* and Tolstoy's *Anna Karenina*. The horse race in Zola's work, described in painstaking detail, is largely accidental to the fortunes of the main protagonist, Nana. One of her many fleeting lovers happens to be ruined by the race and the surprise winner is a horse named Nana, which only underlines the 'tenuous chance association' between the race and the main character (Lukács 1978a: 110). For Lukács, Zola's aesthetic collapses into the symbol – by which he means essentially a particular subsumed under an abstract concept but with only the faintest of any social mediations joining the particular (here a horse race) and the concept (here Nana's rise in polite society). By contrast, in Tolstoy's book Vronksy's fall and the breaking of his horse's back has huge metaphoric-cognitive power because it is so tightly integrated into the social world portrayed. The fall represents the end of Vronsky's social ambitions and forces Anna's feelings for him out into the open with increasingly devastating consequences for her. By contrast, in Zola

> metaphor is over-inflated in the attempt to encompass reality. An arbitrary detail, a chance similarity, a fortuitous attitude, an accidental meeting – all are supposed to provide direct expression of important social relationships.
>
> Lukács (1978a: 115)

In short, Lukács uses exactly a (disguised) Kantian framework to critique Zola for using the aesthetic equivalent of the determinative judgment, here a metaphor that has collapsed into symbol which short-circuits exploration of the social relationships that tie people and events together in increasingly revealing ways (Lukács 1978a: 131). In Della Volpe's terms, naturalism does not achieve a formal structure that can recognize the equivocal discourse of the every day. Whatever one thinks of Lukács analysis of realism and its differentiation from naturalism, the issue here is that once again what is at stake is the affinity or not of the structure of metaphor and the narrative context in which it takes place, to the deeper causal networks of the social. As with the German modernists, Lukács' aesthetics was based on a critique of the merely empirical and empty abstractions he associated with naturalism. For the German modernists metaphor was a cognitively rewarding aesthetic strategy when attuned to fragmentation and the decomposition of organic matter. For Lukács, by contrast, it was a cognitively rewarding aesthetic strategy when it was thoroughly integrated (rather than disintegrated) into the relationships developed within the story world (a more organicist aesthetic model). Despite their differences, in both instances what is at stake for Marxist aesthetics is metaphor and its role in providing cognitively critical images within a reified social order. For Jameson, the crisis of representation today is posed by a global capitalist system whose workings and complexities are simultaneously remote from the phenomenological experience of the individual subject while they also impinge on the subject in innumerable and invisible ways. We therefore need the critical cognitive metaphorical maps offered by the aesthetic as never before.

8

In the Laboratory of Kant's Aesthetic

I have defined the aesthetic as a critical (moral-political) communicative act in a sensuous-imaginative form. Kant's aesthetic turn was thus a way to circumvent the aporias in his own philosophical architecture, which had separated the critical (moral-political) from the sensuous-imaginative and where there was no real space for communication between empirical-historical subjects, merely the subsumption of the empirical subject under the reified a priori of the transcendental subject. In the first *Critique*, we have a powerful tussle going on between two conflicting drives: on the one hand the conceptual and the perceptual are connected and interdependent for cognition and knowledge to be possible; on the other hand they are separate, with the conceptual/rationalist principles of logic being protected from contamination by the contingency of the empirical. For the empirical could not provide the a priori grounds for experience which an increasing awareness of social structure demanded. When empiricism 'audaciously denies whatever is beyond the sphere of its intuitive cognitions, then empiricism itself commits the mistake of immodesty, which is all the more censurable here because it causes irreparable detriment to reason's practical interest' (Kant 1996: 492/B499). True, empiricism cannot ground a priori moral laws any more than it can cognitive ones, and yet Kant's own system ends up grievously threatening reason's practical interest by providing conditions of a possible experience that occlude the possibility of moral reasoning having any substantive effective presence in a world of reified givens. Hence the split between the conceptual and the empirical which protects the former from the contingency of the latter is redoubled with a split between the faculty of the understanding and the faculty of reason which protects the latter from the former's indifference towards freedom. There is, then, a further division between the faculty of the understanding, which maps the world of appearances and the noumena. From the perspective of the noumena, the understanding, for all its objective establishing of the conditions for a possible experience, is in fact as contingent as the empirical world it seeks to order. For the transcendental subject of the understanding can only map what its own logical-empirical apparatus can assimilate into its own structures. Beyond that lies an unknowable X, the noumena, as a forerunner to the concept of the unconscious. The noumena also functions within Kant's philosophical architecture as the counterpart to freedom within us. It is associated with freedom simply because it lies outside what in appearances is given by laws. This odd assumption (that the noumena is analogous to freedom, and not merely a deeper unknowable modality of determination) still implies something important for critical reason: that the given character of empirical appearances becomes de-reified and at least potentially open for change, when we know the non-empirical causes of what appears as given.

> What in an object of the senses is not itself appearance I call *intelligible* … as *intelligible*, according to its action as that of a thing in itself; and as *sensible*, according to the effects of this causality as those of an appearance in the world of sense. Thus regarding such a subject's power we would frame an empirical as well as an intellectual concept of its causality, these concepts occurring together in one and the same effect. Such a two-fold side from which to think the power of an object of the senses contradicts none of the concepts that we have to frame of appearances and of a possible experience … nothing prevents us from attributing to this transcendental object, besides the property through which it appears, also a *causality* that is not appearance although its *effect* is nonetheless encountered in appearance.
>
> Kant (1996: 539/B566)

The proximity of Kant here to Marx's critical theory and ontology is obvious and even the language is a pre-echo of Marx's own critique of the twofold character of labour, divided between abstract labour (the non-sensible totality of capital's relations of accumulation and competition as they bear down on all labour) and concrete labour (the sensuous act of labour occurring at a given point in time and space upon which the sum total of capital's dynamics of abstraction impinge). Yet the first *Critique* comes up against its own limits insofar as the intelligible intuition where supersensible causalities could be rendered palpable through their sensuous effects appears to Kant a flat paradox. However, the seeds of Kant's ability to progress beyond the antinomies of the first *Critique* have been planted, not least in his thinking around the Transcendental Aesthetic. The condition for experiencing the sensuous world is the capacity to figure things *in* time and *in* space. Thus time and space are the pure forms of sensuous intuition. The ability to combine the manifold of empirical appearances requires the ability to combine time and space. As Kant realized, even pure concepts and analytic judgments imply pure intuition as a presupposition for thought to develop through *combination*. The concept of the triangle is really already a combination of other concepts (line, length, angle) and for that combination to occur it presupposes figuration in space. Once the triangle as concept has been formulated, it can then be deployed for a priori synthetic knowledge production proper by the geometrician who via pure intuition (diagrammatic thinking) can generate solutions concerning various mathematical problems (Kant 1996: 670–673/B744–B747). In short, combination, upon which intelligibility and new knowledge rests, presupposes figuration in space and/or time. What the aesthetic does in the third *Critique* is liberate itself from combination according to the schema of universal concepts. Now the organizing of the manifold according to temporal and spatial relations in the first *Critique* uncouples itself from the aim of synthesis that leaves the object of perception to be stamped by the universal concept. Instead this operation is now overlaid with an aesthetic operation that opens up the possibility of other types of combination, for purposes other than the confirmation of so-called universal knowledge. Crucially, this means that the productive imagination, which could only be exercised in relation to pure, non-empirical forms, can now be used in conjunction with sensuous forms drawn from the empirical world of experience.

In the third *Critique*, Kant suggests that natural science adopts the model of the aesthetic in presupposing that nature has a coherent lawfulness that can be discovered, by treating it *as if* it were a work of art, *as if* it were the product of an intention and *as if* all the parts of nature, such as the organs of an organized being, like the eye, function purposively for that being. This is a merely formal purposiveness, a subjective hypothetical trick to make scientific observation and investigation a rational activity. Pre-Darwin, pre-genetic science, Kant had no natural scientific explanation to account for why all the separate cause-effect relations that structure a bird, for example, could come together for the purposes of flight (Kant 1987: 236). Philosophy had to fill the gap until natural science could catch up. The concept of purposiveness allowed science to explore nature as if it were a work of art, that is as if it were designed. Kant insists this is merely a regulative principle, as we have no basis to assume that nature has been designed by a rational being. It is a subjective principle of reflective judgment that allows us to investigate nature as lawful in some way that separate cause-effect mechanisms could not without some unifying principle. This analogy between nature and culture becomes a kind of dialectical switching point that can go in the direction of a philosophy of natural science or a philosophy of the aesthetic. For if nature can be compared with art to subject nature to investigation, art can be compared to an aesthetically apprehended nature in order to investigate art (in the broadest sense of the term, all human practice). Furthermore by introducing subjectivity into nature, Kant is able to think about our relationship to nature in a way that was not possible in the first *Critique*. Aesthetically apprehended nature becomes an image from which antinomies can be overcome. '[A]n idea is an absolute unity of presentation' writes Kant rehearsing the familiar split between deduction and induction, 'whereas matter is a plurality of things that cannot itself supply a determinate unity for its combination' (Kant 1987: 256). Yet in aesthetically apprehended nature, such as the organized being, matter and idea (the principle that organizes the form of the being for particular purposes) seem to fuse and this in turn becomes a metaphor for thinking about our own practices. If one subsequent development of this line of thinking leads to sociobiology, in another it leads to the concept of praxis. Whereas before judgment gives up freedom when assisting the faculty of the understanding and it gives up the sensuous empirical when assisting the faculty of reason, now (reflective) judgment operates in the aesthetic as a point of mediation between this antinomy of bourgeois thought.

Considering nature as if it were art works as a presupposition and analytical strategy for natural science, and it also opens up the prospect that the subject may have a relationship to nature other than merely obeying its natural lawfulness. This is the play of forms by the imagination in its relationship with the understanding. Form determination in the mode of the aesthetic combines an inductive engagement with particulars with the language of analogy, giving it the power to make connections and establish non-contiguous relations that avoid ossifying into reified structures. Analogical meaning is inherently provisional and specific because it depends on what is being compared with what, or what aspect of a thing is being compared within another aspect of a thing. This provisionality and specificity gives a renewed emphasis in Kant's philosophy to the *experience* of aesthetic pleasure:

> If we judge objects merely in terms of concepts, then we lose all presentation of beauty. This is why there can be no rule by which someone could be compelled to acknowledge that something is beautiful. No-one can use reasons or principles to talk us into a judgment on whether some garment, house, or flower is beautiful.

We want to submit the object to our own eyes, just as if our liking of it depended
on that sensation.

Kant (1987: 59)

Yet while the sensuous apprehension of beauty is indispensable, it is only *as if*
our liking depends on the sensuous experience itself. For the sensuous in beauty,
unlike the merely agreeable, has a *form*, an arrangement, a set of relations, a *play*
of elements that we relate to as a relay to our non-sensuous relationships with
others. In the opening of Howard Hawks' *The Big Sleep* (1946) we see Marlow
press the bell at the entrance to the Sternwood mansion. A cross-dissolve takes
us to the interior and we see the butler striding towards the door, open it and
allow Marlow (Bogart) entry. Why that cross-dissolve, why that particular play
of forms? Because a straightforward cut would have eliminated the suggestion
of a small interval of time between the bell being rung and the butler arriving
and that would have eliminated the sense that the Sternwood home is large, large
enough for a passage of time to have elapsed between the bell being rung and the
door being opened. In that humble cross-dissolve not only is a spatial-temporal
relation evoked but a whole set of social relations regarding size, wealth and
power are at work. So our liking does not just depend on the sensuous, nor
even on the play of forms (here the cross-dissolve between two shots) but on
the social relations that we communicate in discussing aesthetic pleasure or
the social relations that are communicated to us in the reception of aesthetic
forms. It is for this reason that an aesthetic judgment is at once based on the
subject's 'own feeling of pleasure in an object, independently of the object's
concept' and at the same time we can judge 'this pleasure as one attaching to
the presentation of that same object *in all other subjects* ... a priori, i.e., without
being allowed to wait for other people's assent' (Kant 1987: 153). In other words,
aesthetic pleasure is at once intensely peculiar to the individual's encounter with
an object perceived aesthetically and yet this is no solipsistic experience but is
a priori assumed to be a pleasure that is shared (whatever nuances there will be
in the 'reading' or meaning of the play of forms) by *all other subjects*. This is the
'deductive' or transcendental component of Kant's aesthetic judgment, but it is
now, in the third *Critique*, edging towards a more socially conceived sense of
intersubjectivity.

What has a claim to universality are not individual judgments of taste
themselves but the capacity to make judgments of this kind, the assumption that
there is necessarily an a priori *social bond* that makes the aesthetic intelligible.

Kant's position is that a judgment of taste is singular, that is it is the conjoining point between something that has to be experienced by the person in order to make a judgment, but without subsuming it under the universal which is here not given. As Kant puts it,

> ... all judgments of taste are singular judgments, because they do not connect their predicate, the liking, with a concept but connect it with a singular empirical presentation that is given.
>
> Kant (1987: 154)

Singularity uncouples experience from its hitherto dominant conceptual framework and thus offers the chance to revivify some experiential engagement with the sensuous object of taste. Yet the singular experience and judgment is not just empirical, nor private nor merely an individual experience. Uncoupled from the universal concept it has the chance to be *more genuinely* social than the reified social world mapped out by pseudo-universal concepts. On the social nature of the 'singular intuitive presentation referred to the feeling of pleasure' Kant states that:

> there can be no doubt that in a judgment of taste the presentation of the object (and at the same time of the subject as well) is referred more broadly [i.e., beyond ourselves] and this broader reference is our basis for extending such judgments [and treating them] as necessary for everyone.
>
> Kant (1987: 212)

The basis of this 'extension' or social bond must be some concept, Kant argues, 'unless we assumed that a judgment of taste relies on some concept or other, we could not save its claim to universality' (Kant 1987: 212). But it is not a concept as the understanding usually deploys in relation to empirical phenomena that has been gathered together by the reproductive imagination. For taste is not open to proofs in the manner of empirically verifiable phenomena from the natural sciences. Taste is part of Kant's attempt to go beyond the empirical, but it is also part of his attempt to go beyond – again by a proto-dialectical mediation – the merely rational. Because if taste implies a social, a priori bond, it also insists on the importance of experience, which rationalism tends to downplay or even dismiss. The experience of the object on which judgment is to be made is essential and cannot be substituted by abstract principles or theory. Taste is thus a mediation between the antinomies of bourgeois thought: ordinary experience which occludes the wider structuring conditions of that experience and abstract principles (of a cognitive or moral kind) which occlude actual concrete experience.

The aesthetic *encounter* is, then, the germ of a dialectical mediation between the experiential and the structural (the supersensible). To find pleasure or displeasure in the encounter is the basis for the beginning of a judgment and an implicit or actual discussion with others. The aesthetic experience reopens the potential malleability of the social order. Receivers share with producers the imaginative remodelling of the known world. The latent creativity in the act of production or reception of the aesthetic experience allows reflection on ordinary experience where creativity has been expunged due to the exercise of class power and the congealing of those power relations into reified things from which all trace of the underlying social relations has been banished.

The beautiful is that which it is pleasurable to communicate because it is the affective trace of objective social relationships. This reading of the beautiful as profoundly social was of course subsequently disavowed by much of the bourgeois scholarship, including the left intelligentsia, which regressed on Kant's attempts to socialize the aesthetic, and instead drives the aesthetic experience back into various models of individualism. In order to do this it was crucial that a consensus on Kant's work was allowed to settle. The consensus was that the Kantian aesthetic was essentially non-conceptual. Both the bourgeois scholars and the Marxist critics have very largely accepted this reading of Kant's aesthetic. No distinction was made between the concepts of the understanding that were mapped out in the first *Critique* and the aesthetically inflected concepts that Kant was struggling to articulate with the notion of aesthetic ideas 'which are essentially distinct from rational ideas of determinate purposes' (Kant 1987: 225).

The aesthetic suspends the universal and this is its most important *critical* feature: it proceeds in an exploratory manner on the basis that the universal is *not given*. Instead of subsuming the particular under the universal as given, we have an arrangement or presentation of the senses that in its form exceeds in its communicative possibilities what the 'universal' concepts of the dominant order can acknowledge and classify. The 'indeterminancy' of the aesthetic is not to be thought of as some refusal to engage or commit, nor is it a forerunner to the more modern notion of open-ended polysemy, a concept highly congruent with a liberal politics. Instead, it is more precisely an engagement with that which the historically determinate universe of concepts represses. It is closer (as the aesthetic counterpart to the noumena) to the concept of the unconscious rather than indeterminate openness. Beauty is thus fundamentally an encounter with otherness (Siebers 1998). In the aesthetic 'something … prompts the imagination to spread over a multitude of kindred presentations that arouse more thought than can be expressed in a concept determined by words' (Kant 1987: 183). These 'kindred presentations' serve as a substitute 'for a logical exhibition' for the very good reason that what counts as socially defined 'logic' is based on domination and identity. Thus the 'proper function' of the aesthetic is essentially critical:

> to quicken [*beleben*] the mind by opening up for it a view into an immense realm of kindred presentations ... that give the imagination a momentum which makes it think more in response to these objects [*dabei*], though in an undeveloped way, than can be comprehended within one concept and hence in one determinate linguistic expression.
>
> Kant (1987: 183–184)

In his essay 'Aesthetic Separation, Aesthetic Community', Jacques Rancière argues that the aesthetic effect begins by working on the sensuous arrangement of common sense and producing a dissensus from that community. This takes the form of a dis-identification on the part of the individual, which separates them from the community of sense of which they are apart. The aesthetic effect thus produces a dissensus with the existing arrangement and organization of the senses. Rancière's mid-nineteenth-century worker-artisan who has an aesthetic interlude at work 'overthrows the "right" relationship between what a body "can" do and what it cannot' (Rancière 2011: 71). The aesthetic separation from life holds out the prospect of a new configuration of sense and a new community of the senses which must be experienced by the individual – so that they are separated from the community as it is in order to be put in touch with an aesthetic community that is fragile and spectral in the sense of Marx's famous ghost haunting Europe at the beginning of *The Communist Manifesto*, that is pointing forward to a future that has yet to come: 'The artwork is the people to come and it is a monument to its expectation, a monument to its absence' (Rancière 2011: 59). There is much in Rancière's presentation to agree with. But we must part company with Rancière on the all-important question of the social nature of the aesthetic, for he is too quick to characterize the aesthetic effect as a dis-identification with the community of which the individual is necessarily apart. Such a dis-identification means that the new community that is prefigured in the aesthetic has no grounding in the spectator's historical moment or collective being. Utopian thought is at its strongest when it finds some basis in the now which provides a point of leverage into some transfigured future. But with Rancière all leverage is lost with dis-identification and the valorization instead of a solitary but free subjectivity (2011: 54). In the case of Rancière's favourite example, it leads to the dis-identification of the worker-artisan from their class identity and this is part and parcel of Rancière's overall hostility to sociological classifications as reproducing the very power relations they ostensibly set out to analyse. Behind this reading of the aesthetic effect lies a conventional understanding of Kant's notion of the disinterested pleasure that characterizes a pure aesthetic judgment of taste – one which sets aside all worldly and social interest and valorizes a decontextualized subjectivity.

We can rearrange the process of aesthetic efficacy and the terminological pieces Rancière uses (consensus, dissenus, dis-identification, community) with a different reading of Kant that puts the question of class interests back on the agenda. The movement which produces the aesthetic effect does not involve the separation of the individual from their existing community but through a rearrangement of sense there is identification with group affiliation(s) that emerges in the inscription of difference, of otherness via aesthetic form. The aesthetic experience brings the subject into a new kind of awareness of difference which the 'universal' (really pseudo-universal) concept disavowed. The aesthetic effect, if we are to associate it with a critical intervention into sense organization, emerges if there is a dis-identification not with group or community membership per se but with the implications of the terms of the difference set up between groups (in-groups and out-groups, dominant and subordinate, etc.) which in turn implies some utopian invitation to imagine the world *as if* its specific arrangements were not so or ought not to be so. A real universal to come is glimpsed in the parallax between perspectives that are simultaneously social and individual. Bourdieu meanwhile is right that class identity is certainly inscribed into cultural and aesthetic form and its reception, but the aesthetic is that play of forms that rounds on and suspends the universal given of such relations, calling them into question by inscribing an awareness of unequal difference into themselves.

Of course it is possible to read or appropriate Kant's aesthetic for a hegemonic project in the field of taste. I would not argue that there is no basis for a bourgeois Kant in Kant. What I am arguing is that Kant's philosophy of the aesthetic is sufficiently contradictory, sufficiently polyphonic, sufficiently open to other historical horizons, that this is not the only or the most productive way of reading Kant today. Thus the Kantian disinterest can be read as the cognitive-affective *enlargement* it offers on our social understanding precisely by inscribing difference reflectively into its form. By coming into contact with others (classed, raced, gendered, etc.), the relational nature of individual and group interests is explored. The social is at once an a priori bond that makes the aesthetic intelligible and it stands revealed as divided, as wounded. The aesthetic relativizes the interests in which we are ordinarily sunk and opens up the prospect of a real universal, one that can be glimpsed in a utopian sensuous-imaginative form. Disinterest is a point of mediation between the pathological conditioning by stimuli (the mere sensuousness of the agreeable) and the moral command of reason (the good). The aesthetic is thus a space that is institutionally constructed between economics (need) and politics (the existing moral order). Disinterest is not the transcendence of egotistical interests or group interests but a reflection on interests and the structures that shape them.

This definition of disinterest reconciles the Kantian aesthetic with consciously pursued political aesthetics. Since interests are associated with the pursuit of cause-effect relations in Kant, disinterest in a conventional interpretation can be associated with the rejection of consciously pursued aesthetic strategies for political effect. For Rancière, recycling a quite conventional Kantianism, this bars explicitly political intentions being successful in the aesthetic since these presuppose a determinate link between cause and effect. For Rancière there is an exhaustion of left aesthetic politics which he claims reproduces the calculated manipulation of consumer aesthetics in its plotting of presupposed outcomes (political understanding of this or that situation) which are anyway highly questionable: 'There is no straightforward road from the fact of looking at a spectacle to the fact of understanding the state of the world; no direct road from intellectual awareness to political action' (2011: 75). Few would have been foolish enough to claim that there was. Of course 'good' politics or politicized aesthetic strategies does not necessarily make for good aesthetic experiences but neither should left politics be barred from producing aesthetic effects. This is not the Kant we want to resurrect. Rancière suggests that left aesthetic politics is preaching to the converted, telling people what they already know (2011: 76). But who is this 'we' that already knows? In a world of deepening inequalities in access to a range of information and perspectives, in a world with increasingly stratified opportunities for productive educational experiences, in a world where many truths are systematically denied expression in our media and established institutions, in a world where the expansion of the market sees the full-scale retreat of reason, where the social base of capital is retrenching to a tiny oligarchical elite, and where confronted with the reified universe of capital, disavowal and denial are rampant, where knowledge and knowing is in crisis precisely because it can only have efficacy when compatible with the imperatives of the business world and where known truths are driven back into the quiet of the individual's inner dialogue, in such a world Rancière's 'we know' seems remarkably complacent and indeed elitist. Re-presenting what we already 'know' but are encouraged to forget or discount and above all making these repressed elements of our lives experientially vivid remains an important part of what is critical about the aesthetic. We know from numerous sociological studies that dominant ideological discourses reproduced by various institutions, such as the media, are more prone to fracture and be questioned when an appeal to direct experience that problematizes or offers alternative understandings can be made. This was a point that Gramsci also made with his comments on the contradictory consciousness torn between that which is grounded in experience and that which is inherited from dominant social groups (Gramsci 1967: 66–67). In the aesthetic (when it is working aesthetically), experiences that we are remote from because of social stratification, cultural difference, temporal distanciation or structural repression become accessible to us in a form in which they are detached from the dominant universal concepts. The aesthetic opens up the pores of our receptivity which the every day has atrophied or clogged up. In this we can agree with bourgeois criticism: the aesthetic marks a breach with the every day.

> Because of the greater complexity of the object in synoptic apprehension the faculty of awareness (the mind in direct awareness) is exercised to a fuller capacity and held in this mode, than is necessary or possible to the needs of daily life. Awareness is expanded. The attendant pleasure is the sort of pleasure proper to the exercise of a skilled aptitude which in ordinary life is apt to be submerged beneath the more urgent claims of practical and theoretical interests.
>
> Osborne (1979: 141)

What bourgeois criticism seems remarkably uncurious about is why ordinary life is as it is that makes the aesthetic so precious that the best thing that can be done with it is to cut it off from life and save it from contamination by the every day. We have seen that in the beautiful the play of forms are not locked into an isolated monad as bourgeois criticism would have it, or a fragmented a-social subject as the left wing of the bourgeois intelligentsia would have it. Rather the beautiful tells us something about our relationships with others. What is compressed and compacted in those forms is our social relationships, and this is the 'content' of the aesthetic.

The aesthetic turns out to be a model and stimulant for the faculty of reason, from which the aesthetic has borrowed key principles, such as purposive unity or totality, freedom and ought-utopian impulses. The play of the imagination with the understanding in the beautiful presupposes that the imagination has already been in play with reason. The disavowal of some special conceptuality at play in the Kantian aesthetic simultaneously blinds criticism to this always already existing relationship between the understanding and the imagination on the one hand and reason in the case of the beautiful. Kant, of course, tries to initially differentiate the beautiful and the sublime on the basis that the latter involves 'a reasoning contemplation governed by ideas' about our 'supersensible vocation' as moral beings while the beautiful involves a 'pleasure of mere reflection' (Kant 1987: 158). But here Kant's specific statements are in contradiction with the overall architecture of his philosophy and the pressure of that architecture (that reason must be involved in the playful relationship between imagination and the understanding) eventually breaks through decisively in his explicit statements. In §59, 'On Beauty as the Symbol of Morality', Kant makes the connections between beauty and reason clear. The beautiful, like the morally good, has an inevitable ought character to it and this is the basis that 'our liking for it include a claim to everyone else's assent' (Kant 1987: 228). This claim is not the universal assent which the concepts of the understanding can make in everyday cognition, but something closer to the free lawfulness of reason.

> Judgment does not find itself subjected to a heteronomy from empirical laws, as it does elsewhere in empirical judging – concerning objects of such a pure liking it legislates to itself, just as reason does regarding the power of desire.
>
> Kant (1987: 229)

The analogous relations between beauty and moral reason explains, Kant suggests (1987: 230), why sensuous images are often judged by terms that imply moral judgments (such as 'majestic', 'magnificent', 'cheerful', or 'humble').

The turn to the sublime, in which Kant explicitly considers the role of reason in the aesthetic, but which he tries to separate off from beauty, really functions to prepare the ground for this later emphatic acknowledgement that the beautiful is political. That is to say its double function is to perform the usual operations of schematizing within the understanding and to then appropriate that process (schematizing without the schema) to produce a 'symbol of morality'. Kant's turn to the sublime not only brings out what is latent in terms of reason's necessary relationship with the beautiful, it also brings out something only very latent in thinking the beautiful as a socially communicative act: namely that if the aesthetic (of the beautiful) is a meditation on our social being, then it must, like our social being, be open to change. The beautiful advances Kant's philosophical search for a more genuinely social form by suspending the universal as given. But with the sublime, it is aesthetic form itself as a subjective purposive form that is suspended as it opens itself up to register the pressures not just of the social, but of the social undergoing large-scale change and perhaps also, large-scale crisis. Both the beautiful and the sublime involve a reorganization of everyday seeing, but the sublime involves a challenge to aesthetic seeing as well, hence it's self-reflexive dimension. In the sublime, the principles that the imagination has borrowed from reason for the beautiful now enter into crisis as a radical new sense of temporality enters the aesthetic. A linear and evolutionary sense of time is cancelled in the sublime and this is conveyed by the breakdown in the sensuous apprehension of the form of the object. In both the beautiful and the sublime, nature is subjectively purposive for our powers of judgment, but in the sublime this purposiveness is paradoxically contra-purposive to our power to exhibit ideas according to the standard of sense. Hence the association of the sublime with negation, ambivalence and contradiction. The crisis of form, the opening up of the aesthetic to social change, is thus also a calling of reason into question, since it was in the palpable forms of beauty that reason finds some materialization in the first place. The architecture of Kant's thought is therefore in contradiction with his explicit statements that give reason a serene a-historical quality and Enlightenment hubris. Both the beautiful and the sublime are concerned with totality (and both depend on reason to put this principle in play with sensuous forms) but with the sublime, the crisis of the totality and the limits of sensuous apprehension vis-à-vis the scale of the crisis are now registered in aesthetic form itself. Thus beauty and the sublime are really different dimensions of the same process whereby aesthetic form perpetually crystallizes and then breaks down in its ongoing and changing relationship to a changing social reality.

The power and scale of nature in the sublime is for Kant a metaphor for our own powers and this lays the basis for the technological sublime, and for thinking of the sublime from the start as a relationship with our productive powers and social relations. Less than sixty years after the third *Critique*, Marx would be writing in *The Communist Manifesto* of how:

> The bourgeoisie, during its rule of scarce one hundred years, has created more massive and more colossal productive forces than have all preceding generations together.
>
> Marx and Engels (1985: 85)

The constant revolutionizing of the instruments of production and the pressure that puts on the relations of production to undergo perpetual transformation is an image already anticipated in Kant's sublime. But although the relations of production are transformed they are also transformed *within* the capitalist mode of production, so that the productive forces continue to store up immense powers and potentialities that both cut against capital (as in the case of overproduction or widening access to cultural goods) and are simultaneously used and absorbed by capital against human needs in the service of exchange value. The fundamental ambivalence of the sublime and its relationship to commodity aesthetics is thus already evident in Kant's concept of subreption, a forerunner to Marx's concept of commodity fetishism. Here the sublime object secretly seizes and appropriates for itself the powers that belong to the collective social body, just as private ownership of the means of production does as a whole. In exchange for that secret seizure, the isolated bourgeois monadic subject is promised some fantasy quotient of power by the society of the spectacle, that is no more than a mess of pottage. Yet at the same time the sublime is suffused with utopian images that tap into the potentialities of the productive forces and the transfigured social relations that those potentialities hint at. The best of mass culture must often – from within the spectacle itself – take the risk of engaging with commodity fetishism in order to critique it.

Of course in an age when the term 'aesthetic' can be routinely appropriated for the spectacle of consumer capitalism, such as cosmetic surgery clinics, there is a temptation to reject the term 'aesthetic' altogether as already too badly compromised. For some defenders of the radical avant-garde and its 'negations', there is a preference for a narrower term, modern *art* as a means of throwing up a protective barrier against the penetration of commodity aesthetics into every aspect of the sensorium. For John Roberts, the 'negations' of the avant-garde, its 'asociality' (an unfortunate term) or autonomy is of a double and dialectical kind. Art must establish a disjuncture with its immediate conditions of existence (pressures ranging from commodification to censorship to bureaucratic and elitist administration) and this requires that it open itself up to broader socio-political dynamics beyond the world of art (Roberts 2010: 291). At the same time, art, Roberts argues, cannot dissolve itself into everyday life. Although opening up the receptivity of art to the everyday remains an important formal, thematic and political ambition for the radical avant-garde ever since Picasso integrated bits of newspaper into his paintings, art's relationship to the every day must remain as a mediated and critical relationship and as the complimentary other side of art's confrontation with the materials and traditions that constitute the world of art (Roberts 2010: 292). When art dissolves itself completely into the every day in the name of an emancipatory politics, as with, for example, Augusto Boal's phenomenally successful forum theatre, whatever merits that practice has in terms of identifying functional solutions to problems in everyday life, in increasing the confidence of marginalized people or as a kind of art therapy, it cannot be assumed that what is valuable in the aesthetic necessarily survives such a radical dissolution of boundaries. For Roberts, as for Rancière, and indeed Adorno, art emerges when practices are non-identical with their conditions – both their immediate conditions (which involves opening the aesthetic up to the broader socio-political antagonisms *beyond* the aesthetic) and also non-identical in turn with that broader socio-political terrain as art must work through its own historically developed languages and practices, its own materials that are necessarily disjunctive with the every day. These are the 'two vanishing points' of art and the aesthetic more generally: 'art becoming mere life or art becoming mere art' within which the politics of the aesthetic plays itself out (Rancière 2002: 150). But without dissolving the real institutional differences between them, this resistance to the every day through the assertion of its own distinct forms on the one hand while also resisting collapse into mere distraction and entertainment on the other is also the mark of the aesthetic of mass culture as well as modern art.

What is at stake here is the whole question of *production*. Kant's work stages the movement of the concept of production from mind to material nature. The productive imagination of the first *Critique* could only be conceived as operating at the level of pure intuition, but by the third *Critique*, thanks to the aesthetic, the productive imagination could now be reconciled with sensuous beauty and even artistic labour. From there, via Hegel and Marx, production would finally be grounded in ordinary work and a historical conception of labour. In Kant, aesthetically apprehended nature – not nature as presented by the understanding in the first *Critique*, as mere mechanical cause-effect relations – played a crucial role to help begin this process of materializing production. In exploring the concept of purposiveness via aesthetically apprehended nature, Kant notes how the growth of a tree involves an extraordinary process of generative production:

> ... the matter that the tree assimilates is first processed by it until the matter has the quality peculiar to the species ... the tree continues to develop itself by means of a material that in its composition is the tree's own product ... the separation and recombination of this raw material show that these natural beings have a separating and forming ability of very great originality ....
>
> Kant (1987: 250)

Kant's aesthetically apprehended vision of nature is thus crucial in the development of an image of production that would help the passage from idealism to materialism. Kant makes his own turn towards production in his discussion of craft labour and fine art. Here it is Kant's explicit statements that point beyond his philosophical architecture as he considers art as a mode of labour and labour as having a crucial artistic dimension, but one that is largely disavowed within capitalism. There is a schema within Marxism, whereby we associate 'production' with material economic production at the base of the social order and something like the aesthetic as helping the reproduction of the system as part of the superstructures. But there is a sense in which this could be reversed.

Material production is more properly thought of as routinely the place where the reproductive imagination exercises itself, as it reproduces the prototypes of products or services, for example. For such material reproduction to exist in the distinctly human form that it does, it presupposes the productive imagination that exceeds the immediate material conditions that are its foundations so that the prototypes of the qualitatively new can come into existence in the first place. If production, then, is routinely really reproduction of prototypes, then the aesthetic becomes the more authentic example of the productive imagination insofar as the aesthetic product is to some extent always its own prototype no matter how much it owes to generic rules. An aspect, then, of culture, normally seen as the means of reproducing the conditions of material production, may, in the aesthetic at least, be seen as productive in the sense that it is an example of the imagination producing something qualitatively new and opening up possibilities for our social being that mere reproduction does not.

What links the productive imagination at the heart of human labour and the productive imagination in aesthetic labour is *technic*. The more culture expands and becomes interwoven with material production, the more scope there is for the productive imagination to be exercised more routinely through *technic*, the production of forms that discovers the new potentialities within a given set of resources (technologies, techniques and rules). *Technic* is Kant's concept for a non-instrumental exploratory and open-ended practice but it also emerges from the satisfaction of use values more generally. The standards inherent in the purposiveness of nature or the nature that we make are the testing ground for honing those judgments that provide the foundations of the beautiful. In the beautiful there develops a complex communicative architecture, 'the form that is purposive for our observation and judging' (Kant 1987: 195) that can get us thinking and feeling about purposiveness in the non-aesthetic sphere and cultivate a utopian desire to remake our objective relationships to nature and the nature that we make. There is, then, a continual dialectic between non-aesthetic and aesthetic purposiveness. For Kant aesthetic pleasure rests in the enhancement of the power of judgment and the play of the cognitive powers (understanding and imagination) which is simultaneously an individual and social enhancement. Is this not quite close to Marx's notion from *The Communist Manifesto* that 'the free development of each is the condition for the free development of all' (Marx and Engels 1985: 105)? Within Chinese aesthetic Marxism, the proximity of Kant and Marx has been better understood:

> Since Kant's goal was to prove that humans are the final purpose of nature in its complete freedom, only aesthetic judgment could fulfill this objective. Aesthetic judgment is the moment whereby people's meditation of their own purposiveness without utilitarian purpose is fully realized. This realization amounts to nothing less than the eventual fulfillment of humanity's self-regulating, self-referential, autonomous, and free subjectivity, which coincides perfectly with the final purpose of nature.
>
> Kang (2000: 172–173)

So while the aesthetic has a strong affinity with the ontology of labour, its technologies, techniques and rules, its exchange with nature and its ineradicable sociality, the aesthetic is also a repository of the creativity of labour that is used and abused by capitalism. In the *aesthetic prototype*, we can recover what is lost to consciousness and narrowed in our practices in order to keep alive the outlines of a qualitatively different future. Whereas the 'industrial' prototype, from the axe to the airplane, modifies social relations *within* a mode of production, the aesthetic prototype may harbour utopian energies that point more powerfully *beyond* the mode of production.

The social surplus that is the condition for aesthetic production and reception in the first place is inscribed into the aesthetic prototype as a rebuke to arbitrary social limitations. The aesthetic as a creative act of labour inevitably speaks to an ought-utopian dimension. This ought-utopian dimension emerges from an awareness of the contradictions between our ontological requirements and capacities and our specific historical organizations and institutions that configure those requirements and capacities in relatively diverse and particular ways. The aesthetic therefore produces *onto-historical* images. Our ontological requirements and capacities pertain to the kind of social creatures that we are. For we have certain needs: to live in social relationships that must strike up a productive relationship with nature, for example. And we have various cultural, psychological, sexual, physical and emotional needs and capacities within these arrangements. These ontological dimensions are, as Mészáros has very usefully argued, the primary mediations of human life and as such are trans-historical, but they are never manifest outside a given set of specific historically determinate modes of social relations (1995: 139–140). These 'second-order' mediations under capitalism build on and develop these ontological foundations (as any mode of production must do) but increasingly develop them in destructively antagonistic ways. The aesthetic lives the contradictions between our trans-historical ontological or primary mediations and the necessarily historically specific second-order mediations, which have a particular structure in the epoch of capitalism. It is in the felt discrepancies between the ontological and historical dimensions of life that provide the onto-historical images of the aesthetic with their ought-utopian powers of critique. The aesthetic is attuned to onto-historical images by its sensitivity to crisis, to those moments when particular configurations of ontological needs and capacities are about to or are threatened with change. This dramatic imperative, which begins the process of relativization of what is, also manifests itself in all those intimations of past or future images. To be sure, what Dorfman and Mattelart once termed 'the historical nostalgia of the bourgeoisie' (1984: 59) has always meant that the past, for example, can function as a bucolic escape from the present while at the same time marked in every degree by the values associated with the intolerable system that narrative adventures are offering an escape from. Yet clearly even the most superficial activation of the ought-utopian principle in such images of the past or the future may stir up something risky and antithetical to the dominant value system, such as those 'properly imperishable desires' (Jameson 1992: 25) for a better set of social arrangements that meet our deepest human needs.

Capitalism's violation of our species-being nature is founded, as with all class societies, on the expropriation of the wealth and creativity of the worker and its conversion into surplus value in the form of capital. The act of labour as an 'act of arising freedom' (Lukács 1980: 117) is inverted into an act of diminishing freedom. Aesthetic labour is also an act of arising freedom as it emerges from various levels of determinate possibilities and constraints, from the specific technology, techniques and rules it works with all the way through to the broader institutional complexes it is embedded in and then up again to the broader socio-political and historical contexts of its time. And in many ways this act of arising freedom (better preserved in the aesthetic than in routine material production) constitutes the form and theme of the aesthetic across the entire epoch of the capitalist mode of production and its various axes of inequality (class, gender, race, sexuality, nation etc.) where the aesthetic dramatizes the contradictions around and between freedom and determination peculiar to this epoch. If positing the aesthetic as an allegory of the act of arising freedom sounds too abstract and universal, then that is because it must be counterpointed with the concept of singularity. Kant used the concept of singularity at the point of reception to think about what makes the nature of the aesthetic experience differentiated from the universal concepts of the understanding that assert their unyielding facticity. But we can also think about singularity at the point of production. The heightened sensitivity of the aesthetic to the world going on around it, its receptivity to trends, shifts or currents often going on below the radar of the official world of public discourse, means that the arising act of freedom always has as its theme and form very historically specific manifestations. This is the *temporal window* within which the aesthetic act can result in the artefact that we have come to know and be the thing that it is and no other. Sometimes, especially for popular culture, which has a remarkable attunement to such vicissitudes, the temporal window can be as little as a single year.

We have seen that Kant's own attempt to correct the latent reification of the first *Critique* in the third was by introducing the concept of reflective judgment, and at the heart of this operation was the concept of metaphor. We can therefore situate the cognitive linguistics of Johnson and Lakoff as working out a parallel project in response to the limitations of the Anglo-American tradition of analytic philosophy. Enlarging the role of metaphor in our routine day-to-day ways of cognizing reintroduces the subject and its powers of imaginative figuration, projection and inference-making back into the process of signification which the analytic tradition, with its stress on logical relations correlating with empirical reality, tends to diminish. Rather than repudiate the materialist basis of rationalism which rationalism itself negates, I see in their work the prospect of recovering a dialectic between the physical and physiological world of embodied realism and the real of social relations. From this perspective, their discussion of the relationship (on a spectrum) between emergent concepts and metaphorical concepts is particularly interesting. Concepts emerge from our sensory-motor interactions with our environment and are always already overlaid with traces of metaphorical thinking:

> We are physical beings bounded and set off from the rest of the world by the surface of our skins, and we experience the rest of the world as outside us. Each of us is a container, with a bounding surface and an in-out orientation. We project our own in-out orientation onto other physical objects that are bounded by surfaces. Thus we also view them as containers with an inside and an outside.
>
> Johnson and Lakoff (1980: 29)

As we develop, both individually with language acquisition and socially and culturally with more complexly differentiated relationships and means of communication, the capacity and need for metaphorical thinking across domains of experience grows accordingly. Metaphorical elaborations have profound entailments or consequences for what we think about and how we think about it. In Patricio Guzman's documentary *Nostalgia for the Light* (2010), the emergent concept of bodies is elaborated metaphorically across two radically dissimilar domains. The astronomers based in Chile's Atacama Desert investigate the heavenly bodies of the stars, always in effect studying the past, given the vast distances which the light from these cosmic phenomena must travel. Meanwhile, in another kind of archaeological recovery of the past, the women of Chile's 'disappeared', search for the remains of their relatives buried in the same desert, murdered during Pinochet's fascist dictatorship. The bodies in the ground can be inferentially connected with the stars above by virtue of the fact that we can think of both phenomena as bounded objects in space and existing in a temporal relationship with us. From this emergent concept the correspondence between predicates of radically different kinds of 'bodies' (although both are made up of calcium, for example) produces a new way of cognizing. By connecting the recovered remains in the ground with the stars, the sublime functions here to relativize the personal trauma caused by the fascists and even dwindle (the miniaturization strategy of the sublime once more) the historic significance of the fascist coup to the pathetic act it really was by making it the antithesis of reason, scientific enquiry and imaginative wonder and hope with which the film (and the socialist project it recalls) is imbued and which is the counterpart to the immensity and complexity of the natural universe we find ourselves in.

In making metaphor central to our cognitive capacities and grounding it in our bodily relations with our environment, Johnson and Lakoff offer the opportunity for the development of a materialist linguistics that has yet to be developed. The problem with their approach is twofold, however. Firstly, while metaphor is quite properly conceived as a routine operation of cognition, they are themselves quite uninterested in the aesthetic as a special zone of cognitive-metaphorical practice from which a cultural politics can be launched. Secondly, merely extending their philosophical framework to the aesthetic would not solve the problem because there is no critique of the relation between rationalism, formal logic and capitalism in their work.

Della Volpe, for example, does differentiate aesthetic discourse from both everyday discourse and natural scientific and philosophical discourse. But as with Johnson and Lakoff he has no critique of reification, while his uncritical positivism typical of the neo-Kantian-Marxist tradition marginalizes the social and historical dimension of the aesthetic. Implicitly equating critical philosophical discourse with natural scientific semantic formations means Della Volpe can have no critique of the socially determined overextension of natural science to social phenomena and therefore the aesthetic plays no role in critiquing the universal, in posing it as not given. In this Della Volpe was radically different from the tradition of German Marxists represented by Adorno, Kracauer and Benjamin. Very tacitly, they took the philosophical inheritance bequeathed by Kant in another direction and one closer, I think, to the spirit of his concept of reflective judgment.

For Benjamin and Kracauer, the body, whose emergent concept as a bounded container we have just explored, was reworked by reflective judgment in a constellation of metaphorical cross-references with other objects (particularly commodities) and bodily conditions, such as death, decay and decomposition on the one hand, in a dialectical relationship with preservation (hence the importance of the fossil as an image of natural history) and reassembling (hence the importance of montage or detective-like narratives of piecing together clues). The fostering of a historical consciousness that critiqued capitalism's 'eternal present' was aided in their work by such concepts and images of fragmentation and reconstitution within a critical framework (the collector for Benjamin). Bodies of people and objects were the means by which to try and think the reciprocal and historical relations which reification severs. A critical hermeneutic meant an act of recovery and reassembly, to smash what had been falsely synthesized into a pseudo-universal whole and to make whole again that which has been smashed by the wrongful victors of history, a theme that connects Benjamin and Kracauer to *Nostalgia for the Light*. The final images of that extraordinary film show us for the first time, Santiago – the capital city where the political drama of the Allende Presidency was played out to its fatal conclusion. It is night and the city is lit with a million pinpricks of light curving out to the black horizon as if we were looking at the night sky. The camera's affinity to the nature that we make (the city) and the nature that has made us (the cosmic formation of stars and planets) allows it to construct an affinity between the two natures, exploring resemblances and differences. Guzman's voice-over tells us that memory is like a gravitational force that keeps attracting us. Those who live without memory do not really live and of course those words spoken over the images of Santiago at night throw down the gauntlet to a nation to overcome its amnesia and feel the gravitational force of memory. This, then, is an example of the aesthetic living the tensions in our onto-historical relations and concretizing them into an image.

For Marx, however, bodies determined by gravity had other metaphorical possibilities. They could be imaginatively compared to commodities determined by the 'gravitational force' of value relations (rather than the tug of repressed memories) in order to encourage us to think the coercive operations of capital at the level of the global totality. Reflective judgment here gets us to imagine the concept of value to a power that certainly does not come naturally within the appearance forms of capitalism. In the medium of Marx's critical social science, the universal that is 'not given' is precisely the pseudo-freedom of discrete exchange between contractually free exchangers independent of any supersensible determinate forces. But to really grasp the concept of value in all its scope, we also need to imagine it by comparison with something as vast as gravity.

Adorno meanwhile resurrected Kant's concept of natural beauty, emphasizing its dialectical possibilities, to pose the question of our reciprocal relations via our relations to nature. Evoking Benjamin in his discussion of natural beauty, Adorno poetically conjures up 'illuminated edges of clouds [that] seem to give duration to lightning flashes'. (Adorno 2004: 92). The meanings or truths of aesthetic images ought to be given just enough duration before they disappear or are reconfigured into a new pattern. 'Natural beauty is suspended history, a moment of becoming at a standstill' (Adorno 2004: 93), argues Adorno, evoking once again Benjamin's famous definition of the dialectical image. 'Thinking involves not only the flow of thoughts, but their arrest as well', notes Benjamin. 'Where thinking suddenly stops in a configuration pregnant with tensions, it gives that configuration a shock' (Benjamin 1999a: 254). Thus natural beauty or the dialectical image is a combination of stasis and transience, where the movement of the dialectic is arrested in a vivid form that illuminates a totality but from a position that is a *momentary arrangement* (the aesthetic experience itself) gone before it can congeal into a reified monolith or new pseudo-universal concept. Yet it leaves behind it (in the form of the aesthetic practice and the seeds it has sown in consciousness) traces that can be reconfigured in future work/future receptions (and also social change) rather than be lost forever.

In socializing the aesthetic as a philosophical concept, we have also understood how the aesthetic helps socialize us, how that is it encourages our sociality in a society that thwarts it by division and domination. For many generations, scholars have stood Kant on his head. But Kant himself demands that we stand him on his feet, materialize and historicize his philosophy of the aesthetic, reconstruct the genealogical relationships between Kant and Marx(ism) and thereby shade in a Red Kant that also helps us reconstruct our understanding of the aesthetic as something special and precious.

Bibliography

Adorno, T.W. (1973), *Negative Dialectics*. New York: Seabury Press.

———. (1991a), 'The Curious Realist: On Siegfried Kracauer', *New German Critique*, 54, 159–177.

———. (1991b), *The Culture Industry*. London: Routledge.

———. (2001a), *Kant's Critique of Pure Reason*. Stanford, California: Stanford University Press.

———. (2001b), *Metaphysics, Concept and Problems*. Stanford, California: Stanford University Press.

———. (2004), *Aesthetic Theory*. London: Continuum.

———. (2005), *Minima Moralia, Reflections on a Damaged Life*. London: Verso.

——— and Horkheimer, M. (1997), *Dialectic of Enlightenment*. London: Verso.

Alberro, A. (2004), 'Beauty Knows No Pain', *Art Journal*, 63 (2), 36–43.

Althusser, L. (1982), *Montesquieu, Rousseau, Marx*. London: Verso.

Anderson, P. (1964), 'Origins of the Present Crisis', *New Left Review*, I (23), 26–53.

Archer, M., Bhaskar, R., Collier, A., Lawson, T., and Norrie, A. (1998), *Critical Realism*. Abingdon: Routledge.

Arnheim, R. (1972), *Visual Thinking*. Berkeley, Los Angeles: University of California Press.

Benjamin, W. (1999a), *Illuminations*. London: Pimlico Press.

———. (1999b), *The Arcades Project*. Translated by Howard Eiland and Kevin McLaughlin. Cambridge, Massachusetts: Harvard University Press.

Bloch, E. (1970), 'Entfremdung, Verfremdung: Alienation, Estrangement', *The Drama Review*, 15 (1), 120–125.

———. (1995), *The Principle of Hope*. Cambridge, Massachusetts: MIT Press.

Bologh, R.W. (1979), *Dialectical Phenomenology: Marx's Method*. London: Routledge and Keegan Paul.

Bordwell, D. (1996), 'Convention, Construction, and Cinematic Vision' in D. Bordwell and N.Carroll (eds), *Post-Theory, Reconstructing Film Studies*. Madison, Wisconsin: University of Wisconsin Press, 87–107.

———. (2002), 'The Art Cinema as a Mode of Film Practice', in C. Fowler (ed), *The European Cinema Reader*. London: Routledge, 94–102.

Bourdieu, P. (1985), 'The Social Space and the Genesis of Groups', *Theory and Society*, 14 (6), 723–744.

———. (1987), 'The Historical Genesis of a Pure Aesthetic', *The Journal of Aesthetics and Art Criticism*, 46, 201–210.

——. (1989), 'Social Space and Symbolic Power', *Sociology Theory*, 7 (1), 14–25.

——. (1996), *Distinction, A Social Critique of the Judgment of Taste*. London: Routledge.

Bowie, A. (2003), *Introduction to German Philosophy from Kant to Habermas*. Cambridge: Polity Press.

Bukharin, N.I. (1978), *Historical Materialism: A System of Sociology*. New York: University of Michigan Press.

Burwick, F. (1996), *Poetic Madness and the Romantic Imagination*. Pennsylvannia: Pensylvannia State University.

Colletti, L. (1972), *From Rousseau to Lenin: Studies in Ideology and Society*. London: New Left Books.

——. (1974), 'A Political and Philosophical Interview', *New Left Review*, 86, 3–28.

——. (1979), *Marxism and Hegel*. London: Verso.

Crowther, P. (1989), 'The Kantian Sublime, the Avant-Garde, and the Postmodern', *New Formations*, 7 (1), 67–75.

Currie, G. (1995), *Image and Mind, Film, Philosophy, and Cognitive Science*. Cambridge: Cambridge University Press.

Darden, L. (1982), 'Artificial Intelligence and Philosophy of Science: Reasoning by Analogy in Theory Construction', *Philosophy of Science Association*, 2, 147–165.

Day, G. (1999), 'Allegory: Between Deconstruction and Dialectics', *Oxford Art Journal*, 22 (1), 103–118.

Deleuze, G. (1998), 'A Philosophical Concept …', *Topos*, 7, 111–112.

——. (2000), 'The Idea of Genesis in Kant's Aesthetics', *Angelaki*, 5 (3), 57–70.

——. (2005), *Cinema 1*. London: Continuum.

Della Volpe, G. (1978), *Critique of Taste*. Translated by Michael Caesar. London: New Left Books.

Dillon, B. (2005), 'Fragments from a History of Ruin', *Cabinet*, 20, 55–60.

Dorfmann, A. and Mattelart, A. (1984), *How to Read Donald Duck, Imperialist Ideology in the Disney Comic*. New York: International General.

Eagleton, T. (1988), 'The Ideology of the Aesthetic', *Poetics Today*, 9 (2), 327–338.

——. (1997), *The Ideology of the Aesthetic*. Oxford: Basil Blackwell.

Eco, U. (1985), '*Casablanca*, Cult Movies and Intertextual Collage', *SubStance*, 14 (2), 3–12.

Evans, L.T. (1984), 'Darwin's Use of the Analogy Between Artificial and Natural Selection', *Journal of the History of Biology*, 17 (1), 113–140.

Fisher, E. (2010), *The Necessity of Art*. London: Verso.

Foucault, M. (1982), *This is Not a Pipe*. Translated by James Harkness. London: University of California Press.

García Espinosa, J. (1997), 'For an Imperfect Cinema' in M.T. Martin (ed), *New Latin American Cinema, Theory, Practices, and Transcontinental Articulations*. Detroit: Wayne State University Press, 83–85.

Goldmann, L. (2011), *Immanuel Kant*. London: Verso.

Gramsci, A. (1967), *The Modern Prince and Other Writings*. London: Lawrence and Wishart.

Guyer, P. (1992), 'Introduction: The Starry Heavens and the Moral Law' in P. Guyer (ed), *The Cambridge Companion to Kant*. Cambridge: Cambridge University Press, 1–25.

Habermas, J. (1987), *The Philosophical Discourse of Modernity*. Cambridge: Polity Press.

Hebdige, D. (1979), *Subculture: The Meaning of Style*. London: Routledge.

Hegel, G.W.F. (1988), *Hegel's Aesthetics, Lectures on Fine Art*. Translated by T.M. Knox. Oxford: Oxford University Press.

Heidegger, M. (1977), *The Question Concerning Technology and Other Essays*. Translated by William Lovitt. New York: Garland Publishing.

Helfer, M.B. (1996), *The Retreat of Representation, The Concept of Darstellung in German Critical Discourse*. New York: State University of New York Press.

Jameson, F. (1986), 'Third-World Literature in the Era of Multinational Capitalism', *Social Text*, 15, 65–88.

———. (1992), *Signatures of the Visible*. New York: Routledge.

———. (1998), *The Cultural Turn: Selected Writings on the Postmodern, 1983–1998*. London: Verso.

———. (2007), *Late Marxism: Adorno or the Persistence of the Dialectic*. London: Verso.

———. (2010), *Valences of the Dialectic*. London: Verso.

Jay, M. (2002), 'Cultural Relativism and the Visual Turn', *Journal of Visual Culture*, 1 (3), 267–278.

Johnson, M. (1987), *The Body in the Mind, The Bodily Basis of Meaning, Imagination and Reason*. Chicago: University of Chicago Press.

Johnson, J. and Lakoff, G. (1980), *Metaphors We Live By*. Chicago: University of Chicago.

Johnson, M. and Lakoff, G. (1999), *Philosophy in the Flesh*. New York: Basic Books.

Kang, L. (2000), *Aesthetics and Marxism, Chinese Aesthetic Marxists and Their Western Contemporaries*. Durham: Duke University Press.

Kant, I. (1987), *Critique of Judgment*. Translated by Werner S. Pluhar. Cambridge, Indianapolis: Hackett Publishing Company.

———. (1996), *Critique of Pure Reason*. Translated by Werner S. Pluhar. Cambridge, Indianapolis: Hackett Publishing Company.

———. (2002), *Critique of Practical Reason*. Translated by Werner S. Pluhar. Cambridge, Indianapolis: Hackett Publishing Company.

Karatani, K. (2005), *Transcritique: On Kant and Marx*. Massachusetts: MIT Press.

Kaufman, R. (2000), 'Red Kant, or the Persistence of the Third "Critique" in Adorno and Jameson', *Critical Inquiry*, 26 (4), 682–724.

Klinger, C. (2009), 'The Sublime, a Discourse of Crisis and of Power, or: "A Gamble on Transcendence" ' in L. White and C. Pajaczkowska (eds), *The Sublime Now*. Newcastle Upon Tyne: Cambridge Scholars Publishing, 91–111.

Kolakowski, L. (1978), *Main Currents of Marxism Vol. 2: The Golden Age*. Oxford: Oxford University Press.

Kracauer, S. (1995), *The Mass Ornament, Weimar Essays*. Translated by Thomas Y. Levin. Cambridge, Massachusetts: Harvard University Press.

———. (1997), *Theory of Film: The Redemption of Physical Reality*. Princeton: Princeton University Press.

Latour, B. (1999), *Pandora's Hope, Essays on the Reality of Science Studies*. Cambridge, Massachusetts: Harvard University Press.

Leslie, E. (2000), *Walter Benjamin, Overpowering Conformism*. London: Pluto Press.

———. (2009), 'Icy Scenes From Three Centuries', in L. White and C. Pajaczkowska (eds), *The Sublime Now*. Newcastle Upon Tyne: Cambridge Scholars Publishing, 35–48.

Lukács, G. (1971), *History and Class Consciousness: Studies in Marxist Dialectics*. London: Merlin Press.

———. (1978a), *Writer and Critic*. London: Merlin Press.

———. (1978b), *The Ontology of Social Being: Marx*. London: Merlin Press.

———. (1980), *The Ontology of Social Being III: Labour*. London: Merlin Press.

Lyotard, F. (1994), *Lessons on the Analytic of the Sublime*. Stanford, California: Stanford University Press.

Makkreel, R. (1990), *Imagination and Interpretation in Kant, the Hermeneutical Import of the Critique of Judgment*. Chicago: Chicago University Press.

Marcuse, H. (1982), 'Some Social Implications of Modern Technology' in A. Arato and E. Gebhardt (eds), *The Essential Frankfurt School Reader*. New York: Continuum, 138–162.

Marx, K. (1983), *Capital*. London: Lawrence and Wishart.

———. (1980), *The Thought of Karl Marx*. Edited by David McLellan. Basingstoke: Macmillan Press.

———. (1993), *Grundrisse*. London: Penguin.

Marx, K. and Engels, F. (1977), *Selected Works, Volume One*. London: Lawrence and Wishart.

———. (1985), *The Communist Manifesto*. Harmondsworth: Penguin Books.

———. (1989), *The German Ideology*. London: Lawrence and Wishart.

McGrath, J. (1996), *A Good Night Out, Popular Theatre: Audience, Class and Form*. London: Nick Hern Books.

McMullin, E. (2001), 'The Impact of Newton's Principia on the Philosophy of Science', *Philosophy of Science*, 68 (3), 279–310.

Mészáros, I. (1995), *Beyond Capital, Towards a Theory of Transition*. London: Merlin Press.

———. (2006), *Marx's Theory of Alienation*. Delhi: Aakar Books.

Munt, S. (2000), *Cultural Studies and the Working Class, Subject to Change*. London: Cassell.

Osborne, H. (1979), 'Some Theories of Aesthetic Judgment', *The Journal of Aesthetics and Art Criticism*, 38 (2), 135–144.

Osborne, P. (2004), 'Art Beyond Aesthetics: Philosophical Criticism, Art History and Contemporary Art', *Art History*, 27 (4), 651–670.

Palmer, B.D. (1991), 'Review of Jacques Rancière's *The Nights of Labour: The Workers' Dream in Nineteenth-Century France*', *Labour/LeTravail*, 27, 340–342.

Rancière, R. (2000), 'Dissenting Words: A Conversation with Jacques Rancière', *Diacritics*, 30 (2), 113–126.

———. (2002), 'The Aesthetic Revolution and Its Outcomes', *New Left Review II*, 14, 133–151.

———. (2004), 'The Sublime from Lyotard to Schller', *Radical Philosophy*, 126, 8–15.

———. (2007), *The Politics of Aesthetics*. London: Continuum.

———. (2009), 'The Aesthetic Dimension: Aesthetics, Politics, Knowledge', *Critical Inquiry*, 36 (1), 1–19.

———. (2011), *The Emancipated Spectator*. London: Verso.

Raunig, G., Ray, G. and Wuggenig, U.(eds). (2011), *Critique of Creativity, Precarity, Subjectivity and Resistance in the 'Creative Industries'*. London: MayFly books.

Ray, G. (2009), 'From Trauma and the Sublime to Radical Critique', *Third Text*, 23 (2), 135–149.

———. (2011), 'Culture Industry and the Administration of Terror', in G. Raunig, G. Ray and U. Wuggenig (eds), *Critique of Creativity, Precarity, Subjectivity and Resistance in the 'Creative Industries'*. London: MayFly books, 167–182.

Ricour, P. (1978), *The Rule of Metaphor*. London: Routledge and Kegan Paul.

Roberts, J. (2010), 'Art and Its Negations', *Third Text*, 24 (3), 289–303.

Rose, J. (2001), *The Intellectual Life of the British Working Class*. New Haven: Yale University Press.

Said, E. (1995), *Orientalism, Western Conceptions of the Orient*. London: Penguin.

Scott, A.J. (2005), *Hollywood, the Place, the Industry*. Princeton: Princeton University Press.

Shaviro, S. (2002), 'Beauty Lies in the Eye' in B. Massimo (ed), *A Shock to Thought, Expression after Deleuze and Guattari*. London: Routledge, 9–19.

———. (2009), *Without Criteria: Kant, Whitehead, Deleuze, and Aesthetics*. Cambridge, Massachusetts: MIT Press.

———. (2010), *Post-Cinematic Affect*. Hants: John Hunt Publishing.

Siebers, T. (1998), 'Kant and the Politics of Beauty', *Philosophy and Literature*, 221 (1), 31–50.

Suvin, D. (1967), 'The Mirror and the Dynamo: On Brecht's Aesthetic Point of View', *The Drama Review*, 12 (1), 56–67.

Tambling, J. (2010), *Allegory*. London: Routledge.

Toynbee, J. (2013), 'How Special? Cultural Work, Copyright, Politics' in M. Banks, R. Gill and S. Taylor (eds), *Theorizing Cultural Work, Labour, Continuity and Change in the Cultural and Creative Industries*. London: Routledge, 86–100.

Tuchman, G. (1978), *The Symbolic Annihilation of Women by the Mass Media*. Oxford: Oxford University Press.

Voronsky, A.K. (1998), *Art as the Cognition of Life*. Michigan: Mehring Books.

Walkerdine, V. and Lucey, H. (1989), *Democracy in the Kitchen: Regulating Mothers and Socializing Daughters*. London: Virago.

Wayne, M. (2003), *Marxism and Media Studies, Key Concepts and Contemporary Trends*. London: Pluto.

———. (2013), 'Transcoding Kant: Kracauer's Weimar Marxism and After', *Historical Materialism*, 21 (3), 57–85.

Willis, P. (1981), *Learning to Labour: How Working Class Kids Get Working Class Jobs*. New York: Columbia University Press.

Index

Lightning Source UK Ltd.
Milton Keynes UK
UKOW06n1825100415

249451UK00001B/33/P

9 781472 511348